Practical OpenTelemetry

Adopting Open Observability Standards Across Your Organization

Daniel Gomez Blanco

Foreword by Ted Young, OpenTelemetry Co-founder

Apress®

Practical OpenTelemetry: Adopting Open Observability Standards Across Your Organization

Daniel Gomez Blanco
Edinburgh, UK

ISBN-13 (pbk): 978-1-4842-9074-3   ISBN-13 (electronic): 978-1-4842-9075-0
https://doi.org/10.1007/978-1-4842-9075-0

Managing Director, Apress Media LLC: Welmoed Spahr
Acquisitions Editor: Jonathan Gennick
Development Editor: Laura Berendson
Editorial Assistant: Shaul Elson

Cover image by Daniel Lerman on Unsplash

Distributed to the book trade worldwide by Springer Science+Business Media New York, 1 New York Plaza, Suite 4600, New York, NY 10004-1562, USA. Phone 1-800-SPRINGER, fax (201) 348-4505, e-mail orders-ny@springer-sbm.com, or visit www.springeronline.com. Apress Media, LLC is a California LLC and the sole member (owner) is Springer Science + Business Media Finance Inc (SSBM Finance Inc). SSBM Finance Inc is a **Delaware** corporation.

For information on translations, please e-mail booktranslations@springernature.com; for reprint, paperback, or audio rights, please e-mail bookpermissions@springernature.com.

Apress titles may be purchased in bulk for academic, corporate, or promotional use. eBook versions and licenses are also available for most titles. For more information, reference our Print and eBook Bulk Sales web page at http://www.apress.com/bulk-sales.

Any source code or other supplementary material referenced by the author in this book is available to readers on GitHub via the book's product page, located at www.apress.com. For more detailed information, please visit https://www.apress.com/us/services/source-code.

Printed on acid-free paper

Table of Contents

About the Author ix

About the Technical Reviewer xi

Acknowledgments xiii

Foreword xv

Introduction xvii

Part I: The Need for Observability with OpenTelemetry 1

Chapter 1: The Need for Observability 3

   Why Observability Matters 3

   Context and Correlation 7

   Summary 12

Chapter 2: How OpenTelemetry Enables Observability 15

   OpenTelemetry's Mission 15

   The Power of Open Standards 17

   The Shift in Vendor Added Value 21

   Summary 24

Part II: OpenTelemetry Components and Best Practices 25

Chapter 3: OpenTelemetry Fundamentals 27

   OpenTelemetry Specification 27

      Signals and Components 29

      Stability and Design Principles 31

      Tracing 33

      Metrics 35

Logs 38

Baggage 39

Context Propagation 39

Instrumentation Libraries 40

Resource 40

Collector 41

OTLP Protocol 41

Semantic Conventions 42

Resource Conventions 43

Tracing Conventions 45

Metrics Conventions 46

Logs Conventions 47

Telemetry Schemas 48

Summary 48

Chapter 4: Auto-Instrumentation 51

Resource SDK 51

Instrumentation Libraries 53

Java Agent 58

Java Standalone Instrumentation 66

Summary 68

Chapter 5: Context, Baggage, and Propagators 69

Telemetry Context and the Context API 69

Baggage API 74

Propagation Using W3C Baggage Specification 76

Cross-Service Context and the Propagators API 77

Configuring Propagators 82

Summary 83

Chapter 6: Tracing **85**

What Is a Distributed Trace? 85

Tracing API 87

Tracers and Tracer Providers 88

Span Creation and Context Interaction 89

Adding Properties to an Existing Span 95

Representing Errors and Exceptions 98

Tracing Asynchronous Tasks 99

Tracing SDK 103

Span Processors and Exporters 105

Trace Context Propagation 107

W3C TraceContext 108

Summary 110

Chapter 7: Metrics **111**

Measurements, Metrics, and Time Series 111

Metrics API 114

Meters and Meter Providers 115

Instrument Registration 116

Instrument Types 120

Metrics SDK 125

Aggregation 126

Views 131

Exemplars 134

Metric Readers and Exporters 136

Summary 142

Chapter 8: Logging **143**

The Purpose of Logs for Observability 143

Logging API 147

Logs API Interface.. 149

Events API Interface... 150

Logging SDK.. 151

Log Processors and Exporters 152

Integration with Logging Frameworks 154

Summary.. 156

Chapter 9: Protocol and Collector.. **157**

Protocol... 157

OTLP/gRPC... 159

OTLP/HTTP 160

Exporter Configuration... 161

Collector.. 162

Deployment 166

Receivers.. 168

Processors.. 169

Exporters 171

Extensions 174

Service 174

Summary.. 178

Chapter 10: Sampling and Common Deployment Models.................. **179**

Common Deployment Models 179

Collector-Less Model 180

Node Agent Model 182

Sidecar Agent Model 185

Gateway Model... 187

Trace Sampling 189

    Probability Sampling 191

    Tail-Based Sampling 197

  Summary.. 202

Part III: Rolling Out OpenTelemetry Across Your Organization 203

Chapter 11: Maximizing Adoption by Minimizing Friction 205

Investing in Telemetry Enablement 205

Adopting OpenTelemetry... 209

    Greenfield Environments 209

    Compatibility with OpenTracing.. 210

    Compatibility with OpenCensus.. 212

    Other Telemetry Clients 214

Summary.. 215

Chapter 12: Adopting Observability.. 217

Shifting Debugging Workflows.. 217

Expanding Context 222

Keeping Telemetry Valuable 226

Summary.. 229

Index.. 231

About the Author

 **Daniel Gomez Blanco** is a Principal Engineer at Skyscanner, leading their observability transformation across hundreds of services, to ensure that travelers get a reliable and performant experience when booking their next holiday. He is an advocate of open standards and CNCF projects such as OpenTelemetry to back the instrumentation and collection of operational data. Daniel has experience working in organizations of all sizes, from international institutions such as CERN in Geneva to London startups such as SKIPJAQ. His main focus has always been building software and adopting solutions to minimize the cognitive load required for engineers to support and operate production services.

About the Technical Reviewer

Dave McAllister was named one of the top ten pioneers in open source by Computer Business Review, having cut his teeth on Linux and compilers before the phrase "open source" was coined. Dave works with DevOps, developers, and architects to understand the advantages of modern architectures and orchestration to solve large-scale distributed systems challenges, using open source and its innovative aspects. Dave has been a champion for open systems and open source from the early days of Linux to today's world of OpenTelemetry and observability. When he's not talking, you can find him hiking with his trusty camera, trying to keep up with his wife.

Acknowledgments

I believe that successfully writing a book is driven by three main factors: experience, motivation, and support. You need something to write about, a desire to tell others about it, and the backing and encouragement required to deliver it. Fortunately, I have people to thank in each of those areas.

First, I must recognize Skyscanner for creating an environment where innovation is encouraged, and the value of open source is realized, at scale, to provide a reliable service for millions of users each month. This allowed me to gain experience from tackling some of the challenges presented by complex distributed systems and to learn from many other talented engineers. I'd like to thank Doug Borland, Stuart Davidson, and Paul Gillespie in particular. Their trust and support have allowed me to lead an entire organization toward open standards in telemetry transport and instrumentation and to help implement observability best practices across dozens of teams.

I'd also like to thank Ted Young, Michael Hausenblas, and Paul Bruce for our ever-insightful conversations. They have motivated me and many others to be advocates of open standards in telemetry instrumentation, fostering a culture of learning and collaboration. OpenTelemetry has built a very special community, and that's all thanks to people like them.

I'm immensely grateful to Apress for giving me the opportunity to write this book and to Jonathan Gennick, who originally proposed the idea to me. I must admit it was not one of my 2022 resolutions, but I regret none of it!

Finally, thanks to my family, both in Spain and in Scotland. Their support has been invaluable, especially as life events have put an extra load on the already-demanding endeavor of writing a book in one's spare time. And of course, thanks to my partner, Nicola Black, for all her love and support (including her own personal data point in a graph within this book). A person I truly admire and who motivates me to be a better person day after day. I couldn't have done it without you.

Foreword

Technology comes in waves, and the topic of observability is going through a sea change at the moment.

I have been writing and running Internet services since 2005. In that time, I have watched us as an industry move from capacity planning and racking servers to scaling virtual machines on demand. We are currently in the process of developing distributed operating systems to help manage these complex deployments, with Kubernetes being the current OS *du jour*. It still feels like desktop operating systems before the advent of plug and play, but that is changing.

What hasn't been changing, over all that time, is how we observe these systems. Our technology stack has grown leaps and bounds and undergone a dramatic transformation. But when I look at the current offerings in the market of monitoring and observability products, I don't see anything that looks fundamentally different from the duct-taped stack of Nagios, Munin, and syslog I was using 20 years ago. The dashboards might be a little prettier, but not really.

This is why, in 2019, I helped to co-found the OpenTelemetry project. After 20 years, we know what the limitations are, and we know that we can do better.

So forget the old shaggy dog story about "three pillars" and all that. Let's begin from scratch, by splitting observability into two stages: telemetry and analysis. Telemetry is how we describe our systems, combined with how we transmit those descriptions. Analysis is what we do with the data once we have it.

If we want to analyze all of the available data together, coherently, then the data needs to be put together… coherently. To correlate across data streams effectively, without resorting to guesswork and heuristics, you must collect those different data streams at the same time, as a single data stream.

Not only do we need to understand how to instrument our systems, we have to understand how to manage that data. Data volumes are so high, and have so many requirements put on them, that the telemetry pipeline itself can become a beast to manage.

This is where OpenTelemetry comes in. OTel is specifically designed to allow logs, traces, and metrics to be correlated with each other in meaningful ways. And it provides some incredibly useful tools and services for transforming and transmitting data.

But there is another reason we created OpenTelemetry, beyond the technical need for a ground-up redesign. And that is standardization. Without a robust, shared standard for describing systems, we are stuck in a fragmented world of vendor lock-in. Telemetry is a cross-cutting concern, and instrumentation needs to be everywhere. That means changing telemetry systems is an expensive and difficult proposition. We don't want to have to do this every time we switch analysis tools. Better yet, we want our software to come with telemetry baked in, so we don't have to do anything at all.

Today, with over 7,000 contributors from over 700 organizations, OpenTelemetry has succeeded in this mission and has become a widely accepted industry standard.

So that's why you should consider using OpenTelemetry. And if you're holding this book, you probably are! So the real question is... how?

The reality is that high-quality observability requires an up-front investment, and it requires an organization-wide plan of action. Most systems that have been in production for some time are heterogeneous, with a mishmash of different telemetry tools already installed. Safely turning this telemetry hairball into a clean, uniform, and highly effective system can be a daunting task.

But, whom better to learn these strategies from than a real, experienced practitioner? Which is what you have here. Daniel is an OpenTelemetry contributor, but more importantly, he is an OpenTelemetry user. He has used it in anger, and he has used it extensively. And he has successfully accomplished many of the large organizational shifts that you, dear reader, may be about to embark upon.

Enjoy the book!

Ted Young

Co-founder, OpenTelemetry

Introduction

Telemetry forms part of everyday life in the modern world. We are constantly evaluating data that describes the current state of concepts, or objects, around us. This allows us to make informed decisions to optimize our behavior. Checking the weather forecast before going out for a run helps us choose suitable clothing and gear, while tracking our pace and vital signs during exercise can be incredibly useful to adjust our training plan. When used appropriately, telemetry can make our lives easier and safer. It allows us to build mechanisms that can automatically react to certain conditions, such as the temperature of a room (thermostats), or the rotational speed of a wheel (traction control systems).

In a similar fashion, telemetry in software systems allows us to efficiently operate complex architectures to ensure high performance and reliability. Unstructured log statements, the most rudimental form of telemetry, may allow an engineer to debug a script run locally, but they won't get them very far when operating distributed systems across multiple clusters in production. This is where standards and out-of-the-box instrumentation become crucial, not only to improve the quality of telemetry collected directly from systems but also to provide a foundation for observability tooling to correlate data originating from multiple components within the stack. Modern applications don't work in isolation, and neither should the telemetry they produce. Thus, effective observability must present a holistic analysis of a system, rather than isolated views of the so-called three pillars of observability (traces, metrics, and logs). The result: a system that describes itself in a way that allows us to detect and debug regressions, in production, backed by evidence and not intuition.

This book provides a detailed explanation of the need for implementing open standards across telemetry signals, the added value from doing so when operating production services at scale, and how OpenTelemetry, a CNCF project, can help achieve effective observability by providing a set of open-source vendor-neutral APIs, SDKs, protocols, and tooling to instrument, export, and transport telemetry data. All of this is done with the support of a large community of observability vendors, open-source projects, and individual contributors.

The OpenTelemetry project is not only changing how applications are instrumented but also shifting the value proposition of observability vendors. As active contributors to open-source components, they can now collectively improve telemetry instrumentation via vendor-neutral components, delivering their unique value via the insights they can extract from standard, well-structured data. Understanding this change can influence buy-vs.-build decisions for organizations wanting to maximize observability and reduce the time taken to resolve incidents while minimizing engineering effort and remaining vendor neutral at the instrumentation layer.

In order to implement observability in software systems, it is important to understand the design and purpose of each of the building blocks of OpenTelemetry and how they relate to each other. The core of this book covers these components from a practitioner's perspective, offering tips and recommendations acquired from years of experience in observability and operational monitoring, with the intention to guide the reader to use the right signal for the right purpose. This starts with a general walk-through of the OpenTelemetry specification and semantic conventions, which bind together all telemetry signals under a set of standards that help all observability tooling speak the same common language.

For each type of signal, that is, baggage, traces, metrics, and logs, this book explores their APIs, SDKs, and best practices needed to instrument applications both manually and automatically via instrumentation libraries. Common use cases for these signals are illustrated with examples in Java, providing short code snippets aimed at explaining individual concepts. These snippets are meant to be considered in isolation, they do not form part of yet another full-fledged OpenTelemetry demo environment, and their source code has not been made available as supplementary material for this book. This is intentional, as the project provides its official OpenTelemetry Demo (available at `https://github.com/open-telemetry/opentelemetry-demo`) for this purpose. The OpenTelemetry Demo is maintained by the OpenTelemetry community and integrated with many observability vendors to showcase instrumentation in multiple supported languages. It is the best way for readers to explore the concepts discussed in this book in practice and to evaluate the telemetry produced in the observability platform with which they are most familiar. However, Chapter 4 showcases the power of OpenTelemetry to automatically instrument an existing application not integrated with OpenTelemetry. To help readers stand up this sample stack quickly, the source code and configuration has been made available on GitHub via the book's product page, located at www.apress.com. For more detailed information, please visit `https://www.apress.com/us/services/source-code`.

The OpenTelemetry specification, APIs, and SDKs are backed by strong stability and backward compatibility gurantees as we'll see in later chapters. Nonetheless, the project and its components have been designed to evolve. Practical Opentelemetry has been written to be compliant with the following component versions:

- Specification v1.16.0

- Java (and Java Instrumentation) v1.21.0

- Collector (and Contrib) v0.68.0/v1.0.0-RC2

- Collector Helm Chart v0.44.0

At an organizational level, observability best practices transcend those related to instrumenting each service in isolation. The value of observability scales exponentially with the number of services sharing telemetry context as part of common units of work. To facilitate adoption, OpenTelemetry provides functionality to easily integrate with existing APIs and frameworks, but, ultimately, it is the responsibility of service owners to configure the necessary components and ensure that their applications produce valuable telemetry. Toward the end of this book, we cover how organizations can benefit from having a telemetry enablement function to guarantee that adoption happens seamlessly across multiple systems, minimizing friction during migrations, and promoting good practices within teams instrumenting production workloads. When applied to large-scale deployments, these best practices also ensure that transfer and storage costs associated with telemetry are optimized without compromising observability.

Even the best and most complete telemetry instrumentation and observability tooling would not be very useful if engineers don't use it to its full potential. The final part of this book focuses on how engineering leads may promote change in the monitoring and debugging practices of teams supporting distributed systems, to maximize the value of observability. As the old saying goes, "if your only tool is a hammer, then everything looks like a nail." Over the years, the way we design and deploy systems has changed, and the way we observe them must adapt accordingly. OpenTelemetry delivers the tools, but we must learn how to use them appropriately.

PART I

The Need for Observability with OpenTelemetry

CHAPTER 1

The Need for Observability

The term *observability* has been increasing in popularity over the last few years in the tech industry. Before we delve deeper into OpenTelemetry and how it can help to make our systems more observable, we should first understand what observability is and, most importantly, why we need it, especially in modern distributed systems.

Why Observability Matters

For most of us, observability starts early in our software development careers, normally in the form of print statements dotted around a script outputting messages like `"I'm here"` when code execution enters a specific function or branch. We make some changes, run the script again, and we expect to see something different. This is the simplest and probably the most inefficient form of debugging, and it clearly would not scale to anything larger than a few lines of code run locally, but it does expose some internal insights from within the script execution, and these are (somewhat) useful to understand what the code is doing and how our changes affect it. In general terms, observability is the quality of a system that measures in what degree its internal state can be inferred from observations of its external outputs. It was first described by Rudolf E. Kálmán as a concept within control systems theory in 1960, as part of his paper "On the general theory of control systems," available at *https://ieeexplore.ieee.org/document/1104873*. A system is observable if, at any point in time, we can assert with confidence how its constituent components are behaving by evaluating the telemetry they produce. Without observability, there is no controllability, as observability allows us to close the feedback loop between change and desired effect.

© Daniel Gomez Blanco 2023
D. Gomez Blanco, *Practical OpenTelemetry*, https://doi.org/10.1007/978-1-4842-9075-0_1

Depending on the type of system under consideration, the key signals to monitor may differ, but the definition remains the same. In order to apply changes in a reliable way, we require confidence in the telemetry produced to assert the state of said system so we can react appropriately in case of unwanted side effects. For instance, if we consider transactional systems, we are normally interested in highly granular insights to debug regressions on key performance indicators like error rate or response time, which reflect the quality of service that their clients (either end users or other dependent subsystems) are experiencing. Efficient observability allows real-time evaluation of how subsystems are performing, and *when* key indicators fall out of acceptable thresholds, it provides the necessary context and signal correlation to confidently debug highly complex distributed systems as fast as possible.

Hopefully, the reader has noticed the intentional use of *when* rather than *if* referring to regressions in system reliability in the last paragraph. A system will eventually fail as a side effect of changes implemented on its components, instability in the hosting infrastructure, human error, or even cosmic rays (as J. F. Ziegler explains in his paper available at *www.srim.org/SER/SERTrends.htm*). Understanding that failure is a constant makes tracking metrics like Mean Time to Recovery/Resolution (MTTR) the first step toward improving incident response. Efforts to increase the reliability of the systems we manage must always contemplate improving the time taken to debug and fix regressions, rather than simply focusing on avoiding them.

From the observability point of view, it is important to make a distinction between Mean Time to Recovery (MTTRec) and Mean Time to Resolution (MTTRes). These two terms are sometimes used interchangeably as MTTR, but if we consider resiliency best practices, we can see how decoupling them allows us to focus on different parts of the incident response life cycle. For instance, consider an N+1 redundant system. This resiliency pattern ensures that the system can recover from a single component failure. Regardless of implementation, either active-passive or active-active, it normally relies on taking one component out of circulation to let one or more components handle the load. In this case, we can see how this type of system could potentially recover, serving traffic as normal, before we can consider the incident fully resolved and either found the root cause and fixed the failing component or replaced it completely. As such, we can define these terms as follows:

- **Mean Time to Recovery (MTTRec)**: The time period between the start of the incident and the system returning to normal operation.

- **Mean Time to Resolution (MTTRes)**: The time period between the start of the incident and the time the root cause is found, and a fix is deployed.

These are the most significant metrics within the incident response life cycle. After all, they tell us when the system is back to normal operation, but they are not granular enough to be able to optimize incident management practices alone. For this purpose, we can subdivide MTTRes as follows:

- **Mean Time to Detect (MTTD)**: Also called Mean Time to Identify (MTTI), it refers to the time period between the start of the incident and when the incident is detected either by a human or an automated alert.

- **Mean Time to Know (MTTK)**: Time period between the detection of the regression and the time when the root cause of the incident is found.

- **Mean Time to Fix (MTTF)**: Time spent between when the root cause is identified and a fix is deployed.

- **Mean Time to Verify (MTTV)**: Time period between a fix deployed and the solution has been verified as successful.

Figure 1-1 illustrates how these key metrics may relate to each other in a scenario where the system may self-heal by temporarily routing traffic away from failing components and where observability can make an impact in optimizing incident response.

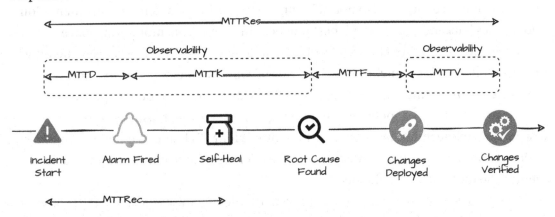

Figure 1-1. *Observability in the incident response timeline*

Observability tooling focuses on reducing MTTD, MTTK, and MTTV. It tries to answer two major questions:

- Is my system behaving as expected? (MTTD, MTTV)

- Why is my system not behaving as expected? (MTTK)

These two questions may sound similar, but the telemetry requirements to be able to answer them are considerably different. Until recently, most efforts had been focused on producing vast amounts of telemetry data to assess if our systems are behaving as expected, leaving the debugging experience untouched at best and often making it more complex, relying on prior knowledge of dependent subsystems. With new observability standards and tooling, effort is now being put into making sure that all this telemetry data can be correlated to provide the context needed to find out "what changed" when something goes wrong.

The popularization of microservice architectures and continuous deployment pipelines has had the effect of improving resiliency and speeding up feedback loops. We can automatically deploy and validate changes faster than ever. Considering defective changes can normally be rolled back as fast as they were deployed in the first place, and often with no human intervention, MTTF has been drastically reduced. Long gone are the days of weekly or monthly deployments that would take hours to roll out or roll back. We can now fail fast and recover fast, and that is a key quality of highly reliable systems and fast velocity teams.

The monitoring field has spent considerable efforts in optimizing MTTD and MTTV to support these faster feedback loops. These are necessary to maintain reliability, as failing fast requires to be notified as efficiently as possible when regressions occur and to know when services are back to normal. Improvements in open-source instrumentation and metrics backends, paired with best practices in operational monitoring, have enabled teams to monitor key aspects of their system and to reduce alert spam, helping organizations to achieve higher velocity. And yet, when an incident occurs, most teams are still left with rudimental debugging workflows involving component-specific metric dashboards and a sea of application logs being produced by increasingly complex distributed architectures. It is now time to optimize for MTTK and to empower engineers to debug complex distributed systems with the telemetry context necessary to easily identify the root cause of incidents.

The main goal of observability is to provide this debugging context out of the box using standardized telemetry conventions. To automatically correlate anomalies from different signals like metrics, logs, and traces, exported from multiple services, under one single holistic debugging experience. This allows us to understand how regressions in different components affect other dependencies and, ultimately, lower the cognitive load associated with answering the question "why is my system not behaving as expected?"

Context and Correlation

As explained in the previous section, observability starts with monitoring the current state of a system, and we have gotten quite good at it over the years! Initially, custom instrumentation was not easy to implement. Most metrics were not application specific, provided by the underlying host itself (CPU, memory, network, etc.), and you could consider yourself fortunate if you had a way to produce and query structured logs. At this point, Application Performance Monitoring (APM) vendors saw the value in providing automatic instrumentation and a unified experience to query system and application insights. Then, with the popularization of open-source metrics and logging frameworks, along with the release of a vast array of technologies to collect, transport, and query this data, everything changed. The fact that we could now start to easily instrument specific key aspects of our applications, paired with the increasing adoption of microservice architectures, resulted in an explosion in log volumes and metric cardinality. From a model where we had one source of telemetry with well-defined system boundaries and relatively well-known failure modes, we moved onto architectures with many more moving parts, each with their own failure modes and interdependencies, each producing their own unique telemetry. The toil and cognitive load to operate these systems increased exponentially.

Faced with this problem, teams that would instrument and create alerts for every known failure mode for a given application started to realize that this is a counter-productive pattern, especially in well-designed distributed systems implementing self-healing and resiliency best practices. Alert spam became a reality, having very damaging effects on MTTRes, as unactionable alerts would get in the way of business-critical alerts that risked going unnoticed. Thankfully, the adoption of Service Level Agreements (SLAs) and Service Level Objectives (SLOs), and the focus on alerting on regressions that would affect progress toward these, created healthier incident response workflows, as they allowed teams to focus on meaningful regressions. Nevertheless, the vast volumes of metrics and application logs instrumented and stored kept increasing. After all, the only way that one could debug a service in production is by asking the right questions from telemetry backends to bring out the information needed to identify the root cause of an incident. The more data stored, the more questions that can be answered. This a well-known troubleshooting pattern: we look at manually crafted dashboards displaying metrics that allow us to follow the USE (Usage Saturation Error) method, popularized by Brendan Gregg and explained in detail at *www.brendangregg.com/usemethod.html*. This may lead us to investigations into other metrics or application logs to explore high-granularity events that may exhibit some degree of correlation.

One can think of the following questions when following the pattern described previously on large-scale distributed systems:

- Are the metrics in our dashboard the most significant?

- Could there be other deviating signals we are missing?

- Is the issue caused by our service, or is it a direct or indirect dependency?

- How are our service failures affecting other services, or our end users?

- What are the most meaningful error messages to look for that may correlate to this regression?

- How can we be sure that the error messages we obtained correlate to the regression?

- How much of the telemetry data being produced is noise and does not add any value to this investigation?

Answering all these questions requires extensive knowledge of the system under operation. For example, an experienced engineer may know that increased response time in their service may be related to more garbage collections happening, or to specific exceptions they may be able to find in logs. This may be okay in simple, almost monolithic systems, providing you can afford all the necessary learning and training for new engineers being onboarded in the team, but cognitive load has limits. Consider the illustration in Figure 1-2, representing the dependencies between different services in a very minimalistic distributed system. Even for the most well-versed engineer, with broad experience in the platform it operates, it would be extremely difficult to know every single failure mode that the system, as a whole, may encounter. This is where observability comes to the rescue, with the two most crucial features it delivers: *context* and *correlation*.

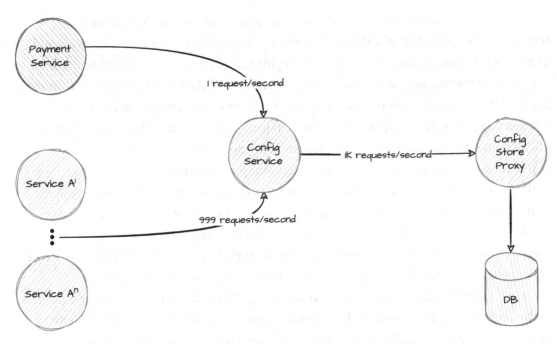

Figure 1-2. *Performance regression in a distributed system*

Distributed systems have delivered higher degrees of resilience, designed for failure and self-healing, but they have brought with them new and unpredicted failure modes. Consider the following scenario based on the diagram shown in Figure 1-2: a response time regression on Payment Service is detected with payments taking considerably longer than expected. In terms of throughput, this service is a small client of the Config Service, which receives requests from many other services and relies on Config Store Proxy to fulfill transactions. From the point of view of Payment Service, all transactions are slower, and its owners, which happen to be a different team to Config Service, have manually correlated this to their requests to Config Service taking longer than expected. They contact Config Service owners, but as Payment Service is not a major contributor in terms of throughput, the owners of Config Service have not had any alerts fired. Their 95th percentile latency remained constant in their dashboards. All lights are green. The owners of Config Service start investigating, and they indeed see a small increase in latency to Config Store Proxy for certain types of requests that may be related to how the data is indexed in the DB. How can the owners of Config Service assert with confidence that the regression in Payment Service is caused by increased latency in Config Store Proxy? This is a simple scenario, but consider this across a large-scale distributed system with hundreds of services and transactions involving dozens of services. To debug these scenarios, we need *context*.

In the previous example, if we were to propagate telemetry context between services in the form of standard transactional attributes like a transaction ID, we could identify individual transactions that made Payment Service slower and find patterns within these transactions alone (i.e., without considering the rest of requests in Config Service) that unequivocally demonstrate where the root of the regression lies. For instance, a specific type of query with poor DB indexing. Providing this context is the role of context propagation in distributed tracing. You can think of it as turbocharged application logging, where we no longer need independent streams of logs per service replica, but instead we're able to look at high-granularity telemetry present in individual transactions (i.e., traces) across services and replicas, instrumented with timings for every meaningful operation (i.e, span). An incident that used to involve multiple teams investigating on a call can now be identified by a single person with no prior knowledge of the system simply by looking at anomalies emanating from tracing data.

This alone is a major improvement in reducing MTTK, but let's take one step back in the incident timeline. In our failure scenario earlier, we mentioned that Payment Service engineers manually identified that their response time regression was due to slowness in the Config Service. Normally, this is something that an on-call engineer does by looking at different metrics and visually comparing that some of them – payment response and config response time in this case – are moving in the wrong direction at the same time. I have personally had to move graphs around in the screen to check that they visually align more often than I'd like to admit! This, as mentioned previously, requires prior knowledge of the system and an experienced engineer to know what metrics are relevant. For instance, we may instinctively go and check CPU throttling or garbage collection metrics if we see the tail latency for a service increases. Wouldn't it be considerably faster for the person debugging an incident if their observability tooling could, out of the box, not only tell them that these two metrics are related but also bring out individual examples of transactions that contributed to this anomaly?

Automatic *correlation* can drastically reduce the time needed to identify the source of anomalies, but it is not magic. It relies on different components sharing the same context to be instrumented following a certain set of semantic conventions that allow for telemetry data to be joined across multiple dimensions. Agreeing on these semantic conventions and then enforcing them across services and teams is something with which organizations have struggled for a long time. Observability tooling must make it easy to instrument and consume telemetry data that follows these pre-agreed conventions and to maximize the potential for automatic correlation when anomalies are detected.

In addition to enabling faster MTTK, telemetry context and automatic correlation also allow to reduce what can be referred to as *telemetry noise*. This is the type of telemetry data that does not aid in the monitoring or debugging of production incidents, and it just sits in the background consuming resources and incurring in higher infrastructure or transfer costs. Never queried, never alerted on, never seen by human eyes. It also risks increasing response time for queries to the underlying telemetry backends affected by the extra load, and, in the same way as alert noise, it may hinder incident response by polluting results with irrelevant information. Considering the distributed system example presented previously, one could go through the effort of manually propagating a transaction ID through these services and store application logs or metrics for every client and server request with its attributes and timings, in every service replica. In any medium to large-scale organization, this may become prohibitively expensive if low delay and fast access to this data are needed, as it is the case of incident response. Furthermore, if we were to follow that approach, more than 95% of the data would probably be of no debugging interest. It wouldn't be related to erroneous or slow user transactions, and it would be a lot larger of a sample size than it's needed to evaluate what "good" transactions look like. This could naively be solved by logging only error and slow requests, plus a certain random percentage of the rest, but a service replica alone would not have the necessary information to assess if the current request is part of a good or a bad transaction in order to make that decision. It can only see what's currently part of its service boundaries. Observability tooling and telemetry standards enable smarter ways of sampling this data, being able to consider complete transactions when making decisions, using this context to store only the information that is relevant to debug regressions at a system level.

This concept of not storing as much telemetry data as technically possible may sound counterintuitive to many, especially when we consider that high-granularity data is a requirement for efficient observability. With storage and compute resources becoming cheaper, there has been a trend over the years to just "store everything in case you need it later". This made sense at a point where debugging regressions required prior and extensive knowledge of the systems under operation to ask the right questions from telemetry backends. After all, we would not know what questions we may need to ask in the middle of an incident. We have previously established that it is no longer feasible for humans, as experienced as they can be, to predict every single failure mode a large distributed system may encounter, and if we rely on observability systems to tell us what is wrong, we should also rely on them to discard any information that is not required for debugging.

This brings up an interesting topic: the separation between observability data and auditing or business data. The requirements for these are vastly different, and yet, due to the historic need to store as much telemetry data as possible, they were often produced, transported, and stored using the same data pipelines. Even though possible at small scale, simultaneously meeting requirements like low delay and completeness becomes exponentially more difficult (and expensive) as systems become larger and their complexity increases. The focus of observability systems is to provide fast retrieval of recent telemetry data and to automatically bring out insights that can facilitate debugging. For this purpose, delayed telemetry is as good as no telemetry. In a certain way, operating a software system is similar to driving a car, as we need telemetry to inform our decisions. I think we would all rather drive a car that tells us our current speed 99.9% of the time than one that tells us our speed 100% of the time with a ten-minute delay.

Observability helps organizations to separate use cases and requirements for different types of data. For instance, request auditing requires completeness in its datasets to be able to find individual records that match a given condition. Missing records could have a damaging impact. However, it is normally acceptable to receive this data with a certain delay and for query performance to not be a primary concern. This type of data can then be optimized for consistency and cheaper storage, rather than the low delay and automatic correlation provided by observability systems.

Understanding the different types of telemetry signals (i.e., metrics, traces, logs), and their features, constraints, and uses cases, is also a crucial part of maintaining a healthy observability function. By being able to correlate these signals under one single set of standards, observability can help reduce telemetry redundancy, minimize cost, and maximize performance. It enables engineers to resolve incidents faster by using the right tool for the right job.

Summary

Over the years, our systems have evolved to provide higher degrees of performance and reliability, but as all software systems, they're not free from failure. In today's modern distributed microservice architectures, the monitoring and debugging practices of yesterday are no longer enough to effectively operate systems at scale. In order to minimize the time taken to react and debug regressions in production, we need observability practices that incorporate the use of multiple telemetry signals, each for the right purpose, and observability tooling that can correlate these signals across services to provide engineers with the necessary context to pinpoint root causes in a timely manner, with minimal cognitive load.

As we will see along the chapters in this book, OpenTelemetry provides the tooling necessary to implement these best practices in a standard way across languages and frameworks, empowering developers to easily instrument software and enhance system observability.

## CHAPTER 2

How OpenTelemetry Enables Observability

In the previous chapter, we covered the *why* of observability and the value of key concepts like telemetry context and correlation to speed up incident debugging in production systems. It is now time to dive into OpenTelemetry, and the best way to start is to explain *how* this Cloud Native Computing Foundation (CNCF) project is changing the way we think about instrumenting our services to enable best practices in observability.

OpenTelemetry's Mission

Visiting *https://opentelemetry.io/community/mission/* is a great way to get introduced to the core values of OpenTelemetry and especially its mission statement:

> *To enable effective observability by making high-quality, portable telemetry ubiquitous*

Albeit short, it is packed with meaning. Starting with *effective observability*, we have seen in Chapter 1 that in modern distributed systems, this requires a holistic approach to monitoring and debugging systems, correlating different signals across services to promptly alert on regressions and then provide the necessary debugging context to efficiently find the root cause. OpenTelemetry enables this by providing open standards and tooling to instrument, collect, and transport the three main types of telemetry signals: metrics, traces, and logs. It also standardizes the way that telemetry context is propagated across signals and services and proposes a set of naming conventions to make sure that telemetry emanating from different applications can be correlated out of the box by observability frameworks and vendors.

© Daniel Gomez Blanco 2023
D. Gomez Blanco, *Practical OpenTelemetry*, https://doi.org/10.1007/978-1-4842-9075-0_2

For observability to be effective, developers must also learn to use the right type of signal for the right purpose when instrumenting and debugging systems. For instance, monitoring and alerting on SLOs becomes more reliable when dashboards and alerts are driven from low-granularity metrics rather than application logs. Nevertheless, metrics are not always the solution to aid debugging, as a high number of unique attribute values can have unwanted side effects on metrics backends. We will cover these concepts, use cases, and best practices on individual chapters across this book, giving the reader a good picture of what signal to use for what purpose. The reality is that instrumenting an application efficiently is not a trivial task. Until now, this task relied mostly on the application owner, making it especially difficult to add (and most importantly maintain) instrumentation for libraries written by third parties.

When instrumentation is tightly coupled to the telemetry platform and export pipelines that support those metrics, traces, or logs (which are often separate systems), library developers had to either choose one or multiple frameworks or simply rely on users of their library to instrument it themselves. Let's say the owner of an HTTP client wanted to produce some request and response metrics for their library; they'd have to decide on an SDK to use for those metrics (i.e., StatsD, Prometheus, etc.). The SDK of choice would not normally be compatible with other metrics backends, so users would be limited to whatever frameworks library maintainers decided to support, or library owners forced to support a myriad of different SDKs. With the proliferation of open-source frameworks in modern cloud-native systems, this can become unmanageable both for library maintainers and for their users.

By providing a set of stable, backward-compatible, loosely coupled APIs for telemetry instrumentation, OpenTelemetry enables library maintainers and application owners to instrument once and export everywhere. Developers using OpenTelemetry APIs in their libraries can rely on the fact that the telemetry they produce will be compatible with whatever SDK or protocols are used to export and transport the data. The decision on what SDK or telemetry platform to use can be deferred to whenever the application is configured and deployed. This results in code being instrumented by the right person to do it, the one that wrote it.

For these reasons, with increased adoption of OpenTelemetry in open-source and other third-party libraries and frameworks, telemetry becomes *ubiquitous*. Application owners can leverage automatic instrumentation, drastically reducing toil and engineering effort taken to obtain relevant insights from the applications they maintain.

The Power of Open Standards

Providing a set of APIs and protocols to instrument and transport telemetry does not, by itself, result in *high-quality* data. Empowering developers to rely on open, backward-compatible APIs certainly puts the responsibility of instrumenting systems in the right hands, but can you imagine what it would be like if each HTTP client library author decided to name or label metrics, like request duration for instance, differently? Or to use library-specific headers to propagate information identifying the current transaction? Building tooling to automatically correlate signals and offer rich debugging context using data produced this way would be nearly impossible to maintain as new libraries and frameworks become available. Unfortunately, you don't have to imagine it. This is the world we've been living in for many years, resulting in disjointed metrics, traces, and logs. OpenTelemetry would fail in its mission without a set of standards that APIs and developers must adhere to.

Standards shape our understanding of the world around us, and they facilitate communication between independent groups of people that would otherwise find it almost impossible to collaborate. For instance, when we consider the International System of Units (SI) definitions, these enable a research team in Spain to easily collaborate with a research team in India. Although both may speak different languages, they both understand what a second, or a meter, represent. They can build on these standards and easily talk about other concepts like speed, or acceleration, because they can be expressed using commonly understood units: meters and seconds. Technology that relies on these standards can be easily assimilated by its users, as there is a common set of assumptions to define measurements. Most importantly, standards make our lives safer. Miscommunicating measurements can lead to very damaging side effects. One of the most notable cases was the loss of the Mars Climate Orbiter on September 23, 1999, when the spacecraft vanished as it approached Mars closer than expected while inserting into its target orbit and either disintegrated into the planet's atmosphere or escaped its gravitational pull. The fate of the orbiter remains unknown to this date. The failure in measurement was attributed to a mismatch in units used by two different software systems: one by NASA using SI units and the other one by Lockheed Martin using US customary units.

The adoption of SI units as a standard in all scientific fields has boosted research collaboration, leading to faster and safer advancements in technology. Unfortunately, standards in software telemetry are in a much more delicate situation, and we don't have to contemplate interactions at a global scale to see these flaws. Miscommunication during incident response can happen between teams within the same organization. It is not uncommon in incident calls for engineers to manually try to find correlations between different metrics or logs, each using different naming and attributes, resulting in longer times to identify and resolve the root cause.

OpenTelemetry provides a set of standard naming conventions, protocols, and signal and context propagation formats so that

- Developers have a clear contract to instrument applications knowing telemetry will be supported by most frameworks and vendors

- Clients and servers can propagate telemetry context between each other using commonly supported specifications

- Application owners can debug complex distributed systems with minimal added cognitive load, minimizing misunderstandings during incident response

- Observability vendors and open-source telemetry platforms can provide automatic analysis tooling to facilitate debugging based on the same open standards

We will cover these standards in detail in the next chapters, but for now, let's consider the Payment Service regression detailed in Chapter 1, and we'll evaluate how a system instrumented with OpenTelemetry could drastically reduce MTTK. Figure 2-1 annotates the previous use case with some key signals to consider.

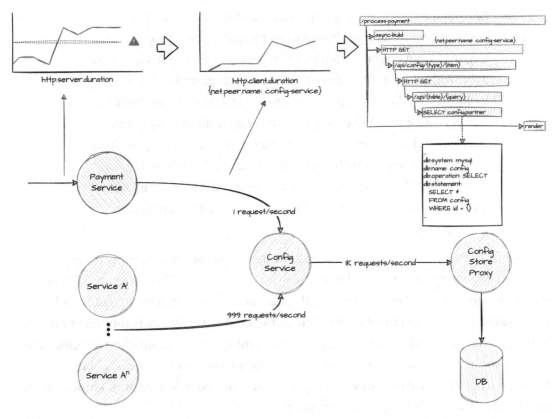

Figure 2-1. *Distributed system using semantic conventions*

With this in mind, let's see how a possible debugging workflow could benefit from using open standards:

1. Payment Service engineers get alerted for a regression on an `http.server.duration` metric that's generated out of the box by their HTTP server, measuring the response time of their application.

2. Their observability tooling can quickly show a correlation to their `http.client.duration` metric, automatically instrumented by their HTTP client, with a `net.peer.name: config-service` attribute describing requests made to Config Service. Both metrics seem to follow a similar regression pattern. This can also be linked to individual transactions involving Payment Service that contain `HTTP GET` operations decorated with the same `net.peer.name: config-service` attribute.

3. Although Payment Service only amounts for 0.1% of the requests going to Config Service, thanks to automatic context propagation, engineers can directly examine problematic transactions and look at individual operations annotated with high-granularity data, including the database queries executed by Config Store Proxy, which is not a direct dependency. They can immediately see that queries to a particular table are the root cause of these regressions without the need to involve any other team in the debugging process. Database owners can then examine the query and adjust indexing appropriately on the table or add caching to optimize query performance.

This is a very simple scenario, but without standards for naming conventions and context propagation, it would have involved two or three different teams having to coordinate their response and manually correlate all these signals. In real-world distributed systems, the tree of dependencies for a service is normally multiple times wider and deeper, making this task exponentially more complex and often unachievable for humans in a reasonable timeframe. Hence, the goal of effective observability is to lower the cognitive load of debugging regressions to the point where prior knowledge of the systems involved is not generally needed.

Small subsystems like the one presented in Figure 2-1 can, by themselves, reap the benefits of using OpenTelemetry within their boundaries, but it's easy to see how the value of these open standards increases with the number of components instrumented in large, distributed architectures. After all, standards are only useful if they're widely adopted. Otherwise, they risk becoming just another competing standard, contributing to the problem they originally sought to solve.

In addition to making adoption as easy as possible, OpenTelemetry was designed, from conception, to avoid the problem of becoming another competing standard, as it was created as a merge of two other widely used standards, now deprecated. The need for telemetry standardization was already recognized in the cloud community long before the OpenTelemetry project started, and two competing solutions with similar goals were gaining popularity: OpenTracing (a CNCF project) and OpenCensus (a Google Open Source community project). In May 2019, maintainers of these projects decided to merge them into a single one, using the lessons and experience acquired from them to kickstart OpenTelemetry. Readers that are already familiar with any of these projects will see that OpenTelemetry has incorporated elements of both projects into its design.

The Shift in Vendor Added Value

The final key aspect to discuss when analyzing OpenTelemetry's mission in detail is the goal to make telemetry *portable*, enabling engineers and organizations to remain vendor neutral when instrumenting their systems, allowing to easily move between telemetry platforms. We have discussed the positive implications for developers when instrumenting their services, now able to defer the decision on what backend or protocols to use until the application configuration stage. However, the consequences for organizations wanting to adopt a given open-source telemetry platform or third-party vendor for their observability tooling are equally important.

As it is the case with instrumentation standards, OpenTelemetry would not achieve its goals of being a true observability standard without wide adoption from telemetry backends and observability platforms. Being part of CNCF gives OpenTelemetry the support of a large community of developers, users, and service providers that collaborate on a large array of popular open-source projects to develop, deploy, and operate scalable systems on cloud computing platforms. At the start of August 2022, this included 825 members totalling $22T in market cap and $51.6B funding, collaborating in 1,125 projects (up-to-date information is available at *https://landscape.cncf.io*). Many of these members are observability vendors contributing to OpenTelemetry like Grafana Labs, New Relic, Splunk, Lightstep, and many others, but there are also other tech giants like Microsoft, Google, Amazon, or Red Hat actively contributing to the project. Virtually, all organizations working in observability have nowadays integrated OpenTelemetry support as part of their product offering, and many have started to rely solely in this project to ingest telemetry from their customers. At the same time, open-source projects that are part of CNCF like Prometheus, Jaeger, Pixie, or Grafana Tempo, among others, have also integrated OpenTelemetry to handle different types of signals.

CNCF projects have maturity levels of sandbox, incubating, and graduated, which correspond to the innovators, early adopters, and early majority tiers in the diagram contained in Figure 2-2, originally proposed by Geoffrey A. Moore in his 1991 marketing book *Crossing the Chasm*. Thanks to the support from CNCF members, the wider open-source community, and early adopters running OpenTelemetry at scale in production workloads, OpenTelemetry reached *incubating* state in August 2021.

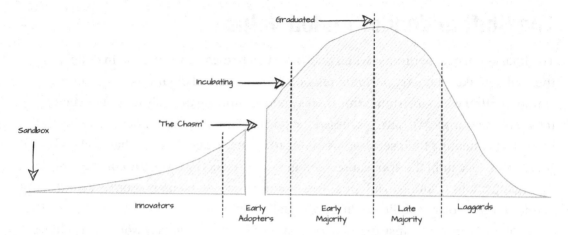

Figure 2-2. *The technology adoption life cycle corresponding to CNCF project maturity levels as seen in* `www.cncf.io/projects`

To achieve this maturity level, a CNCF project must demonstrate to CNCF's Technical Oversight Committee that

- It's being used successfully in production at a certain level of quality and scope

- It has a healthy number of contributors and contributions

- It has a clear versioning scheme and security processes in place

- Its specifications have at least one public reference implementation

Having achieved these milestones means that the project has attained a maturity level past the early adoption phase and into the early majority adoption stage. As such, adopting OpenTelemetry is a decision no longer associated with the intrinsic risk of a CNCF sandbox project. The project is stable, and this changes the playing field for companies wanting to improve their observability tooling.

There are many articles, blog posts, and books in the public domain on the topic of "buy vs. build" and how organizations may decide on one or the other depending on multiple factors. We do not intend to discuss the advantages of one over the other in this book, but we can evaluate how OpenTelemetry may influence this decision. Until recently, organizations were presented with two choices:

- Use an observability vendor, including their instrumentation agents and integrations of vendor-specific SDKs and protocols to produce, export, and transport telemetry data.

- Use open-source telemetry platforms and allocate engineering effort
  to maintain infrastructure, instrumentation, and pipelines, normally
  backed by multiple backends.

The value of observability vendors was clear: providing automatic instrumentation
for supported systems and libraries via postcompilation agents and a unified way to
access all telemetry data. The engineering effort to instrument services was reduced, and
the debugging experience improved, at least theoretically. The price to pay, however,
was too high for some, and not just in terms of financial cost. Relying on vendor-specific
agents, SDKs, and protocols across a large organization normally results in vendor lock-
in, as migrating to another vendor or to an open-source solution would require teams
to install different agents and, even worse, change their custom instrumentation code.
This is not a trivial task when multiple teams are involved, requiring coordination across
a whole organization. Additionally, any automatic instrumentation would rely on the
chosen observability vendor to support it and to keep up to date with upstream changes
in open-source libraries. For early adopters of multiple cloud-native technologies, this
could hinder their adoption progress.

On the other hand, we have previously seen the issues arising from disjointed
telemetry when it comes to quickly finding the root cause of an incident. Organizations
implementing open-source telemetry observability solutions would spend most of the
engineering effort in maintaining infrastructure, pipelines, and internal tooling, often
not having enough time or engineering budget to spend on helping teams to instrument
their services to produce high-quality telemetry data that can be correlated across
services and signals. Custom instrumentation would not be vendor-locked, but it would
nevertheless be coupled to the open-source SDK of choice, making it difficult for teams
to migrate to other solutions.

As illustrated in Figure 2-3, OpenTelemetry drastically changes the telemetry
landscape, providing a new angle to approach the "buy vs. build" decision. For
observability vendors, this means that they can rely on library developers and platform
providers to instrument their systems using open standards, focusing their efforts
instead on providing advanced analysis and correlation over well-structured, standard
telemetry data. In a similar fashion, open-source telemetry platforms can build on top of
the same open standards to provide uniform access across telemetry signals.

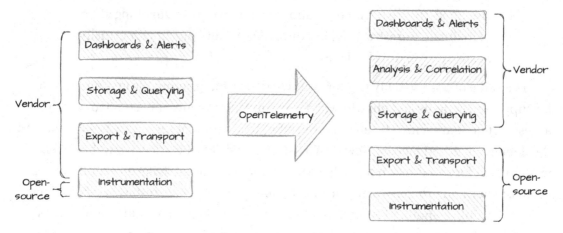

Figure 2-3. *The shift in vendor vs. open-source boundaries*

For organizations desiring to improve observability, this means freedom of choice and the assurance that the instrumentation and transport layers can remain unaffected on large, company-wide migrations between different vendors or open-source solutions. Adopting OpenTelemetry puts organizations in a more advantageous position as they work on defining their long-term observability strategy, focused on open standards to produce high-quality telemetry data, wherever that data needs to be exported to.

Summary

OpenTelemetry has changed the way we think about instrumenting services and exporting data to telemetry backends, going from isolated services and signals to correlated views that describe distributed systems with high-quality, contextualized data. As a merge of OpenTracing and OpenCensus, two popular telemetry projects, it stands on the shoulders of giants. Thanks to a strong community of observability vendors, tech companies, and individual contributors, it has become one of the most active CNCF projects, passed its early adopter phase and into its early majority stage within the technology adoption life cycle.

In Chapter 3, we'll explore some of the concepts and building blocks that help OpenTelemetry deliver on its mission to provide open standards to instrument, export, and transport telemetry in a vendor-agnostic manner.

PART II

OpenTelemetry Components and Best Practices

CHAPTER 3

OpenTelemetry Fundamentals

After having discussed the challenges of implementing observability using traditional operational monitoring practices and how OpenTelemetry proposes a different approach to solve those, it is finally time to dive into the project fundamentals. In this chapter, we'll cover key concepts that will help the reader get a general grasp of the project structure and how different OpenTelemetry components relate to each other. We will then go through details of semantic conventions, as one of the key cross-signal aspects of portable, high-quality telemetry data.

OpenTelemetry Specification

Providing cross-language and cross-platform support for telemetry data is one of the key values of OpenTelemetry. This would be difficult to achieve in an efficient, reliable, and standard way without having a set of agreed guidelines, requirements, and expectations that developers must adhere to when instrumenting systems or providing telemetry client support.

The OpenTelemetry specification is a living document that captures the requirements that any component must meet in order to consider its implementation compliant. This includes API, SDK, data structures, semantic conventions, protocols, and other cross-language components. It ensures a level of uniformity and stability between OpenTelemetry packages in different languages and frameworks, and it guarantees support across telemetry backends and observability tooling. It also proposes design principles and best practices to be considered by OpenTelemetry maintainers and end users instrumenting their services.

© Daniel Gomez Blanco 2023
D. Gomez Blanco, *Practical OpenTelemetry*, https://doi.org/10.1007/978-1-4842-9075-0_3

In February 2021, version 1.0.0 of the specification was released, marking the API and SDK specifications for Tracing, Context, and Baggage stable. This was a huge milestone for the project, as it meant that trace clients could be implemented to be OpenTelemetry compliant. Shortly after, release candidates were made available for Java, Python, Go, Node.js, Erlang, and .Net, which later turned into 1.0 releases, respectively.

As a living document, the specification is constantly being reviewed, improved, and extended as needed. Bug fixes and other small changes can be contributed via the usual open-source processes for projects hosted in GitHub, opening issues or pull requests, and getting them reviewed and merged in collaboration with maintainers. Larger pieces of work, especially changes that would add, modify, or extend functionality across languages and components, require a more formal process involving the creation and approval of OpenTelemetry Enhancement Proposals (OTEP) under *https://github.com/open-telemetry/oteps*. This process, based on other preexisting processes like the Kubernetes Enhancement Proposal or the Rust RFC, ensures that all necessary aspects are considered to either approve or reject strategic changes that could affect the project direction in a meaningful way.

For instance, OTEP (*https://github.com/open-telemetry/oteps/pull/111*) illustrates an addition to the OpenTelemetry specification to standardize the use of automatic resource detection mechanisms that, as we'll see later in the chapter, add default attributes to all telemetry exported by a producer, crucial for debugging purposes. The proposal takes preexisting solutions existing in OpenCensus and certain OpenTelemetry language implementations and proposes a common approach for all.

After an OTEP is approved and integrated into the specification, issues are created in the relevant components affected by the proposal, and when the requested changes are implemented, their status is updated accordingly to indicate their compliance against a specific version of the specification.

Specification documents may also have a *status*, normally at the top of the document, to indicate their current life cycle stage. The possible values are as follows:

- **No explicit status**: Equivalent to Experimental (see the following text).

- **Experimental:** Breaking changes are allowed to the specification and, consequently, to its implementations.

- **Stable**: Breaking changes are not allowed, enabling long-term dependencies on its implementations.

- **Deprecated**: Only editorial changes are allowed.

In addition to these, a document may also be in *feature-freeze* state, which can apply to any life cycle state. This indicates that maintainers are not accepting new features to it, normally to allow the specification community to focus on certain other aspects.

Note   The up-to-date version of the OpenTelemetry specification, including current status, is publicly hosted at `https://opentelemetry.io/docs/reference/specification`.

Signals and Components

OpenTelemetry is structured around the concept of signals, with each signal being a type of telemetry in a particular area of observability. Some signals, like metrics and logs, have been used in the software industry for many years; others are a more recent addition to the observability toolkit, as is the case of traces and baggage. In addition to signals, OpenTelemetry also provides a common subsystem called context, shared by all signals to propagate in-band data as part of a distributed transaction, needed to correlate telemetry across services and languages, which is key to any system implementing observability.

Historically, developers did not always have the full telemetry toolkit at their disposal when instrumenting services, as clients had to be compatible with the backend where data was exported. By providing unified access to different types of telemetry in a standard manner, OpenTelemetry empowers developers to choose the most appropriate signal for each use case.

Regardless of the signal under consideration, telemetry instrumentation is a cross-cutting concern by design. It requires applications to depend on instrumentation clients in some way across vast parts of the code base. For instance, in order to generate metrics from a given function execution, we need to use a metrics client within or around that function code. The same metrics client is used to instrument parts of the application that share no responsibilities between each other. This lack of separation of concerns is not generally a good software design principle, but there are certain cases, such as providing an application-wide feature like telemetry, where it is unavoidable. As we have seen in previous chapters, with most metrics clients, this can have unwanted side effects if these cross-cutting dependencies are also coupled to the implementation and transport layers.

To minimize the impact of this unavoidable lack of separation of concerns, each signal in OpenTelemetry is carefully designed to decouple cross-cutting packages from their implementations. Each signal has four main packages:

- **API**: Public interfaces for cross-cutting concerns, along with minimal implementation. Applications and libraries can directly depend on it for their telemetry instrumentation.

- **Semantic conventions**: Attributes used to name and decorate telemetry in a standard way across signals and languages for common concepts like cloud providers, deployments, protocols, and many others.

- **SDK**: Reference implementation for the API, provided by the OpenTelemetry project. Although it also provides public interfaces, these are not part of the API, as they're used to control self-contained *constructors* and *plugin interfaces*. For example, we can use a plugin interface to control what trace exporter to use (e.g., Jaeger exporter) and a constructor to obtain an instance of a tracer for manual instrumentation. The SDK also includes certain core plugins, like OTLP exporters or TraceContext propagators, required by the OpenTelemetry specification.

- **Contrib packages**: Plugins and instrumentation packages for popular open-source projects, maintained by the OpenTelemetry community. These are optional packages that application owners may decide to depend on in order to automatically instrument their applications, or to export telemetry to their backends of choice.

Figure 3-1 illustrates the main OpenTelemetry packages and the split between cross-cutting packages, with minimal implementation, and self-contained packages, providing most of the implementation.

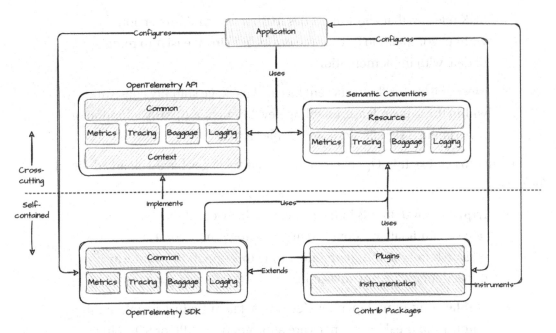

Figure 3-1. *OpenTelemetry architecture overview*

By decoupling API and semantic conventions from their implementations, OpenTelemetry can provide strong stability guarantees. This, however, requires instrumentation authors, both on third-party libraries and end-user applications, to write code that depends solely on the API and avoid coupling their instrumentation code with SDK or contrib packages that do not have the same stability requirements.

Tip   Minimizing SDK touch points within applications is a good way of increasing stability, keeping only API usage as a cross-cutting concern. This will be covered in detail in Chapter 11.

Stability and Design Principles

The design of telemetry clients discussed previously would not be very valuable without a set of guarantees on which application owners can rely when instrumenting their services. OpenTelemetry focuses on providing

- APIs that *always* remain backward compatible to allow libraries and frameworks to be instrumented by their authors without sacrificing long-term stability for the application owner

- SDK releases that allow upgrades to their latest minor version, without compilation or runtime errors, making it easier to remain up to date with implementations

- Mechanisms to allow different levels of package stability coexisting within the same release, enabling development and early adoption of experimental signals alongside stable signals

In order to achieve this, OpenTelemetry signal packages have a clearly defined *life cycle*:

- **Experimental**: In this initial stage, which covers alpha, beta, and release candidate versions, breaking changes may come as a minor version bump on the client integrating this signal, so long-term dependencies are not advisable.

- **Stable**: Long-term dependencies can be taken against signals at this point, as no breaking changes are allowed to the API, or SDK plugin interfaces and constructors, unless a major version bump occurs.

- **Deprecated**: Signals may become deprecated after a replacement signal becomes stable, still respecting the same stability guarantees.

- **Removed**: As a breaking change, removing a signal from the release would require a major version bump.

This signal life cycle gives OpenTelemetry contributors and instrumentation authors the capacity to develop new signals in a less restricted way while allowing teams and organizations to plan their integration as they transition through the life cycle. Individual teams may start testing an experimental client in alpha or beta releases, making sure that they're ready to adopt it in production, but relying on such a client across an organization is not recommended, especially if the API is not considered stable yet. The current status of signals and their main components is available at https:// opentelemetry.io/status.

Note   OpenTelemetry maintainers currently have no intention of releasing a major version of OpenTelemetry past 1.x, so stability is guaranteed long term for stable signals in current 1.x releases.

Although a version 2.x of OpenTelemetry is not planned, the OpenTelemetry specification has a clear definition for long-term support. In the event of a new major release, the previous major release APIs will be supported for a minimum of three years, and SDKs and contrib packages for a minimum of one year.

The stability guarantees covered so far are mostly aimed at dependency management and package compatibility, but the OpenTelemetry specification also covers *design guidelines* for instrumentation authors to provide a reliable runtime experience. Telemetry instrumentation is not usually something critical from the point of view of application business logic. It is preferable to incur in telemetry data loss than to affect the performance or reliability of the systems being instrumented. Without going into specification details, the main goals of these design guidelines include the following:

- No unhandled exceptions are thrown from APIs or SDKs during runtime. Even when used incorrectly, implementations return safe defaults in this case.

- The API returns no-op implementations if no SDK is configured. This allows library authors to safely instrument their code even if users are not configuring OpenTelemetry.

- Implementations are designed with a low performance overhead in mind to never block end-user applications and to never consume unbounded memory. Additionally, rigorous performance benchmarking is carried out on individual packages.

With these guarantees in mind, OpenTelemetry users should be confident that not only their instrumentation will be supported long term but also that it won't degrade their production workloads, regardless of where or how it's used.

Tracing

Our simple Payment Service example from Chapters 1 and 2 showed us that when debugging a distributed system, transactional context propagated across services is key. With high-granularity insights into individual transactions, we can automatically correlate regressions between systems separated by multiple layers of dependencies. This is where tracing really excels.

Note   Across this book, we refer to transactions not as database transactions but rather as logical units of work, normally implemented by multiple operations and services within a distributed system.

In a way, traces are a form of supercharged, standardized, structured application logs. Historically, in order to be able to debug individual transactions, application owners would add attributes like `transaction_id` or `correlation_id` to their logs. With a considerable engineering effort, they may have been able to propagate these between services automatically by adopting custom plugins within their organization to extract and inject these attributes using request headers and decorate logs with them using mechanisms like Mapped Diagnostic Context (MDC) in Java. Even after all this work, engineers debugging incidents would only be able to look at individual transactions, manually joining these logs by running queries against their metrics backend. These backends would not normally be able to handle complex queries to show all logs for all transactions starting at a given service, or any other query joining these logs across services and transactions. At least not in a timely fashion. This is certainly not effective observability.

Distributed tracing, making use of context propagation, automates and standardizes this practice adopted by many organizations. Although it is most commonly used in client-server models, tracing can be used in a variety of ways. The common defining factor is the concept of a set of events that are part of a single common operation, connected by causal relationships between them. In OpenTelemetry, these events are called *Spans*. Although spans are part of a trace, there is no single event that defines a trace, but rather the relationships between spans.

Spans represent single operations within a transaction. One can think of them as individual structured logs measuring time spent in a given operation, decorated with a collection of standard attributes that allow linking them to other spans. In Figure 3-2, we can see an example of a simple distributed trace describing a common operation handled by different services. As spans contain start and end timestamps, it is normally convenient to visualize them within a time dimension.

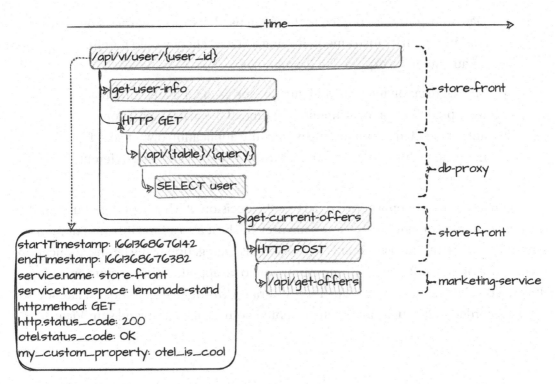

Figure 3-2. *A simple distributed trace over time involving three services:* store-front, db-proxy, *and* marketing-service

Metrics

Metrics are one of the most widely used telemetry signals. They allow us to monitor measurements over time using different aggregation functions in a more stable way than tracing or logs. This, in turn, enables teams to visualize and alert on key performance indicators represented as a collection of time series, that is, sequences of data points over time annotated with a unique combination of attributes.

Generating metrics has become increasingly easier and more powerful in the past few years. Open-source projects like Prometheus, StatsD, Telegraf, Spring Metrics, or Dropwizard Metrics, among many others, have empowered engineers to instrument applications and export metrics using client libraries, container sidecars, or agents. This popularity has often resulted in an overuse of high-cardinality metrics for debugging purposes in scenarios where distributed tracing would be a better fit. Before OpenTelemetry, all existing metrics clients had at least a couple of constraints in common from the perspective of the instrumentation author:

- Data transport was coupled to the client used to export metrics. For example, metrics instrumented using a StatsD client would require an adapter to be exported to Prometheus.

- The aggregation function and dimensions used for a measurement were predefined at instrumentation time. If the instrumentation author decided to create a histogram, the application owner could not change this easily without an extra conversion step in a different component.

OpenTelemetry not only allows deferring the decision of what exporter to use until the application is configured, as we've seen previously. It also allows instrumentation authors to record raw measurements with a default aggregation while letting application owners decide on a different data representation to be applied if they require so. This is illustrated in Figure 3-3, where we can see how raw *Measurements* for request latency can be recorded individually and then presented both as histogram and sum *Views*.

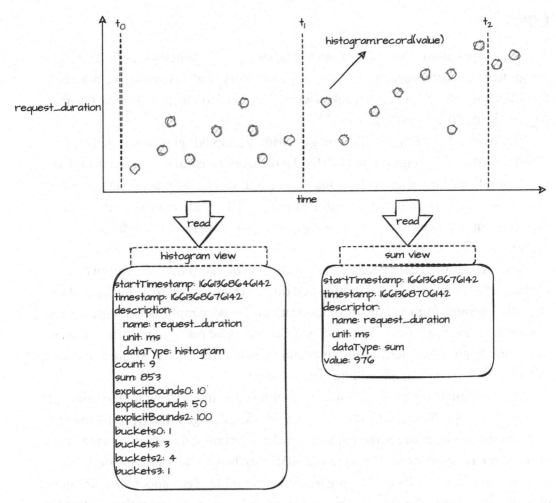

Figure 3-3. *Recoding a histogram with* `histogram.record()` *and reading it with the default aggregation or with a sum aggregation*

In addition to this flexibility to defer decisions on exporters and aggregations, by being integrated within the same shared context propagation ecosystem as distributed traces, OpenTelemetry metrics allow one to decorate metric data points with *Exemplars*, that is, links to other signals like distributed tracing spans, that can be useful to see high-granularity data for the current active telemetry context when the metric event was generated.

Logs

Logs have been around for longer than any other type of telemetry signal. They are so integrated into every language, library, and framework, and so easy to use, that the first thing most developers still think of when they need to measure a single event is `logger.info("This just happened")`.

The Twelve-Factor App methodology, a widely adopted set of best practices for cloud-native deployments crafted by Heroku developers in 2011, already identified the decoupling of applications from log routing and storage as a desirable pattern and recommended writing all logs, unbuffered, to `stdout`, allowing the execution environment to process this stream and export logs to backends accordingly (*https://12factor.net/logs*).

Although easy to generate, the debugging value of traditional logs within a distributed system is massively diminished due to a lack of context, especially when logs are generated from hundreds, or thousands, of service replicas. With the default approach of "log everything" followed by many teams for many years, this results in high infrastructure and networking costs and engineers trying to navigate a sea of uncontextualized data in the middle of an incident.

The Log signal is still experimental at the time of writing (except for the protocol); nevertheless, OpenTelemetry maintainers have acknowledged that OpenTelemetry must integrate with existing logging frameworks and standards rather than making users adopt a new separate API. Although SDK and data models are provided, these seek to integrate with existing logging frameworks via handlers, appenders, or Collector plugins. The focus of the project with regard to logging is to contextualize existing logs, to automatically decorate them with standardized attributes that allow correlating them with other signals.

The use of structured logs, containing standard and custom attributes, results in a thin line separating log records and events. They can both be represented using the same underlying data structures, but their meaning and intention differ. To provide a solution that can cater to both use cases, the Logging API provides a logging interface, not intended to be used by application developers directly (as integration with standard logging frameworks is strongly encouraged), and an events interface, which allows developers to produce events with a particular set of attributes.

Baggage

In certain situations, it is desirable to be able to annotate telemetry produced as part of a common operation with a set of user-defined key-value pairs, propagated across services and execution units. While trace information allows one to correlate operations that are part of a transaction, baggage allows us to correlate signals on custom properties. For instance, we may be interested in looking at certain spans from a backend service across multiple traces that originate in a front-end service, but only when a certain feature flag is enabled. In this case, the front-end service can use the Baggage API to "set" a value in the current context, and have it automatically propagated to its dependencies on network calls. As baggage is propagated, other services can "get" baggage values from the current context and use it accordingly.

Context Propagation

In observability, context is key. It exposes information about the current execution, which can be propagated across threads, processes, or services. This can contain information about the transaction being handled, or other custom properties that can be useful for telemetry instrumentation in multiple components within a single common unit of work. Distributed tracing, for example, relies on information about the current span and trace being propagated across application boundaries.

To manage context within an application, OpenTelemetry provides a cross-signal *Context API* to manage key-value pairs. Although this depends on the language, context is not normally handled explicitly, that is, developers don't need to pass a context object around method invocations. For instance, in Java, it is stored in thread-local storage by default. In this case, the API provides a way to attach, detach, and obtain the context for a current execution.

To propagate context across services, OpenTelemetry defines a *Propagators API* that allows server instrumentation to extract context from incoming requests and client instrumentation to inject context into outgoing requests. For example, in the case of network requests, these are injected and extracted as request headers. Although many header formats are supported (e.g., B3 or Jaeger headers), the default way of doing so is using OpenTelemetry's own TraceContext, a now approved W3C Recommendation (www.w3.org/TR/trace-context).

Instrumentation Libraries

One of the goals of OpenTelemetry is to make telemetry ubiquitous. For many libraries, native OpenTelemetry instrumentation can be added directly by their authors and integrated with the rest of telemetry generated by an application. This is the preferred approach; however, it is not always viable. To help in the mission to get standard telemetry out of the box from applications with minimal user-defined instrumentation, the OpenTelemetry project maintains a series of libraries for every supported language that automatically instrument popular libraries and frameworks.

These libraries are not part of the SDK, but OpenTelemetry makes it easy to enable, disable, or configure them via the most widely adopted instrumentation technique in every language. For example, in Python, libraries dynamically rewrite methods and classes via monkey patching, while in Java, the most popular approach is to use a Java agent that dynamically injects bytecode into instrumented classes.

Resource

When we query telemetry signals, we are normally interested in the service or application that generated those signals. After all, the purpose of telemetry is to identify regressions affecting the performance or reliability of our service. In order to do so, telemetry is decorated with attributes that identify the source of that telemetry (e.g., the hostname) along with other operation-specific attributes (e.g., the HTTP path of a request). Although some telemetry clients prior to OpenTelemetry allowed one to define common attributes for all metrics, traces, or logs produced by an application, there was no logical segmentation between attributes corresponding to the origin of telemetry and attributes corresponding to the operation itself. Additionally, the lack of naming standards across languages, frameworks, or signals within the same application made it difficult for observability tooling to automatically correlate signals. If multiple signals generated by the same service could refer to its service name in different user-defined ways, how could a general-purpose tool identify that they are indeed coming from the same entity?

To standardize and decouple these producer-related properties from other event-specific ones, OpenTelemetry defines the concept of a *Resource*: an immutable set of attributes that represent the entity producing telemetry and that can be easily associated with the telemetry produced. Although not part of the SDK, OpenTelemetry also provides packages that can automatically detect and extract resource information for the runtime environment like container ID, hostname, process, etc.

Collector

By design, OpenTelemetry decouples instrumentation from data representation. This allows developers to choose the most appropriate exporters and protocols to export data directly from their applications. However, there are many cases in which OpenTelemetry cannot be easily integrated into the telemetry producer code, as it is the case for legacy or third-party applications. Even if it can, it may also be beneficial to funnel all telemetry data from multiple services through a common layer, for instance, to implement certain sampling techniques or to apply some data processing globally.

OpenTelemetry Collectors allow us to collect telemetry in multiple formats and protocols (e.g., OTLP, Prometheus, Zipkin); process this data in multiple ways to aggregate, sample, or transform it; and finally export it to multiple telemetry backends, or other collectors. They are effectively the Swiss Army knife of the observability engineer, allowing them to integrate with existing infrastructure, manipulate telemetry data, and provide a frictionless migration path between telemetry tooling.

OTLP Protocol

The OpenTelemetry Protocol (OTLP) is a vendor-agnostic data delivery mechanism, designed to encode and transport telemetry data between telemetry producers and telemetry backends, or collectors. At the time of writing, tracing, metrics, and logs are considered stable under the OpenTelemetry specification, although they may be at different levels of maturity in independent language implementations.

The protocol has been designed to ensure high throughput with minimal serialization/deserialization overhead, to efficiently modify deserialized data, and to be load balancer friendly. It is implemented as Protocol Buffers (Protobuf) over gRPC or HTTP transports, also supporting JSON format over HTTP. OTLP contemplates features like concurrency, retrying policies, or backpressure in its design to allow for efficient delivery on high-throughput environments.

Although OpenTelemetry Collectors can ingest telemetry data in OTLP and convert it to other formats compatible with most telemetry backends, the popularity of this protocol has seen observability backends and major vendors start to support it within their APIs, and some even made it their default way of ingesting data.

Semantic Conventions

Most engineers supporting production workloads in medium to large organizations have probably seen this case many times: metrics or logs produced by multiple services decorated with an attribute or label, for example, cloud provider region, that is expressed in a plethora of different ways depending on the signal, or the service. For instance, region, region_name, cloud.region, cloud_region, and aws_region if deployed to Amazon Web Services, or even legacy attributes like data_center that may still be in use in services that migrated to the cloud but reused that attribute giving it a completely different meaning. They all represent the same thing, but they require domain knowledge to use them. One could not blame an engineer that just joined a team for not being able to find logs that correspond to a particular region if they get alerted on a metric labelled as region: eu-west-1 when the logs, stored in a separate telemetry backend, are labelled as data_center: eu-west-1. They would need to ask their colleagues that would respond with something like "Oh, yeah, we used to run on data centers, but since we migrated to the cloud, we just reused the same label. Changing the label would be too much effort."

We have seen how automatic correlation between multiple signals can be the key differentiator between fast and slow incident resolution, but we cannot simply expect observability tooling to have the necessary domain knowledge and to magically correlate all signals being ingested into a telemetry platform if they don't follow a set of semantic conventions. Although one could think of ways to inform correlation algorithms to handle custom attributes, it would require time and effort to define these relationships and train those algorithms to bring up the necessary context to debug a production incident in a timely fashion. Additionally, any change to these attributes would generate toil to update the backing definitions and could negatively impact correlation.

OpenTelemetry semantic conventions define a set of keys and values for common attributes that describe context around telemetry signals. These represent concepts like runtime environment, protocols, and operations instrumented by telemetry clients. The goal of semantic conventions is to facilitate cross-signal and cross-language telemetry correlation and to empower observability tooling to process telemetry using a commonly understood language. Going back to our previous example, if all telemetry produced refers to a cloud provider's region as cloud.region, this will not only make it easier for a new joiner to find the metrics, logs, or traces they need, but it will also enable observability tooling to process telemetry accordingly and automatically provide better insights.

As a cross-cutting concern, semantic conventions are published as a separate package from the different client APIs and SDKs. To ensure cross-language uniformity, the constants and enums included in those packages are autogenerated from a set of YAML files hosted on the common `opentelemetry-specification` repository.

Although semantic conventions are not considered fully stable at the time of writing, the road map to stability does not contemplate major changes to the attributes currently defined, especially for stable components like Resource or Tracing. As such, there is a wide adoption from observability platforms and instrumentation libraries. Nevertheless, to be able to use them in a Java project, we must include the alpha version of the package in our build. For example, to use them in a Gradle project, where the recommended approach is to use the provided BOM, along with the OpenTelemetry API, we'd need to include the following dependencies:

```
dependencies {
  implementation platform("io.opentelemetry:opentelemetry-bom:1.21.0")
  implementation platform('io.opentelemetry:opentelemetry-bom-
  alpha:1.21.0-alpha')

  implementation('io.opentelemetry:opentelemetry-api')
  implementation('io.opentelemetry:opentelemetry-semconv')
}
```

We will cover how to initialize OpenTelemetry in future chapters, including the package structure in different languages in general, and Java in more detail. For now, it is enough to know that semantic conventions are still not shipped as part of the stable Java packages and require an extra dependency.

Resource Conventions

Resources are the basis of observability standards and semantic conventions. If we cannot unequivocally identify the service that is producing telemetry, we cannot assert if a system is functioning correctly. To achieve effective observability, it must be trivial to know where a given signal is originating from. Resource conventions are normally used to construct a resource, that is, the producer of telemetry, but they can also be used in any situation where there is a need to identify a resource, for example, to refer to a third-party device type.

Attributes are grouped according to the concept that they're describing: service, cloud, operating system, etc., with a set of required attributes that must be present if any of the attributes of the group is used. For instance, the `service.*` group, perhaps the most important as it allows to identify the service producing telemetry, contains the following attribute conventions:

- `service.name`: Logically identifies a service and must be unique within a `service.namespace`. For horizontally scaled workloads, this name must be the same for all replicas. As a required attribute, if not present, the SDK will default to `unknown_service:` followed by executable name, if available (e.g., `uknown_service:java`).

- `service.namespace`: It identifies a group of services logically related, for example, part of the same project or business area, and that are normally managed by the same team.

- `service.instance.id`: The unique ID of an instance of a given service. In horizontally scaled workloads, it helps identify a specific replica producing telemetry.

- `service.version`: The version of an individual application that a given service instance is running.

From this list, only `service.name` is required. One cannot use `service.namespace` without also using `service.name`. Additionally, as we will see in the next chapter, this attribute has a special treatment when configuring an OpenTelemetry Resource.

Tip   Resource conventions can be very useful for other organizational aspects that may seem tangential to observability, like data ownership and cost reporting. We'll cover these aspects in Chapter 12.

Other important resource convention groups include `cloud.*`, `container.*`, `host.*`, `k8s.*`, or `process.*`, to name a few. For a full list of resource conventions published in a human-readable format, one can visit `https://opentelemetry.io/docs/reference/specification/resource/semantic_conventions`.

Resource conventions can be easily used within instrumented code by using OpenTelemetry packages. In Java, they are released as part of the `opentelemetry-semconv` Maven artifact and defined in the `ResourceAttributes` class as `AttributeKey` constants. For example, to create a new Resource identified by service name and the namespace that it belongs to, we can write the following:

```
Resource resource = Resource.create(
  Attributes.of(
    ResourceAttributes.SERVICE_NAME, "juice-service",
    ResourceAttributes.SERVICE_NAMESPACE, "lemonade-stand"));
```

Tracing Conventions

OpenTelemetry spans can be decorated with an arbitrary number of attributes that relate to the operations being instrumented. In the same way as with resource conventions, a great number of these attributes are common across languages, applications, and operations, like those related to HTTP or database client calls.

Spans, by design, contain the most granular telemetry of all signals. Compared to metrics, or even logs, the number of attributes per event is normally much greater, and their telemetry throughput is much, much higher. This means that tracing data is normally more expensive to transport and store and in general more computationally expensive to process. From the perspective of observability, much of the value of tracing comes from the rich debugging context it provides when correlated with other signals. If we see an interesting pattern in a given metric, we normally want to look at traces that expose examples of that pattern, that is, that correlate to them, and also spans that correlate between each other. Therefore, semantic conventions are especially important in tracing data, to provide a background for high-granularity insights and cross-signal analysis.

Tracing conventions consider more aspects than simply attribute keys and values. They also cover best practices specific to tracing such as those related to span kinds, names, or events (concepts that will be covered in detail in Chapter 7). For instance, following general guidelines for span naming, the semantic convention for a SERVER span corresponding to an HTTP request specifies that it should not include URL parameters in its name, as the span name would be too descriptive and cardinality too high. Having a span named /api/customer/1763/pet/3 for an operation to retrieve a customer's pet information would result in spans for different customers and different pets to have different names, making it difficult to assess if the code backing that endpoint is behaving as expected, as each URL would be an independent statistical group. In contrast, if the server instrumentation is capable of extracting variables from the request path, it can name the span /api/customer/{customer_id}/pet/{pet_id}, making all spans for the same operation have the same name, albeit with different properties, thus making the span name more statistically significant.

Like resource conventions, tracing conventions are divided into logical groups depending on the execution context. Some of these are general and used across many instrumentation libraries, like exception.*, net.*, or thread.*, while others are specific to certain libraries, like http.*, rpc.*, or messaging.*. Due to the nature of tracing, as it propagates telemetry context across services, network attributes like net.peer.name are of special importance and widely used across many clients and signals. The full list of semantic conventions for tracing is hosted at https://opentelemetry.io/docs/reference/specification/trace/semantic_conventions.

To provide easy access to semantic conventions for span attributes, the Java implementation provides a SemanticAttributes class, which can be used as follows, for example, to annotate the current span:

```
Span span = Span.current();
span.setAttribute(
  SemanticAttributes.NET_PEER_NAME,
  "my-dependency.example.com");
```

Metrics Conventions

Metrics allow us to get a stable signal for key performance indicators, but when it comes to debugging, they are not the most efficient signal. The strengths of metrics, being able to easily aggregate across dimensions for long time intervals, also become their downside when metric cardinality (i.e., the number of different combinations of attribute values for a given metric name) reaches a certain point and may affect the performance of metrics backends. By following naming conventions compatible with tracing attributes, OpenTelemetry metrics make it possible to correlate metrics with traces and enable engineers to navigate from aggregated metric views to high-granularity trace data.

Additionally, metric conventions aim to solve an issue present in many organizations, which is the lack of standards for metric names. A pattern that is unfortunately common is the creation of metrics with names coupled to the telemetry producer, like service, environment, or technology used, for example, prod.my-svc.okhttp.duration. This hinders debugging and ad hoc analysis as finding the right metric requires domain knowledge. Engineers from different teams, or even companies, should be able to refer to the same concepts using the same names. Thus, metric names must be considered within a global scope, allowing attributes to define the differences between metrics that measure the same concept. For instance, a metric like `http.client.duration` should represent the same regardless of the client implementation, letting OpenTelemetry resource attributes identify the environment, service, or telemetry SDK. OpenTelemetry metric conventions give guidance toward naming metrics within a hierarchy based on usage, similar to attribute groups in trace spans (e.g., `http.*`, `os.*`, `process.*`, `rpc.*`).

The OpenTelemetry specification also gives further guidance on good naming practices and other aspects like metric units, which are part of the data model and should not be included in the metric name, or pluralization, which should be avoided unless the value represented is a countable quantity, for example, errors.

The state of metrics conventions is less mature than resource or tracing conventions and is not yet included as part of the `opentelemetry-semconv` package. Nevertheless, the core principles for consistent naming across signals have been defined. The full list of metrics conventions is available at `https://opentelemetry.io/docs/reference/specification/metrics/semantic_conventions`.

Logs Conventions

It is still early days for semantic conventions affecting log attributes. At the time of writing, the effort from the OpenTelemetry community remains focused on stabilizing the Logs API and SDK. Nonetheless, some conventions have started to materialize for logs and events.

For logs, these include `log.*` attributes (e.g., `log.file.path`) identifying the source of a log, and `feature_flag.*` attributes which can be used to represent evaluations of feature flags happening outside of any transactional context.

The semantic conventions for events include the mandatory attributes required by the events API interface, which ultimately differentiate events from logs in the underlying records produced by the SDK. These are `event.domain`, logically segmenting events from different systems (e.g., `browser`, `device`, or `k8s`), and `event.name`, which identifies a type of event with similar attributes within a given domain.

Both logs and events use the same `exception.*` conventions to describe exceptions during code execution. These are compatible with the semantic conventions for exceptions present in the Tracing API.

The full list of logs conventions can be found at `https://opentelemetry.io/docs/reference/specification/logs/semantic_conventions`.

Telemetry Schemas

Renaming telemetry signals, or their attributes, is hard. If an observability system or tool is relying on telemetry data to have a certain name or include a series of attributes to generate alerts or visualizations, changing these becomes problematic. It can result in long interruptions in access to telemetry data, with very damaging effects. Without telemetry, system operators fly blind, not able to assert the health of their system. To minimize or avoid interruptions, either the source needs to send both versions of telemetry events to allow the consumer to switch without interruption (e.g., old and new metric name), or the consumer needs to account for every single possible variation of these names and attributes. This is not always possible, and it is normally painful for both sides.

OpenTelemetry semantic conventions aim to provide stable naming and event attributes. Nevertheless, although not desirable, the project acknowledges that semantic conventions may need to change over time. To solve the issue presented previously, OpenTelemetry proposes the use of schemas, currently in experimental stage, to be associated with telemetry events. When data is exported, it can contain a `schema_url` pointing to the schema file that describes the transformations necessary to convert telemetry data between versions. This enables certain scenarios that could support semantic changes in telemetry, like having backends and tooling that can resolve telemetry transformations as information is being processed, or using OpenTelemetry Collectors to transform all telemetry to a given target telemetry schema supported by a given backend. Schemas allow for the evolution of semantic conventions, if required, without sacrificing portability.

Summary

OpenTelemetry provides a specification for its different constituent components that allows for a cohesive implementation across languages and frameworks and that evolves following a well-defined process. It also provides design guidelines and conventions to be followed by maintainers and end users to ensure stability and reliability of telemetry instrumentation. As we've seen in this chapter, this specification includes semantic conventions, which establish how telemetry should be named and annotated using multiple attributes to facilitate telemetry correlation between signals and services.

Having a general view of the different OpenTelemetry building blocks helps to understand each of the following chapters within the wider context of the project. In the next chapter, we'll introduce the Resource SDK (briefly mentioned in the "Semantic Conventions" section of this chapter) and the use of instrumentation libraries to enable out-of-the-box observability.

## CHAPTER 4

Auto-Instrumentation

The API design of OpenTelemetry puts telemetry instrumentation in the hands of the most adequate person to instrument a library: the author or maintainer. Although this is a great pattern, it is not always possible to apply it, and it requires application owners to upgrade package dependencies to their instrumented releases. To stay true to its mission of providing ubiquitous telemetry out of the box, the OpenTelemetry project provides a set of packages that automatically add instrumentation for popular libraries and frameworks. In this chapter, we will explore how automatic instrumentation works and how it can be configured in an example Java application.

Resource SDK

Before we study different forms of auto-instrumentation, we must introduce a key concept in OpenTelemetry that binds together all telemetry produced from a given service: the *Resource*. It is a first-class concept in the OpenTelemetry SDK, represented as a set of key-value pair attributes that identify the producer of telemetry, and that is attached to all telemetry exported. For instance, a given service replica deployed in a Kubernetes cluster can be identified by attributes like `k8s.container.name`, `k8s.pod.name`, `k8s.cluster.name`, and other attributes following resource semantic conventions listed in Chapter 3. This decoupling of resource definition from instrumentation means that all telemetry produced can be automatically associated with a given service replica without changing the instrumentation itself. The decision on how to identify a telemetry producer is ultimately in the hands of the application owner, rather than the instrumentation author.

© Daniel Gomez Blanco 2023
D. Gomez Blanco, *Practical OpenTelemetry*, https://doi.org/10.1007/978-1-4842-9075-0_4

Although the Resource SDK is not, by itself, an instrumentation package, it is included in this chapter for two main reasons:

- It is necessary to define a resource in order to configure the OpenTelemetry SDK, even if we only use instrumentation packages.

- OpenTelemetry implementations normally contain resource detectors as SDK extensions or instrumentation libraries. These can automatically detect common attributes related to the execution environment where the application is running (e.g., OS, host, or process).

Resource instances are immutable. In order to modify their attributes, they must be merged with other Resource instances, resulting in a new instance where the values of the updating resource take precedence. For instance, in Java, to update the attributes of the default Resource, we can use

```
Resource resource = Resource.getDefault()
  .merge(Resource.create(
    Attributes.of(
      ResourceAttributes.SERVICE_NAME, "change-service",
      ResourceAttributes.SERVICE_NAMESPACE, "lemonade-stand")));
```

The Resource.getDefault() method called in this example returns a Resource with some default attributes related to the telemetry SDK and mandatory attributes like service.name. The Java SDK uses uknown_service:java as default, as it cannot discover the service name without plugins or user input. Then, when calling merge(), the service name and namespace we specificied overwrite the defaults, resulting in a resource containing the following attributes:

```
service.name: change-service
service.namemspace: lemonade-stand
telemetry.sdk.name: opentelemetry
telemetry.sdk.language: java
telemetry.sdk.version: 1.21.0
```

This resource can also be merged with resources obtained from resource providers included in the `opentelemetry-resources` Maven artifact under the `io.opentelemetry.instrumentation` group. For instance, to automatically add OS, host, and process attributes to the resource, we could do the following:

```
resource = resource
  .merge(OsResource.get())
  .merge(HostResource.get())
  .merge(ProcessResource.get());
```

This produces a resource containing attributes such as `os.type`, `host.name`, or `process.command_line`, among many others. The resource providers used previously do not result in any attribute key collisions. If they did, the attributes from the last merged resource would take precedence.

As we will see in future chapters, a resource is necessary to initialize trace and meter providers. If none is specifically configured, these will use a default resource. Ultimately, depending on the telemetry exporter configuration, resource attributes will be attached either on a per-event or per-export basis to decorate the telemetry produced.

When using instrumentation agents or equivalent solutions that take care of automatically instrumenting applications, there is no need to create a resource manually. Instead, these provide different ways to configure resource attributes via environment variables, system properties, etc. The details are implementation specific, but in general, two environment variables control the resource definition:

- `OTEL_SERVICE_NAME`: Represents the value for `service.name`

- `OTEL_RESOURCE_ATTRIBUTES`: A set of key-value pairs defining resource attributes in W3C Baggage format (i.e., `key1=value1,key2=value2`)

Instrumentation Libraries

The OpenTelemetry project provides a set of libraries that automatically instrument telemetry in many common libraries and frameworks. These are called *instrumentation libraries*. Different mechanisms are used to implement them depending on the language, such as a bytecode injection in Java, wrapping methods in JavaScript, or monkey patching in Python, to name a few.

The official documentation at *https://opentelemetry.io/docs/instrumentation* is full of good resources for each of the OpenTelemetry supported languages, containing quick starts to help application owners instrument their services, including how to use and configure auto-instrumentation libraries.

There are generally two different models supported by language implementations to initialize and configure instrumentation libraries:

- **Zero-touch model**: The instrumented application code is unchanged, and the OpenTelemetry SDK and instrumentation libraries are initialized by a separate component and configured independently from the instrumented code. This model is the easiest one to implement for service owners, but it's not available in every language and normally requires being able to modify the command used to start the application, for example, attaching the Java agent or using Python's `opentelemetry-instrument` command, or having access to configure the runtime environment as in .NET's CLR profiler. In some cases, this model can limit the options to configure or customize certain aspects of instrumentation libraries.

- **Implementation model**: The OpenTelemetry SDK and instrumentation libraries are configured and initialized by the application owner as part of the instrumented application code, normally happening during application startup. This may provide more flexibility to configure instrumentations, but it requires extra effort to install and maintain. In some languages, like Java, this model can have additional drawbacks, as instrumentation libraries that dynamically inject bytecode in the agent model cover a wider set of instrumented libraries and frameworks.

Choosing the right model depends on individual circumstances, and it is ultimately up to the application owner to decide, but in general, a zero-touch model, if provided by the language implementation, results in reduced maintenance effort and easier version upgrades when SDK changes are released.

Although OpenTelemetry languages have a variety of different examples and documentation to demonstrate how to instrument applications in any of the models mentioned previously, it is sometimes clearer to see the benefits of automatic telemetry instrumentation with a well-known project that is not related to OpenTelemetry. For our case, we will use `dropwizard-example`, a Dropwizard demo application available at *https://github.com/dropwizard/dropwizard.* On version v2.1.1, which is the version used in our example, this application has not been instrumented with OpenTelemetry nor it depends on OpenTelemetry in any way.

Having Git and Java installed, running the application according to the docs is fairly straightforward (tests are skipped during build for simplicity):

```
# Clone the repository on version v2.1.1
git clone git@github.com:dropwizard/dropwizard.git \
  --branch v2.1.1 --single-branch
cd dropwizard

# Package the application
./mvnw -Dmaven.test.skip=true package

# Prepare the H2 database
cd dropwizard-example
java -jar target/dropwizard-example-2.1.1.jar \
  db migrate example.yml

# Run the application
java -jar target/dropwizard-example-2.1.1.jar server example.yml
```

After the application starts, some warnings may be present as metrics cannot be reported to Graphite by Dropwizard. This is expected, as it is the internal Dropwizard Metrics reporter that expects a Graphite endpoint. Hitting the *http://localhost:8080/hello-world* endpoint will respond with a nice welcoming message if all is working as expected.

The easiest way to validate the telemetry produced out of the box by our example is to stand up a Docker Compose stack with Jaeger (a popular distributed tracing system), Prometheus (a popular metrics backend), and an OpenTelemetry Collector. The following *docker-compose.yml* definition can be used for that purpose:

```
version: "3"

services:
  jaeger:
    image: jaegertracing/all-in-one:1.37.0
    ports:
      - "16686:16686"
      - "14250"
```

```
  prometheus:
    image: prom/prometheus:v2.38.0
    command:
      - --web.enable-remote-write-receiver
    volumes:
      - /dev/null:/prometheus/prometheus.yml
    ports:
      - "9090:9090"

  otel-collector:
    image: otel/opentelemetry-collector-contrib:0.68.0
    command:
      - --config=/etc/otel-collector.yml
    volumes:
      - ./otel-collector.yml:/etc/otel-collector.yml
    ports:
      - "4317:4317"
    depends_on:
      - jaeger
      - prometheus
```

The otel-collector container requires the following configuration file to be present in the active directory under *otel-collector.yml*:

```
receivers:
  otlp:
    protocols:
      grpc:

processors:
  batch:

exporters:
  jaeger:
    endpoint: jaeger:14250
    tls:
      insecure: true
  prometheusremotewrite:
```

```
      endpoint: http://prometheus:9090/api/v1/write
  logging:
    verbosity: detailed
service:
  pipelines:
    traces:
      receivers: [otlp]
      processors: [batch]
      exporters: [jaeger]
    metrics:
      receivers: [otlp]
      processors: [batch]
      exporters: [prometheusremotewrite]
    logs:
      receivers: [otlp]
      processors: [batch]
      exporters: [logging]
```

The logs pipeline will be unused for now, as the Java agent used later in this chapter does not export logs by default. We will explain how to enable OTLP log exporters in Chapter 8, and we will cover OpenTelemetry Collectors and best practices in detail in Chapters 9 and 10. For now, as illustrated in Figure 4-1, it is enough to know that this simple configuration takes care of defining separate pipelines for metrics and traces that can receive data in OTLP format and export them to Jaeger and Prometheus, respectively.

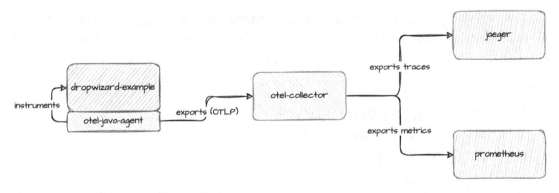

Figure 4-1. *Simple telemetry pipeline for* dropwizard-example

Having Docker installed, the following command will create our stack:

```
docker compose up
```

Now we have a telemetry backend for metrics and traces ready to use.

Caution   The Docker Compose stack and OpenTelemetry configuration used in this example have been chosen for simplicity and clarity. It should not be used in production environments.

Java Agent

Now that we have a simple telemetry backend where we can view our telemetry, it is time to auto-instrument our `dropwizard-example`. In order to do so, we can download the OpenTelemetry Java agent and restart the application as follows:

```
# Download OpenTelemetry Java Agent
curl -o ./opentelemetry-javaagent.jar \
  -L https://github.com/open-telemetry/opentelemetry-java-instrumentation/
releases/download/v1.21.0/opentelemetry-javaagent.jar

# Start the application
java -javaagent:opentelemetry-javaagent.jar \
  -Dotel.service.name=dropwizard-example \
  -jar target/dropwizard-example-2.1.1.jar \
  server example.yml
```

Notice that the only thing we had to change to instrument the application is adding the Java agent and start it with the `otel.service.name` system property (although we could have used the `OTEL_SERVICE_NAME` environment variable instead). With our application running, we can post some data to store in the database:

```
curl -H "Content-Type: application/json" -X POST \
  -d '{"fullName":"Other Person","jobTitle":"Other Title"}' \
  http://localhost:8080/people
```

Now, we can open *http://localhost:8080/people* to verify that the data was saved successfully. This scenario, to store and retrieve an entry from the database, has been automatically instrumented, and we can now see the telemetry produced.

Visiting *http://localhost:16686* will open the Jaeger UI. By selecting the `dropwizard-example` service, we get to see all operations that are automatically instrumented. It is certainly quite a few for such a simple application! As illustrated in Figure 4-2, if we select the `/people` operation and navigate to one of the traces, we can see different operations, down to the database calls, that were part of that single transaction.

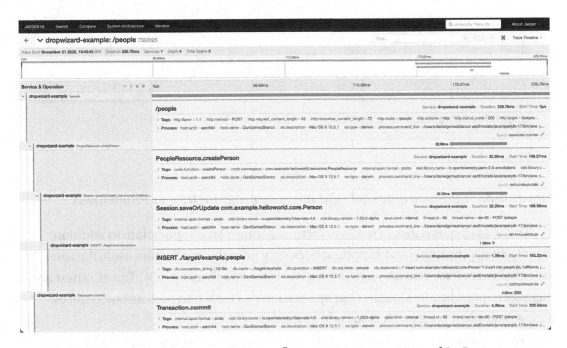

Figure 4-2. *A trace starting at the `/people` operation represented in Jaeger*

In this trace, we can see how individual operations were instrumented by different libraries, like the instrumentations for Jetty, JAX-RS, Hibernate, or JDBC. Each individual span is also annotated with attributes related to the process (or resource) and operation-specific attributes like HTTP status or database statements, all using the relevant semantic conventions.

In a similar fashion, opening *http://localhost:9090* will take us to the Prometheus web interface, where we can see several metrics available for our application. These include db_client_*, http_server_*, and process_runtime_jvm_* metrics for the different instrumented libraries, and metrics related to the OpenTelemetry SDK itself, like otlp_exporter_* metrics. Figure 4-3 showcases one of these metrics.

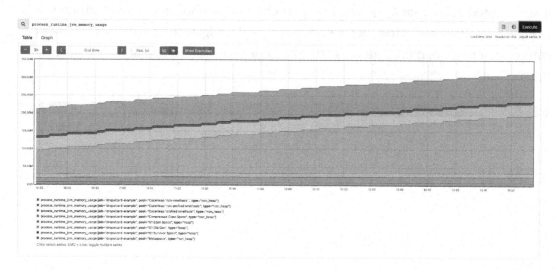

Figure 4-3. *Auto-instrumented JVM memory usage metrics in Prometheus*

This is as easy as it gets in terms of instrumenting a Java application. In addition to collecting, processing and exporting telemetry from the application itself, the agent also configures trace and baggage propagation (by default using W3C TraceContext and Baggage request headers) so that our application can form part of distributed traces across multiple services with zero code changes.

We were able to use the default configuration because this is a simple example and because we deployed a local OpenTelemetry Collector to accept data in OTLP. Nevertheless, the agent allows configuration options to be supplied in multiple ways, in order of priority (highest to lowest):

- System properties

- Environment variables

- Configuration file, containing system properties, specified via the otel.javaagent.configuration-file property or the OTEL_JAVAAGENT_CONFIGURATION_FILE environment variable

- The ConfigPropertySource SPI

The full list of configuration options is available at *https://opentelemetry.io/ docs/instrumentation/java/automatic/agent-config*. We will detail some of the options related to tracing, context propagation, metrics, and other specific components in future chapters as we cover different signals in detail. Nonetheless, there are a few important aspects, common to multiple OpenTelemetry components, that we must be aware of when configuring the agent. We will cover these in the following text.

Extensions

In most cases, the functionality provided by the agent and instrumentation packages is all that's needed to instrument an application. However, specific cases may require custom solutions. For example, consider an application that calls a service providing cache-like features, which returns a 404 status code for HTTP calls on resources that are not cached. Under the OpenTelemetry specification and consequently on the default implementation, a 404 being returned must be marked as an error on the HTTP client side (using `otel.status_code: ERROR`). However, in our cache service case, a 404 is expected by the client in a high percentage of calls and not considered an error. Treating these client spans as errors can affect observability for service owners as the error ratio does not represent actual errors, and it can influence trace sampling algorithms that select traces containing a single error span, resulting in many traces being unnecessarily stored, thus increasing costs.

To solve this issue, we can create a class implementing the `SpanProcessor` interface to process all spans that match a given condition (i.e., client spans with a given `net. peer.name`). Span processors cannot modify spans that have already finished (in this case with 404 response) but we can add an attribute that identifies them as cache client spans when the span is created. This information can be later used in OpenTelemetry Collectors to unset the error status for this type of spans when they correspond to 404 response codes. We will examine the Tracing SDK in detail in Chapter 6, including span processors. For now, let's assume we have a Java class called `CacheClientSpanProcessor` that implements our requirements. To configure the agent to use it, we can use the `AutoConfigurationCustomizerProvider` Java Service Provider Interface (SPI). The OpenTelemetry SDK uses SPIs to automatically discover and load implementations matching interfaces that allow to extend the SDK functionality in a certain way. These are contained in the opentelemetry-sdk-extension-autoconfigure-spi Maven artifact. For our purpose, we can configure our span processor using the following class:

```
public class CacheClientCustomizer
    implements AutoConfigurationCustomizerProvider {

  @Override
  public void customize(AutoConfigurationCustomizer customizer) {
    customizer
      .addTracerProviderCustomizer(
        this::configureTracerProvider);
  }

  private SdkTracerProviderBuilder configureTracerProvider(
      SdkTracerProviderBuilder builder,
      ConfigProperties config) {
    return builder
      .addSpanProcessor(new CacheClientSpanProcessor());
  }
}
```

Our two Java classes can now be compiled into a JAR file along with the SPI configuration file. Projects like Google's AutoService can help generate these files via annotations, but ultimately, SPI requires implementations to be listed in configuration files under *META-INF/services* at the root path of the JAR file. Each SPI implemented is configured in a file matching the SPI interface name, containing all implementation class names. In our example, the contents of the JAR file could look like

```
./META-INF/MANIFEST.MF
./META-INF/services/io.opentelemetry.sdk.autoconfigure.spi.
AutoConfigurationCustomizerProvider
./com/example/CacheClientCustomizer.class
./com/example/CacheClientSpanProcessor.class
```

And the contents of the *io.opentelemetry.sdk.autoconfigure.spi. AutoConfigurationCustomizerProvider* file would be

```
com.example.CacheClientCustomizer
```

Finally, to load this extension, we can use the `otel.javaagent.extensions` system property (or equivalent environment variable), which accepts a list of comma-separated extension JAR files, or a folder containing all extensions to be loaded. In our `dropwizard-example` scenario, we could start the application as follows:

```
java -javaagent:opentelemetry-javaagent.jar \
  -Dotel.service.name=dropwizard-example \
  -Dotel.javaagent.extensions=cache-client-processor.jar \
  -jar target/dropwizard-example-2.1.1.jar \
  server example.yml
```

When the application starts, the agent will merge our custom configuration with other default values and use our span processor to handle cache client spans accordingly.

Note   There are more examples of extensions, including how to programmatically configure the agent, and other uses cases at `https://opentelemetry.io/docs/instrumentation/java/extensions`.

Resource

In our `dropwizard-example` scenario, we have set `otel.service.name` as required and let automatic resource providers extract information from the execution environment. This can be useful to see the full list of attributes that can be discovered out of the box, but depending on the environment and telemetry backend, it may result in too many (or too verbose) attributes stored with every single event, which may incur high transfer or storage costs in large-scale deployments, especially as most telemetry backends store resource attributes along with every span. For example, a Java application configuring many system properties or other arguments when calling the `java` binary may result in a `process.command_line` attribute of considerable length. If the application is deployed in a containerized environment where a given version will always use the same command to start the container, storing the command used to start the application with every span may not give us any useful information that would help us find the root cause for a regression. We could easily cross-reference the version of the service deployed (specified by the `service.version` attribute) with the command used to start the container and save a sizable amount of span storage space.

Ultimately, the choice of resource attributes must represent meaningful observability data that can help during the debugging process or that can be used to extract trends across deployments (e.g., Java version). To support this, the agent can be configured with the following options (or equivalent environment variables):

- `otel.resource.attributes`: A set of key-value pairs defining resource attributes in W3C Baggage format. These will overwrite the values of any other attributes discovered by resource providers.

- `otel.java.enabled.resource-providers`: Comma-separated list of resource provider class names to enable. If unset, all automatic resource providers are used.

- `otel.java.disabled.resource-providers`: Comma-separated list of resource provider class names to disable.

- `otel.experimental.resource.disabled-keys`: Keys to filter out from the detected resource attributes.

The available resource provider classes to enable or disable are part of the `opentelemetry-resources` Maven artifact.

Suppressing Auto-Instrumentation

The number of libraries that can be automatically instrumented by the agent is impressive. At the time of writing, it includes 122 libraries and frameworks and 9 different application servers. The full list is available at *https://github.com/open-telemetry/opentelemetry-java-instrumentation/blob/main/docs/supported-libraries.md*. Having all instrumentation enabled by default when attaching the Java agent to an existing application is very powerful, showcasing the value of OpenTelemetry instrumentation in action, enhancing observability across multiple application layers. However, this is not always desirable. For instance, if the OpenTelemetry agent is bundled as part of a base image that is reused across an organization, it is sometimes safer to only enable specific basic instrumentation and let service owners decide which libraries are important to them if they decided to enable additional ones. This avoids operational surprises due to large increases in data volume when a service enables OpenTelemetry or starts using an instrumented library in an unexpected way. It gives telemetry enablement teams a safer way to roll out OpenTelemetry by default, making sure that instrumentation is well understood and provides value out of the box.

The agent supports multiple options that allow it to supress instrumentation in different ways. These are some of the most important ones:

- `otel.instrumentation.[name].enabled`: Where `[name]` is the instrumentation short name as listed in the official documentation, is a boolean property controlling if a given instrumentation is enabled or not. Instrumentations are enabled or disabled by default depending on the value of `common.default-enabled` described below.

- `otel.instrumentation.common.default-enabled`: Controls if instrumentations are enabled by default. If `false`, instrumentations must be individually enabled. It defaults to `true`.

- `otel.instrumentation.common.experimental.controller-telemetry.enabled`: Defaulting to `true`, controls the behavior of server instrumentations, like JAX-RS, that add internal spans for the controller layer. Completely disabling the instrumentation would disable other desirable aspects like automatically extracting operation names from REST API endpoints and updating the parent server span. Instead, disabling this option leaves server telemetry untouched while avoiding the creation of additional spans.

- `otel.instrumentation.common.experimental.view-telemetry.enabled`: Similar to `controller-telemetry`, this option controls the creation of internal spans for the view layer. It defaults to `true`.

Finally, it is possible to completely disable the agent by using the `otel.javaagent.enabled=false` property or the equivalent environment variable.

Tip   When configuring OpenTelemetry in large deployments, auto-instrumentation and resource discovery can generate high telemetry data volumes. Depending on the type of deployment, the configuration options shared previously for suppressing certain instrumentations and resource attributes, or adjusting attribute values via extensions to improve sampling, can sometimes result in cost savings without affecting observability.

Java Standalone Instrumentation

Using the OpenTelemetry agent is the easiest and most supported way of configuring the OpenTelemetry SDK and other instrumentations in Java, but there are particular scenarios where the agent model cannot be used, or it is not possible to change the java command arguments to attach the agent. To support these cases, the OpenTelemetry project provides a set of instrumentations that can be configured as standalone libraries.

Each standalone library may have a different way of being initialized: filters, interceptors, wrappers, drivers, etc. Let's take the *OkHttp* instrumentation as an example. To be able to initialize this instrumentation library, we first need an instance of the OpenTelemetry API to be registered. When using the agent, this is done as part of the agent startup process, but in this case, we must do it manually. To do so, we need to include the opentelemetry-api and opentelemetry-sdk Maven artifacts in our dependencies, and as we're going to register an OTLP span exporter, we'll also require opentelemetry-exporter-otlp. In Gradle, these dependencies would be declared as follows:

```
dependencies {
    implementation platform("io.opentelemetry:opentelemetry-bom:1.21.0")

    implementation('io.opentelemetry:opentelemetry-api')
    implementation('io.opentelemetry:opentelemetry-sdk')
    implementation('io.opentelemetry:opentelemetry-exporter-otlp')
}
```

Using the Resource we created at the start of this chapter, we can create a trace provider and register it against an OpenTelemetry instance, along with context propagators:

```
SdkTracerProvider tracerProvider = SdkTracerProvider.builder()
  .addSpanProcessor(BatchSpanProcessor.builder(
    OtlpGrpcSpanExporter.builder().build()).build())
  .setResource(resource)
  .build();

OpenTelemetry openTelemetry = OpenTelemetrySdk.builder()
  .setTracerProvider(tracerProvider)
  .setPropagators(ContextPropagators.create(
    W3CTraceContextPropagator.getInstance()))
  .buildAndRegisterGlobal();
```

The call to buildAndRegisterGlobal() returns an instance of the OpenTelemetry API that can be used across the application as a cross-cutting concern. It also registers it as a global singleton, so future calls to GlobalOpenTelemetry.get() will give access to the same OpenTelemetry instance. The use of this get() method, however, is not recommended, as it may be subject to initialization order. It is preferable to construct the instance and pass the reference where needed, or use other patterns to reference a given instance such as Dependency Injection. We will cover trace providers and context propagators in Chapters 5 and 6.

With the OpenTelemetry API configured, we can now instrument OkHttp. To do so, we must first include the dependency in our Gradle dependencies:

```
implementation("io.opentelemetry.instrumentation:opentelemetry-
okhttp-3.0:1.21.0-alpha")
```

The OkHttpTracing instrumentation provides a Call.Factory implementation that wraps the provided OkHttpClient:

```java
public class OkHttpConfiguration {
  public Call.Factory createTracedClient(OpenTelemetry openTelemetry) {
    return OkHttpTracing.builder(openTelemetry).build()
      .newCallFactory(createClient());
  }

  private OkHttpClient createClient() {
    return new OkHttpClient.Builder().build();
  }
}
```

Using the provided Call.Factory for any HTTP calls will automatically create client spans under the active span context and propagate tracing context with the configured context propagators. The generated spans will then be exported via OTLP to a default endpoint (we will explore span exporters in Chapter 6).

Summary

Although some of the concepts in this chapter may seem unfamiliar to the reader, such as collector pipelines, tracer providers, or span processors, we have seen how adding instrumentation to an existing Java application can be as easy as attaching an agent. The implementation details may be different in other languages, but the concept remains intact. Default, out-of-the-box telemetry should be easy to add and to maintain.

Making the entry requirements to instrument an application and discover resource attributes as easy as possible empowers teams to roll out OpenTelemetry by default across organizations. Along with automatic context propagation, this means that distributed systems can start to include services in distributed traces with very limited effort, enriching the transactional context available to debug regressions and better understand system behavior. How this trace context is propagated within and across services will be the focus of our next chapter.

## CHAPTER 5

Context, Baggage, and Propagators

Having standard telemetry being produced by our services out of the box goes a long way toward enabling observability tooling to extract valuable insights that help us monitor and debug our systems in production. However, it'd be virtually impossible to find a modern software system that works in complete isolation, with no external dependencies needed to fulfill a given operation. Having access to more data does not imply observability. To effectively enable observability, we need context to bind all telemetry produced as part of a transaction, across services and signals. This chapter covers how OpenTelemetry standardizes telemetry context and how it implements propagation across services.

Telemetry Context and the Context API

Observability aims to provide the necessary data to understand how changes affect our systems and effortlessly find the root cause of a regression when things don't go according to plan. In such cases, we're mostly interested in finding out what was happening inside our system when a change happened. For instance, within a service replica, we may be interested in looking at individual operations that made a response time metric increase, and we also want to know these details across services that contributed to make certain user transactions behave unexpectedly.

In most real-world distributed systems, individual operations are often handled by different threads, coroutines, or other types of execution units, to deal with multiple client requests simultaneously, or asynchronously. As cross-cutting concerns, telemetry clients need a way to store transactionally scoped information that can propagate across different operations responsible for handling a given transaction. To achieve this, the *Context API* provides a standard way to manage a set of key-value pairs that are related to the operation being handled at a given time by a given application.

The concept of telemetry context has been around for a long time. Java users may be familiar with Mapped Diagnostic Context (MDC) as a way of storing thread-scoped attributes that can then be used within logging frameworks like Logback or Log4j. Instead of manually passing a property, like a user session ID, through all methods invoked as part of serving a request, developers can set this property once in the MDC and rely on logging handlers to populate this field as part of every log line. The OpenTelemetry Context API works in a similar fashion in Java, using ThreadLocal to store key-value pairs. Other language implementations use similar mechanisms that allow developers to propagate context without having to manually pass a context object between function calls. These include Python's Context Variables or JavaScript's Async Hooks. The use of these mechanisms makes the handling of telemetry context in these languages *implicit*. Other languages that do not support a way to store execution-scoped values in a standard way require developers to manually propagate context in an *explicit* manner, for example, as function arguments.

Note   Users of languages that handle context implicitly, like Java, do not normally need to interact with the Context API directly and should use the relevant telemetry signal API to do so, if possible.

The Context API defines a set of functions and a default implementation to create keys and get or set values for a given key in a context. Individual context instances are immutable, so any modification will return a new instance containing the updated key-value pairs, as well as all other keys in the parent context from which it was created. Additionally, in languages that handle context implicitly, the API provides a set of global functions to obtain the context associated with the current execution and to attach or detach context from the current execution scope. This API enables all telemetry signals to share a common underlying system for context propagation within a single code base, abstracted from the underlying implementation.

In Java, this functionality can be accessed using the Context and ContextKey classes in the opentelemetry-context Maven artifact, which is already included as a dependency of opentelemetry-api. As this is a language where context is handled implicitly, to update a key, we normally must obtain the current context first (this will be a default root context if none has been set before) and then create a new context with the updated key, which must be associated with the current execution:

```
// Create a context key
static final ContextKey<String> MY_KEY =
  ContextKey.named("someKey");
...
// Create a new context with the new key
Context myContext = Context.current().with(MY_KEY, "someValue");
Scope myScope = myContext.makeCurrent();
...
// Get value in another method (same thread)
String myValue = Context.current().get(MY_KEY);
...
// Close scope before returning
myScope.close();
```

Each call to makeCurrent() returns a Scope, which represents a context being attached within a specific block of code. It must always be closed before the current execution context finalizes; otherwise, memory leaks may occur, and any telemetry relying on context may become faulty if the wrong context information is used. To make sure scopes are closed, the Scope class implements the AutoCloseable interface, so it can be used within a try-with-resource block:

```
try (Scope ignored = myContext.makeCurrent()) {
    // Methods called here can use the same context
}
```

While it is possible to manage context this way, it is not trivial. Making sure that all scopes are closed properly becomes especially difficult in asynchronous code with multiple executors and thread pools that can take part in handling a single client request. To help in this endeavor, the Context API provides a set of wrappers that makes working with asynchronous tasks easier. As an example, if we want to propagate the current context so that the code inside a Runnable inherits the same execution scope variables, we can wrap it using the following code:

```
Context.current().wrap(new Runnable() {
  public void run() {
```

```
    // Code in this thread inherits the parent thread context
  }
}).run();
```

Similar `wrap()` methods are provided for `Callable`, `Consumer`, `Function`, `Supplier`, and other concurrency classes.

As illustrated in Figure 5-1, using a method like `wrap()`, or manually calling `makeCurrent()` on a context instance, attaches a given context to an execution unit. In this case, if Task 1 calls `Context.current()` while `scopeB` is active, it will find a context with `foo: bar`. After a different context is attached in the same thread in Task 2, the same call within `scopeD` would return a context with `foo: quz`.

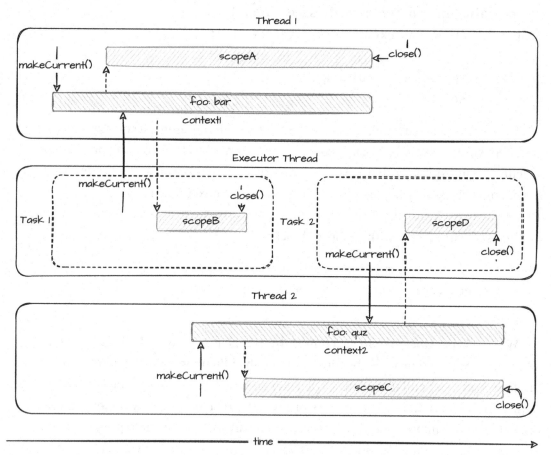

Figure 5-1. *Context being propagated from multiple threads into a single executor thread*

When working with the Executor framework in Java, we often do not have access to the context that tasks should inherit when creating the `Executor` or `ExecutorService`, and the current context at the time is not normally the most appropriate one. For instance, a common pattern is to initialize an executor service at application startup and to use this service in async HTTP clients. Each individual call will be picked up by the service and executed asynchronously in a different thread. When an incoming request is handled, we normally want to propagate the same telemetry context from the incoming request to the outgoing async HTTP calls. Instead of wrapping every runnable picked up by the executor, which may not always be possible, we can instrument the `ExecutorService` as follows:

```
ExecutorService myExecutor =
    Context.taskWrapping(Executors.newFixedThreadPool(10));
```

Any calls to `myExecutor.submit()` (or `myExecutor.execute()`) will automatically inherit the current context at the time of invocation.

Finally, if using the Java agent instrumentation, some common executors are automatically instrumented by the `executors` library, such as the `ForkJoinPool` or Akka's `MessageDispatcher`, among many others. This behavior can be controlled via the following two configuration options:

- `otel.instrumentation.executors.include`: Comma-separated list of `Executor` subclasses to be instrumented.

- `otel.instrumentation.executors.include-all`: Whether to instrument all classes implementing the `Executor` interface. It defaults to false.

Caution   As we will see in Chapter 6, propagating tracing context to async tasks may not always be appropriate to describe the causal relationship between operations, so automatically instrumenting executors should only be used in specific cases where application owners understand the consequences.

The concepts presented in this section can perhaps be slightly abstract and difficult to grasp without concrete, real-world examples that require context to be propagated across execution units and services. These concepts will become clearer as we delve into the Baggage API in the following section and later into the Tracing API in Chapter 6.

Baggage API

While it is possible to interact directly with the Context API to set or retrieve execution-scoped properties, as mentioned in the previous section, this is discouraged for instrumentation authors and developers, especially if context is handled implicitly. Instead, OpenTelemetry provides access to these properties via their respective signal APIs. For instance, the Tracing API will store information related to the current trace using the Context API, but developers should use the Tracing API to interact with these.

To support the need for user-defined properties that relate to the current telemetry context, OpenTelemetry provides the *Baggage API*. This is useful, for instance, to propagate information that may only be available further up the dependency chain in a user transaction (e.g., the web session ID that started a request) as it makes its way down to other services in the stack. Baggage allows to propagate this information and use it in other signals where relevant.

Note   Baggage is independent from other telemetry signals. This means that values are not added as attributes to spans or metrics automatically. They must be retrieved and added to those using the relevant signal APIs.

In a similar way to the Context API, the Baggage API is fully functional without an installed SDK, according to the OpenTelemetry specification. The Baggage API defines the *Baggage* data structure as a set of name-value pairs of type string. It also implements the following collection of functions to interact with a given baggage instance:

- Set a string value, identified by a name/key, and optionally some metadata associated with the value (also of type string).

- Get a value given a name/key, along with its metadata.

- Get all values (and any metadata) and their names/keys.

- Remove a value (and any metadata) given a name/key.

Additionally, the Baggage API provides functionality to interact with the telemetry context, to

- Extract the baggage instance from a given context.

- Attach a baggage instance to a given context.

- Extract or attach the Baggage instance from the current context if context is handled implicitly.

- Clear the baggage from an existing context, which, depending on the implementation, may be done by attaching an empty baggage to a context. This can be useful to make sure no sensitive information is propagated across untrusted boundaries.

In Java, the Baggage API follows a very similar pattern to the Context API. Implementations of the Baggage interface are immutable, with a new object returned when setting a value. To attach a baggage to the current context, a makeCurrent() function is provided, which calls the underlying Context API to create a new context with the given baggage and return a Scope. As it is the case with context, this scope must be closed to avoid memory leaks and faulty instrumentation. In the following example, we set and retrieve values from the current Baggage as follows:

```
// Create a new baggage updating the current baggage
Baggage myBaggage = Baggage.current()
  .toBuilder()
  .put("session.id", webSessionId)
  .put("myKey", "myValue",
      BaggageEntryMetadata.create("some metadata"))
  .build();

// Make the new baggage current in this scope
try (Scope ignored = myBaggage.makeCurrent()) {
  ...
  // Retrieve values in other methods in this scope
  String mySessionId = Baggage.current()
    .getEntryValue("session.id");

  BaggageEntry myValueEntry = Baggage.current()
    .asMap().get("myKey");
  String myValue = myValueEntry.getValue();
  String myMetadata = myValueEntry.getMetadata().getValue();
}
```

```
// Clear baggage
try (Scope ignored = Baggage.empty().makeCurrent()) {
  // Baggage will be empty in this scope
}
```

This example also demonstrates how to retrieve all values with the asMap() method, how to retrieve metadata from a BaggageEntry, or how to clear the baggage in a scope to avoid propagating any values.

Caution   As baggage is propagated to outgoing network requests normally as HTTP headers, it is important not to use baggage for sensitive information, especially when calling third-party endpoints.

Propagation Using W3C Baggage Specification

As explained in detail in the following section related to the Propagators API, OpenTelemetry standardizes how different signals can propagate context across services. The Baggage API provides a way to propagate baggage using what is called a TextMapPropagator, that is, a type of propagator that injects or extracts context from a carrier using string key-value pairs. For instance, instrumentation modules, like HTTP clients/servers, can use the Baggage API to inject/extract baggage values to/from HTTP requests.

The concept of baggage existed previously in tracing libraries like OpenTracing, before it was decoupled from the Tracing API in OpenTelemetry. As OpenTracing did not provide a default implementation for their API, there was a proliferation of different baggage key-value propagation formats that could be used as HTTP headers, for instance:

- Jaeger clients using uberctx-{key}: {value}.

- Lightstep clients using ot-baggage-{key}: {value}.

- Zipkin clients (normally using B3 propagation) do not mandate a specific format, but the majority use baggage-{key}: {value}. See *https://github.com/openzipkin/b3-propagation/issues/22* for more details.

As a default implementation, OpenTelemetry proposes a new standard to represent baggage, accepted as a W3C Working Draft and available at *www.w3.org/TR/baggage*. Instead of encoding each key-value pair as a separate header, W3C Baggage uses one single baggage header (although multiple baggage headers are allowed and can be combined). Each header contains a comma-separated list of baggage items, with each item comprised of a key-value pair separated by an "equals" sign. Additionally, metadata can be appended to each item as a list of semicolon-separated properties. The format specification goes into all necessary details related to leading or trailing spaces, header format, limits, percent encoding, etc., but for our purpose, we can illustrate this with the following example:

```
baggage: key1=value1;property1;property2, key2 = value2, key3=value3;
propertyKey=propertyValue
```

This baggage header would result in the following entries being extracted:

- Entry with key1 as key and value1 as value, along with two metadata properties with property1 and property2 as keys

- Entry with key2 as key and value2 as value, with no metadata

- Entry with key3 as key and value3 as value, with one metadata property with propertyKey as key and propertyValue as value

Cross-Service Context and the Propagators API

As we have seen in the previous sections, propagating telemetry context across execution units within a service is useful, by itself, for many use cases, including features specific to telemetry signals but also to carry user-defined properties related to the same execution scope. However, propagating context across services that are part of the same transaction is what takes observability to the next level. One that, in distributed systems, must be part of the core definition of what constitutes an observable system. If we consider a distributed system handling an individual user request, it can sometimes feel like a black box. The input, i.e. a request, goes in; the service receiving this request calls other internal services, which in turn may call other services; and it all normally results in a response given to the user or some other type of output from the distributed system. We have little information about the path that this transaction followed through a distributed system, which would be quite handy if we were to try to understand how the system is operating. This certainly does not look like observability.

Context propagation provides telemetry clients and observability tools with the necessary information to link together multiple telemetry events occurring as part of a single originating transaction. It allows for high-granularity insights into the transactional behavior of distributed systems.

Over the years, organizations have implemented different solutions to try to solve this problem. Some, using vendor-specific APM agents, relied on internal vendor representations and proprietary context propagation formats that would limit organizations in many ways, as explained in the first chapters of this book. Others, utilizing more open-source approaches, decided to build context propagation themselves, normally in the form of transaction or correlation IDs being propagated across services with custom-built HTTP server/client plugins and header formats, manually extracted and injected from requests into frameworks like MDC in order to be used as part of application logging. This normally resulted not only in maintenance overhead, but in faulty context propagation when a service in the chain of dependencies was running in a system not supported by the provided plugins. Additionally, any existing observability tooling would not be able to easily present this information in a way that could speed up debugging. From personal experience, looking for individual transaction IDs across application logs from multiple services is not a fun activity!

With the popularization of OpenTracing and OpenCensus, some standards started to emerge to propagate context across services. These, however, had some fundamental challenges:

- With OpenTracing not providing a default implementation, many propagation formats started to emerge using headers like b3, X-B3-*, ot-*, uber-*, etc.

- Context would normally be coupled to tracing, so without trace context propagation, there would be no context propagation at all.

- APIs only allowed one propagator to be configured for an application. This made it difficult to propagate context in large distributed systems owned by multiple teams, especially when migrating between implementations, as context would stop being propagated when client and server were configured with different propagators.

To tackle these challenges, we have seen that OpenTelemetry decouples context from trace context in the Context API. It also defines a *Propagators API* that exposes a set of public propagator interfaces that can be used as a cross-cutting concern to inject and extract context to and from what is known as a carrier, that is, a medium or data structure to write values to and read values from. This can be used independently by any signal, like tracing or baggage. The only propagator currently defined in the OpenTelemetry specification is the `TextMapPropagator`, which uses string maps as carriers, although a binary propagator will be provided in the future.

A propagator supports the following operations:

- **Inject**: The propagator obtains the relevant values from a given context and writes them into a given carrier. For instance, a map of HTTP headers for an outgoing request. The carrier in this case is expected to be mutable.

- **Extract**: The propagator reads the relevant values from a given carrier, for instance, a map of HTTP headers of an incoming request, and updates a given context with those values, resulting in a new immutable context being returned.

Additionally, and depending on the language, the propagator may require setter and getter instances, which are to be used to work with values in the given carrier. This helps propagators support a more general use case without coupling data manipulation to any string map implementation.

The OpenTelemetry project defines a list of default propagators that are maintained and distributed either as part of the API or extension packages:

- **W3C Baggage**: As detailed in the previous section, this is the W3C Working Draft to propagate baggage values. It is normally available as part of the API.

- **W3C TraceContext**: The W3C Recommendation to propagate trace context, normally provided along with the API implementation. We will cover this in detail in Chapter 6.

- **B3**: The trace context propagation standard proposed by Zipkin but also widely used in many other distributed tracing implementations, normally included as an extension package.

- **Jaeger**: Used primarily by Jaeger clients to propagate trace context, normally included as an extension package.

Optionally, core OpenTelemetry extensions may include the **OT Trace** propagator, used by OpenTracing basic tracers like the Lightstep tracer. It is also possible for externally maintained packages to provide additional propagators, like the AWS X-Ray context propagator.

To support multiple trace context propagators simultaneously, or to support multiple signals propagating context (e.g., tracing and baggage), any language compliant with the OpenTelemetry specification must also support *Composite Propagators*. These can be created from an ordered list of propagators, or injectors/extractors, which will be called in the order they were specified when creating the composite propagator. The resulting context or carrier processed by a propagator may include a merge of the values read or written by the previous propagator. For instance, if we use Jaeger and W3C Baggage propagators, defined in that order, and the same baggage entry is present in both headers for a given incoming request, the one extracted from W3C Baggage will take precedence, as it is called last.

Tip   When using composite propagators for the same signal, make sure your preferred propagator is the last one in the list, especially if other propagators may result in information loss, for example, padding for trace IDs of different length. This will make sure context is extracted and propagated appropriately to other services.

Normally, propagators are used by client/server or consumer/producer instrumentation packages (e.g., Jetty), obtained from a set of globally configured propagators, and rarely used directly by application owners. As previously mentioned, the carriers are normally objects from network-related frameworks like `HttpURLConnection` for instance, which can use methods like `setRequestProperty()` to inject headers into the outgoing request. Figure 5-2 elaborates from Figure 5-1 and illustrates how context is propagated not only across execution units within the service, but it is also extracted from an incoming request and injected into an outgoing request part of the same transaction. The context extracted from the incoming request is propagated to a different thread, where client instrumentation can use it to inject headers in the outgoing request. Normally, a client instrumentation library will create its own scope from the current context when handling a request. This has been omitted from the diagram for clarity.

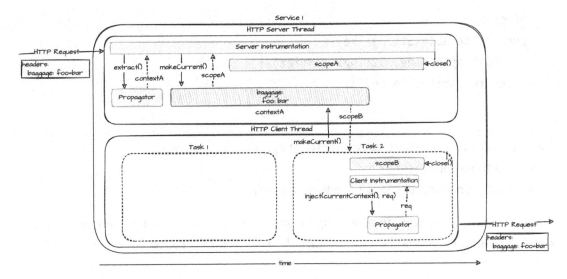

Figure 5-2. *W3C Baggage being extracted and injected into a request being handled by multiple threads in a service*

Although not often used by application owners, but rather auto-instrumentation authors, to demonstrate how the Propagators API works, we can inject the current context into a HashMap using the following code snippet (validation for null values has been removed for simplicity):

```
TextMapSetter<HashMap<String, String>> setter = HashMap::put;
HashMap<String, String> myMap = new HashMap<>();
openTelemetry.getPropagators()
  .getTextMapPropagator()
  .inject(Context.current(), myMap, setter);
```

In this case, the setter implementation simply needs to call put() on the map, with the key and value passed as arguments. Inversely, to extract context from a HashMap, we can use

```
TextMapGetter<HashMap<String, String>> getter =
  new TextMapGetter<HashMap<String, String>>(){
    @Override
    public String get(
        HashMap<String, String> carrier, String key) {
      return carrier.get(key);
    }
```

81

```
  @Override
  public Iterable<String> keys(
      HashMap<String, String> carrier) {
    return carrier.keySet();
  }
};
Context extractedContext = openTelemetry.getPropagators()
  .getTextMapPropagator()
  .extract(Context.current(), myMap, getter);
```

In this case, in addition to providing a way of getting a value from the map for a given key, the getter must provide a way to return the keys as an `Iterable`.

Configuring Propagators

In Chapter 4, we mentioned that the Java agent configures a set of defaults for context propagation, using W3C TraceContext and W3C Baggage as the default propagators. When using the Java agent, the easiest way to configure propagators is to use the `otel.propagators` property (or `OTEL_PROPAGATORS` environment variable), which accepts a comma-separated list of propagator names. The supported values are as follows:

- `tracecontext`: W3C TraceContext, enabled by default

- `baggage`: W3C Baggage, enabled by default

- `b3`: B3 single, a single `b3` header representation standardized in 2018

- `b3multi`: The original B3 context propagation, using `X-B3-*` headers

- `jaeger`: The Jaeger context and baggage propagation

- `xray`: Context propagation for AWS X-Ray

- `ottrace`: Context and baggage propagation for OpenTracing basic tracers

Alternatively, it is also possible to configure propagators programmatically when creating and registering the global OpenTelemetry instance at application startup. To elaborate on our example from Chapter 4, where we only configured a W3C

TraceContext propagator for simplicity, the following snippet will make sure that baggage is also propagated using W3C Baggage, and any dependency using Jaeger headers can also get their context propagated:

```
OpenTelemetrySdk openTelemetry = OpenTelemetrySdk.builder()
  .setTracerProvider(tracerProvider)
  .setMeterProvider(meterProvider)
  .setPropagators(ContextPropagators.create(
    TextMapPropagator.composite(
      JaegerPropagator.getInstance(),
      W3CTraceContextPropagator.getInstance(),
      W3CBaggagePropagator.getInstance())))
  .buildAndRegisterGlobal();
```

The set of core trace context propagators in Java is released as part of the opentelemetry-extension-trace-propagators Maven artifact, excluding W3C TraceContext and W3C Baggage propagators that are part of the API.

Summary

In this chapter, we have detailed the motivation and need for context propagation in distributed systems and how OpenTelemetry's design, influenced by now deprecated projects like OpenTracing and OpenCensus, results in more flexible, modular, and loosely coupled Context and Propagators APIs. The chapter also contains the necessary information for service owners to configure propagators within their applications.

Baggage, covered in this chapter, is one of the telemetry signals that relies on context to fulfill its purpose of propagating user-defined values across execution units and services. In the next chapter, we will examine Tracing, another signal that requires context to be propagated in order to effectively describe the behavior of a system under operation.

CHAPTER 6

Tracing

Considering what has been discussed in previous chapters, it should be evident that telemetry context must be a requirement to implement observability. It is of no surprise that, along with context and propagation, tracing became the main component to focus on in order to achieve the first 1.x release of OpenTelemetry, as it standardizes how causally related operations are represented within a distributed transaction. Although Chapter 5 may have felt slightly abstract, the concepts of context, scope, and propagation will start to materialize more firmly when we apply them to tracing. In this chapter, we'll examine the OpenTelemetry Tracing API and SDK, configuration, trace context propagation, and best practices for manual instrumentation.

What Is a Distributed Trace?

When we explored the concept of telemetry context in Chapter 5, we explained how OpenTelemetry provides a standard way to manage and propagate execution-scoped values between threads and across services that are part of the same common unit of work. As we've seen, some of that telemetry in-band data (i.e., data passed between components as part of business messages) is custom to the system domain and normally represented by baggage. However, there is a certain type of information that is common to all distributed systems. Imagine how confusing it would be if every team, or organization, implemented their own way of representing distributed transactions and their constituent operations and attributes directly using the Context and Propagator APIs. It certainly would not promote collaboration, and it would be near impossible for observability tooling to work with this data and provide valuable analysis and visualizations to help with debugging.

Ultimately, the concept of a transaction is not unique to any domain. Most systems, especially distributed systems, require multiple operations, components, and services to perform a given action. This is where tracing helps. As we discussed in our introduction

© Daniel Gomez Blanco 2023
D. Gomez Blanco, *Practical OpenTelemetry*, https://doi.org/10.1007/978-1-4842-9075-0_6

to tracing in Chapter 3, it provides data representation and tooling to instrument, process, and export this data so that observability platforms can provide high-granularity insights into distributed systems.

For those used to application logging, tracing can be thought of as highly granular access logging with reported duration timings, although in this case access logging does not stop at the HTTP/RPC layer, but it goes deeper into applications to time meaningful operations involved in serving a request. Instead of freeform log messages, tracing provides a structure for each of these events, including default attributes related to the common transaction of which they're part, and their place in it (i.e., what caused a certain operation). In tracing, this structured data representation is called a *Span*, and the logical concept that links all operations under one distributed transaction is called a *Trace*.

This level of granularity provides very valuable insights into distributed systems, but it can become challenging to maintain when deployed at scale. Exporting, processing, and storing the volume of data required to accurately represent a large distributed system can be overwhelming both in technical and in financial terms. Although some of this data is vital to debug systems, similarly to application logging, most of it is not that interesting. It belongs to transactions that behave as expected, containing no errors and having an acceptable duration. Fortunately, the structure and context provided by tracing allow the development of sampling algorithms that help to retain only a fraction of all traces, making sure that the majority of traces that are not valuable for debugging purposes are discarded. Although sampling is mentioned in this chapter, it is a topic that deserves to be discussed independently, along with OpenTelemetry Collector features, in Chapter 10.

The structured nature of spans makes them very powerful. Although they are normally visualized as part of a single trace, they can also be analyzed across traces as individual events representing a unit of work, aggregating their reported durations and grouping across multiple dimensions. Some telemetry backends allow to execute ad hoc queries on spans, for instance, to obtain the mean duration of a given operation. It is also possible to derive metrics from spans in OpenTelemetry Collectors. This often results in an overuse of spans as a substitute for metrics when teams start to adopt tracing. As Dr. Ian Malcolm famously pointed out in Steven Spielberg's film *Jurassic Park*, "Yeah, but your scientists were so preoccupied with whether or not they could, they didn't stop to think if they should." Trace sampling can affect any interpretations extracted directly from spans, as it normally skews distributions toward the worst cases, that is, transactions containing errors or the slowest response times, the ones worth debugging. Even with no sampling in place, the high volumes of data and cardinality processed by trace pipelines in high-throughput systems normally result in signals that are less stable than metrics originating directly from a service. As we'll cover in Chapter 7, due to their lower volume and API design, by aggregating multiple events into a single data point, metrics can benefit from longer export retry loops and other mechanisms that can account for short service interruptions without sacrificing signal stability.

This is not to say that spans should not be used to analyze trends. Quite the contrary. Distributed tracing can and should be used to identify regressions across services and operations, detect anomalies, and link to individual examples, that is, traces, that give evidence of why a regression occurred. It is not, however, the most recommended signal to track a long-term KPI. With OpenTelemetry, we can use the right signal for each use case, and, thanks to a shared context, link between signals that are part of the same transaction.

Tip   The purpose of tracing is to aid debugging by helping to identify anomalies across services and operations and to provide high-granularity exemplars to back root cause investigations with the necessary contextual evidence. However, it is not a substitute for metrics.

Tracing API

Following OpenTelemetry design principles, the Tracing API defines a set of public interfaces and minimal implementation, relying on an SDK to be configured at application startup to provide the desired behavior. This ensures that any instrumentation directly implemented in an application, or any of its third-party library dependencies, has no side effects on said application, even if no SDK is configured. In this situation, the Trace API becomes a no-op API, with the exception of context propagation. If propagators are configured, trace context can be propagated through a service, avoiding disjoined traces, even if no tracer is configured.

Tracers and Tracer Providers

When we initialize the OpenTelemetry SDK and register it against the global OpenTelemetry instance, a `TracerProvider` can be configured. Although using a single instance is the most common use case, it is possible to have more than one `TracerProvider` instance in an application. This may be useful, for example, to use different tracer configurations.

The responsibility of a `TracerProvider`, as the name indicates, is to provide `Tracer` instances. In turn, the responsibility of a `Tracer` is to create spans. To obtain a tracer, the following parameters can be used:

- **Name**: The name of the tracer. This can be the name of an instrumentation library, or for custom instrumentation or instrumentation built natively into libraries, it can be the library name, a class, a package, etc. This is a mandatory parameter. If none is passed, it will default to an empty string.

- **Version**: The version of the instrumentation or instrumented library, if any. This is an optional parameter.

- **Schema URL**: Optional parameter to specify the `schema_url` that should be attached to all events produced by this tracer.

- **Attributes**: An optional set of attributes to associate with the instrumentation scope for any spans emitted.

Together, name, version, and schema URL uniquely identify the *instrumentation scope* for a tracer. The OpenTelemetry specification does not dictate if the same or different `Tracer` instances are returned when obtaining a tracer. Individual languages may implement this behavior differently. For example, in Java, instances are returned from a component registry in a thread-safe way, so two calls to get a tracer with the same parameters will result in the same `Tracer` instance being returned.

In Java, we can obtain a tracer either from a `TracerProvider` or from an `OpenTelemetry` instance (which will use the registered tracer provider):

```
Tracer tracer = openTelemetry
  .tracerBuilder("my-library")
  .setInstrumentationVersion("0.1.0")
  .setSchemaUrl("http://example.com")
  .build();
```

As mentioned in Chapter 4, the `OpenTelemetry` instance can be obtained from `GlobalOpenTelemetry.get()`, but it is encouraged to make the instance available to the instrumented class via other methods like Dependency Injection.

Span Creation and Context Interaction

A `Span` represents an individual unit of work within a trace. Every trace starts at a root span, which normally encapsulates the work required to carry out a given transaction in a distributed system. Each span in a trace can have one or multiple sub-spans, which define the different operations on which the parent span depends to complete its work.

As a structured event, a `Span` has the following properties:

- **Name**: The span name, representing a unit of work. Names must follow OpenTelemetry semantic conventions and be statistically significant in order to facilitate analysis across traces (e.g., a span name containing UIDs or any other high-cardinality values is strongly discouraged).

- **Span context**: Not to be confused with the common telemetry `Context`, the `SpanContext` describes the information from a span that uniquely identifies it (i.e., `TraceId` and `SpanId`), along with other flags and values related to the trace. It is normally stored in a `Context` (the active span in a scope will be the one in the current context) and propagated to other execution units and across services. It conforms to the W3C TraceContext specification, detailed later in this chapter.

- **Parent span**: An optional parent span in the form of a `Span` or a `SpanContext` reference. This holds the causal relationship between spans within the trace tree.

- **Span kind**: The `SpanKind` describes the semantics of parent-child span relationships. It can have one of the following values:

  - `CLIENT`: A synchronous remote call instrumented on the caller side, for example, an HTTP request, where the span should not be considered finished until a response is received. Unless it represents a call to an external system, it is normally the parent of a `SERVER` span.

- SERVER: A synchronous remote call instrumented on the callee side, where the spans should not be considered finished until a response is returned to the caller. Unless it represents a call from an external system, or user, it is normally the child of a CLIENT span.

- PRODUCER: An asynchronous request instrumented on the initiator side, for example, a message in a queue, where the span normally finishes before its CONSUMER child span starts.

- CONSUMER: An asynchronous request instrumented on the receiver side, where the PRODUCER parent span may have finished before this span starts.

- INTERNAL: Represents an internal operation within a service. This is the default value when creating spans.

- **Start timestamp**: Start of the span in Unix epoch time, with a minimum precision of milliseconds and a maximum precision of nanoseconds.

- **End timestamp**: End of the span in Unix epoch time, with a minimum precision of milliseconds and a maximum precision of nanoseconds.

- **Attributes**: A set of key-value pairs where the key must be a non-null, non-empty string and the value either a primitive type (e.g., string, boolean, etc.) or an array of primate values. If possible, attribute keys should follow OpenTelemetry semantic conventions.

- **Links**: A collection of Link instances, where each Link contains a reference to another Span or SpanContext in the same or in a different trace, and an optional set of attributes describing the link. Links can only be added at span creation.

- **Events**: A collection of Event instances, where each Event is described by its name, timestamp, and zero or more attributes describing the event.

- **Status**: Defines the outcome of the unit of work represented by the span. A status contains a status code and an optional description (only used in error cases). The status code can be one of the following:

    - UNSET: The default status, normally indicates the operation completed as expected

    - OK: Indicates a conscious decision by the application owner to mark this span as successful and should not be overwritten

    - ERROR: Indicates the operation contains an error

One important aspect to consider when creating spans is *granularity*. Spans should represent units of work that are statistically significant when evaluating the health of a system. For instance, creating an internal span to instrument a private method that represents less than 1% of the total parent span duration, and that always propagates errors to the caller, is probably not very effective. In addition to the potential increase in transfer and storage costs, it can add noise to traces, making it more difficult to identify key areas of improvement, especially if the instrumented method is called many times as part of a single operation. For some of these cases, span events may be a better fit, providing a leaner way to annotate individual events within an operation. At the other side of the spectrum, relying solely in SERVER and CLIENT spans, which are automatically instrumented in most cases, may be too generic for operations that involve complex internal processing.

Tip   Creating spans that are not too general, yet not too verbose, can improve observability, keeping data volumes at reasonable levels. Keep your spans meaningful by identifying optimization opportunities and key points in your application where capturing errors can prove useful.

A good practice for service owners is to start from SERVER spans for their services and gradually build tracing inward. Figure 6-1 illustrates a simple example of this process. We can see that the endpoint that retrieves PDF documents by document ID takes considerably longer to complete than the CLIENT span to retrieve the document content from a different service. Service owners may have some intuition of what may be happening inside the service, but no evidence backing their claims. In this case, it's useful to break down the main operation and create three children spans: get-content, load-tpl, and render-pdf. Now we can clearly see that most of the time is spent rendering the PDF and that perhaps the template could be loaded concurrently as content is being retrieved if we want to optimize this operation.

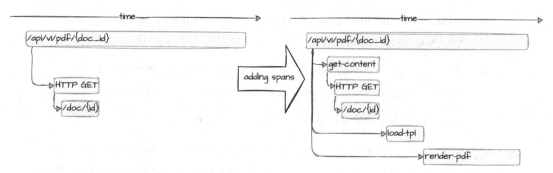

Figure 6-1. *Manually instrumenting a long operation with internal spans*

In order to demonstrate the Tracing API in Java, we can use the Tracer we initialized in the previous section to start a span with a single attribute and then finish it:

```
Span span = tracer.spanBuilder("my first span")
  .setAttribute("isFirst", true)
  .setNoParent()
  .startSpan();
...
span.end();
```

This will generate an INTERNAL span (the default span kind) with start and end timestamps at the moment the startSpan() and end() methods are called. However, the SpanBuilder and Span classes provide methods to use different timestamps if required. As Java handles context implicitly, any span created will automatically be a child of the active span in the current context. This is normally the desired behavior, but it can be overridden by calling setNoParent() or by manually setting the parent when creating the span. In the preceding example, our span would have no parent, making it the root span of a new trace.

Having a span in isolation is not very useful, so let's create a hierarchy of spans, with one span as the child of another. In the following example, the main operation span will be the child of whatever span is active in the current context when myMethod() is called. Then, the inner operation span is created as a child of the main operation span:

```
void myMethod() {
  // Automatically child of the current span in context
  Span parentSpan = tracer.spanBuilder("main operation")
    .startSpan();
  try {
    innerMethod(parentSpan);
  } finally {
    parentSpan.end();
  }
}

void innerMethod(Span parentSpan) {
  Span span = tracer.spanBuilder("inner operation")
    .setParent(Context.current().with(parentSpan))
    .startSpan();
  try {
    // do some work
  } finally {
    span.end();
  }
}
```

This would result in a hierarchy of two spans, but it's easy to see how this would be problematic. We had to pass parentSpan as a parameter to the inner method. This would definitely not scale, and adding instrumentation to an existing code base would be a developer's worst nightmare, requiring changes to method signatures. Fortunately, the Tracing API provides easy access to manage context implicitly in some languages, like Java, Python, or Node. As we saw in the previous chapter, instead of directly using the Context API to manage trace context, it is recommended to handle context via the Tracing API. The following code would achieve the same behavior:

```
void myMethod() {
  // Automatically child of current span in context
  Span parentSpan = tracer.spanBuilder("main operation")
```

```
      .startSpan();
  try(Scope ignored = parentSpan.makeCurrent()) {
    innerMethod();
  } finally {
    parentSpan.end();
  }
}

void innerMethod() {
  // Automatically child of parentSpan
  Span span = tracer.spanBuilder("inner operation")
    .startSpan();
  try(Scope ignored = childSpan.makeCurrent()) {
    // do some work
  } finally {
    span.end();
  }
}
```

The innerMethod() no longer requires the parent span to be passed as a parameter. Instead, by calling makeCurrent() in myMethod(), a scope is created with parentSpan as the span in the current context. When the inner method creates a span within that scope, it automatically uses Span.current() as the parent span, which, in this case, corresponds to parentSpan. The way span context is managed within the Tracing API is the same as baggage is handled in the Baggage API, explained in detail in Chapter 5. Both use values stored in the same context, identified by different keys, using the underlying Context API.

Caution   Ending a span does not imply that the scope where it's running is automatically closed, or that the current context is detached. A span life cycle is independent from the scope or context under which it operates; for example, a span may end but remain as the active span in the current context. Conversely, closing a scope does not end a span, so it's important to ensure that the end() method is always called to avoid memory leaks.

As mentioned previously, spans are created as INTERNAL spans by default. The SpanKind cannot be modified once a span is created, but it can be specified at creation time:

```
Span span = tracer.spanBuilder("/api/v1")
  .setSpanKind(SpanKind.SERVER)
  .startSpan();
```

Another property that can only be configured at span creation is the list of span *links*. Links can be useful to logically connect two or more spans, potentially in different traces, that are somehow related but don't have a causal relationship. For example, if we start an async task but the outcome of said task does not affect the current operation, we may decide to separate it into a different trace and link the span describing the task to the originating operation. To create a span starting a new trace, linking to the current span with a noncausal relationship, we can use

```
Span span = tracer.spanBuilder("linkedSpan")
  .setNoParent()
  .addLink(Span.current().getSpanContext(),
    Attributes.builder().put("submitter", "mainMethod").build())
  .startSpan();
```

The addLink() method can be called more than once, resulting in multiple links to the created span. It can also be called with or without attributes, although adding attributes is recommended to describe the relationship between linked spans.

Working with the Tracing API to create spans is not always necessary, especially for simple use cases. Some languages provide helper mechanisms, like the @tracer.start_ as_current_span decorator in Python, or the @WithSpan annotation in Java. The latter is provided as part of the opentelemetry-instrumentation-annotations Maven artifact. These wrap an annotated method into a span, optionally accepting name, attributes, and span kind as arguments. More information on the Java annotations can be found at *https://opentelemetry.io/docs/instrumentation/java/automatic/annotations*.

Adding Properties to an Existing Span

Creating a new span is not always necessary, or recommended, especially when instrumentation packages are configured. In most cases, adding attributes or events to an existing span is all the necessary instrumentation needed to account for domain-specific use cases. If we take the auto-instrumentation example from Chapter 4 where a POST request is sent to the *http://localhost:8080/people* endpoint to insert a new username with name and job title, we may be interested in annotating the spans with the job title. To do so, we can obtain the current span in the method that serves that resource and add the job title passed as parameter as an *attribute*:

```
@POST
@UnitOfWork
public Person createPerson(@Valid Person person) {
  Span span = Span.current();
  span.setAttribute("job.title", person.getJobTitle());
  return peopleDAO.create(person);
}
```

Figure 6-2 shows a trace in the Jaeger UI after rebuilding the dropwizard-example-2.1.1.jar file as detailed in Chapter 4 containing the preceding changes and then sending the same POST request to the /people endpoint on the application running with the OpenTelemetry Java agent. We can see that the PeopleResource.createPerson span is now annotated with a job.title attribute.

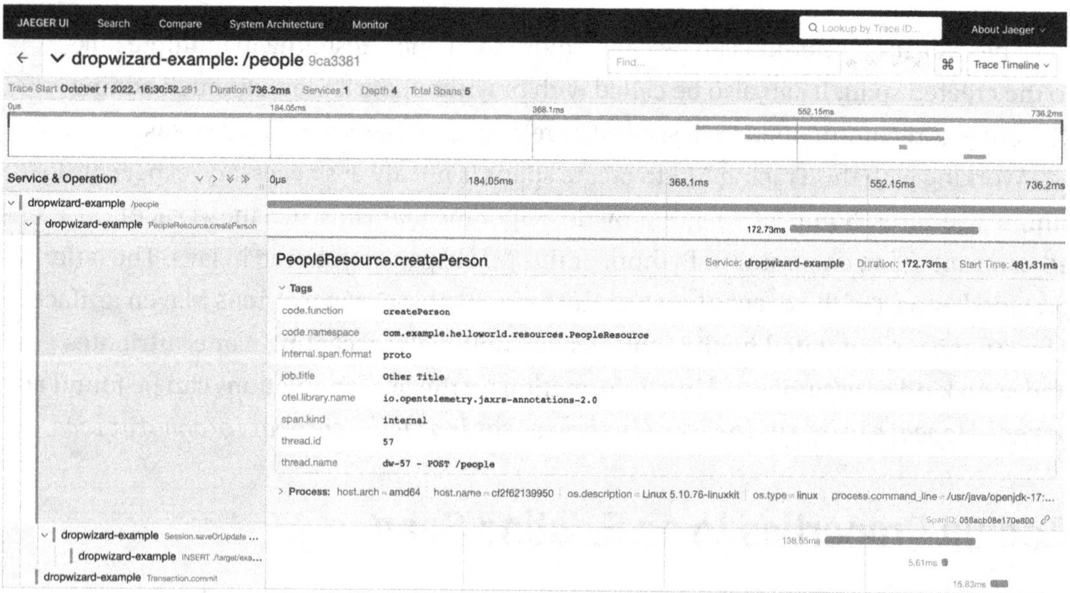

Figure 6-2. *Annotating spans in dropwizard-example with job.title*

Calling setAttribute() overwrites any attribute already present in the span for the same key. In Java, it is also possible to set multiple attributes at the same time by using the setAllAttributes() method.

In addition to attributes, on certain occasions, we may be interested in tracking individual markers during an operation, for which we don't require a full-fledged span. This is the case of sub-operations that are not that meaningful on their own, but knowing when, or if, they happened would enhance the debugging context provided as part of span. To support this use case, spans can be decorated with a list of *events* as follows:

```
span.addEvent("something happened");
span.addEvent("something happened earlier",
  Instant.ofEpochMilli(1664640662000L));
span.addEvent("something else happened",
  Attributes.builder().put("eventKey", 42).build());
```

Events consist of a name, a timestamp, and an optional set of attributes. By default, events will take the current timestamp when the event is added to the span, but it is possible to specify the timestamp if required.

In the vast majority of occasions, the name given to a span when created is sufficient. However, there are certain cases that require the *span name* to be adjusted at a later stage, when more information is available to build a meaningful name. This is the case of SERVER spans, for example. OpenTelemetry semantic conventions discourage the use of unbound cardinality in span names, so an HTTP server instrumentation library may create a span called HTTP GET for a URL like /api/people/12, as using the URL would result in a different span name per person ID. Later, a controller or middleware instrumentation library, using information available to them within that layer, can update the span name to something like /api/people/{person_id}, which better represents the operation while keeping cardinality at bay. For example:

```
span.updateName("/api/people/{person_id}");
```

Caution   Any sampling behavior based on span names may be affected by updating the span name, as samplers may only consider the name given during span creation.

Representing Errors and Exceptions

Spans offer a standard way of representing the outcome of an operation. By default, and unless modified, the status code of a span is UNSET. This means that the operation captured by the span completed normally.

To represent error cases, we can change the status code of a span to ERROR, optionally allowing for a description of the error, for example:

```
@WithSpan
void myMethod() {
  try {
    // some work
  } catch (Exception e) {
    Span.current().setStatus(StatusCode.ERROR,
                              "an error ocurred");
  }
}
```

Although we could add the exception name or message as the description, the Tracing API provides a recordException() method to handle exceptions:

```
@WithSpan
void myMethod() {
  try {
    // some work
  } catch (Exception e) {
    Span.current().setStatus(StatusCode.ERROR,
                              "an error occurred");
    Span.current().recordException(e);
  }
}
```

This provides a simplified and standard way of representing exceptions following OpenTelemetry semantic conventions. It creates a new event on the span with name exception and attributes exception.type, exception.message, and exception. stacktrace obtained from the Throwable object passed as a parameter. Additionally, this method allows passing extra attributes that will be appended to the exception event.

There is a third status code, OK, which has a special significance. In general, instrumentation libraries and manually created spans should leave the status as UNSET if no errors occur. However, there are certain cases where the application owner wants to override the status of a span set by some other library, or wants to indicate that a specific case should be considered as successful. For instance, an HTTP client library instrumentation may set the status of a span to ERROR when a 404 status code is returned, but the application owner may be expecting a 404 to be returned. In that case, the span status can be changed to OK:

```
span.setStatus(StatusCode.OK);
```

Tracing Asynchronous Tasks

The relationship between parent and child spans should be one of causality and dependence. The operation described by a parent span causes the one described by the child, and it also depends, in some capacity, on its outcome. This is of particular importance when we consider asynchronous code execution. As we've seen in Chapter 5, the Context API provides functionality that allows to propagate context between execution units, that is, threads, in languages that manage context implicitly. Let's consider the following simple example, where a mainOp() method calls a slumber() method asynchronously and then waits for its response in order to log how long the slumber was:

```
void mainOp() throws Exception {
  Span span = tracer.spanBuilder("mainOp").startSpan();
  try(Scope ignored = span.makeCurrent()) {
    // Wait for slumber to return
    long millis = CompletableFuture
      .supplyAsync(Context.current()
        .wrapSupplier(()-> slumber()))
      .get();
    LOGGER.info("Back from a {} ms slumber", millis);
  } finally {
    span.end();
  }
}
```

```
long slumber() {
  // Generate random number between 100 and 1000
  long millis = (long) (Math.random() * (1000 - 100) + 100);
  Span span = tracer.spanBuilder("slumber").startSpan();
  try(Scope ignored = span.makeCurrent()) {
    Thread.sleep(millis);
  } catch (InterruptedException e) {
    span.setStatus(StatusCode.ERROR,
                  "slumber interrupted");
  } finally {
    span.end();
  }
  return millis;
}
```

Using the Context API `wrapSupplier()` functionality, we can propagate trace context and have both spans form part of the same trace, depicted in Figure 6-3 (a SERVER span called /api/v1/main was added as parent of mainOp). In this case, although the task is executed asynchronously, the main method depends on its sub-operation to complete its work, so it's correctly represented under the same trace.

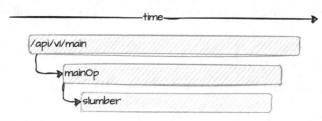

Figure 6-3. *Propagating span context between threads*

To simplify the preceding example, if we are using the Java agent, we can rely on the executor instrumentation to automatically propagate tasks submitted to the ForkJoinPool executor (enabled by default). We can also include the opentelemetry-instrumentation-annotations package in our dependencies to make use of annotations. With these instrumentations in place, the equivalent resulting code would look like

```
@WithSpan("mainOp")
void mainOp() throws Exception {
```

```
// Wait for slumber to return
long millis = CompletableFuture
  .supplyAsync(()-> slumber())
  .get();
LOGGER.info("Back from a {} ms slumber", millis);
}

@WithSpan("slumber")
long slumber() {
  // Generate random number between 100 and 1000
  long millis = (long) (Math.random() * (1000 - 100) + 100);
  try {
    Thread.sleep(millis);
  } catch (InterruptedException e) {
    Span.current().setStatus(StatusCode.ERROR,
                             "slumber interrupted");
  }
  return millis;
}
```

As application owners, we may decide that waiting for the slumber() method to return is no longer required, and we can avoid blocking the thread when calling get() on the CompletableFuture, converting it into a fire-and-forget async task execution using runAsync(). This breaks the dependency between the mainOp span and the slumber span, as the parent span no longer depends on the child span to finish its execution. Figure 6-4 shows the effect that this would have in a trace, with the parent span potentially finishing before the child span starts, and how splitting this fire-and-forget operation in two traces may provide a better representation.

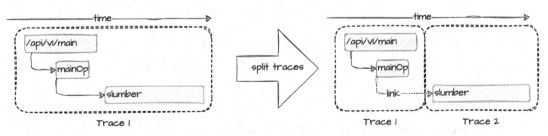

Figure 6-4. Splitting traces for fire-and-forget tasks

Having all spans in the same trace may not seem like an issue at first sight, but ultimately the trace no longer represents the dependency between operations accurately. When we consider a public API, we're normally interested in representing the behavior experienced by the client. The slumber() method could take orders of magnitude longer to complete than its parent, or it could fail, and the response to the client would be unaffected. When analyzing traces by root span to understand the behavior of our system, this could result in a wrong interpretation of traces commencing at /api/v1/main. This is especially important when traces are sampled. A common sampling methodology is to consider the whole trace and keep traces that contain errors, or that take longer to complete than a specific threshold. Retaining slumber as part of a trace would affect the sampling result, as we would keep traces where the slumber() method took longer to complete, rather than traces where the client got a slow response, which is normally what service owners are interested in.

Tip   Representing async tasks spawned from an operation as child spans may not always be desired behavior in fire-and-forget operations, especially when using certain types of trace sampling.

To solve this issue, we can split the trace in two, with a new trace being created where slumber is the root span, linking back to the mainOp span via a span link, as represented in Figure 6-4:

```
@WithSpan("mainOp")
void mainOp() {
  // Do not wait for slumber to return (fire-and-forget)
  CompletableFuture.runAsync(()-> slumber());
}

long slumber() {
  // Generate random number between 100 and 1000
  long millis = (long) (Math.random() * (1000 - 100) + 100);
  Span span = tracer.spanBuilder("slumber")
    .setNoParent()
    .addLink(Span.current().getSpanContext())
    .startSpan();
```

```
try(Scope ignored = span.makeCurrent()) {
  Thread.sleep(millis);
} catch (InterruptedException e) {
  span.setStatus(StatusCode.ERROR,
              "slumber interrupted");
} finally {
  span.end();
}
return millis;
}
```

Users of OpenTracing may recognize this type of relationship, represented as a link between spans, as the equivalent of a FOLLOWS_FROM reference.

Tracing SDK

In the previous section, we mentioned that TracerProvider, Tracer, and Span contain limited functionality in the Tracing API to provide a no-op behavior if no SDK is configured. As a standard implementation of the API, the Tracing SDK implements those interfaces to represent spans in memory, process them, and export them to tracing backends.

In addition to providing Tracer instances, the TracerProvider implementation within the OpenTelemetry SDK contains all span handling configuration. This includes the following:

- **Span processors**: List of hooks called when spans are started or ended, including exporters. By default, no processors are defined.

- **ID generator**: Defines how to generate span and trace IDs. By default, random 16-byte trace IDs and 8-byte span IDs are returned.

- **Span limits**: Helps ensure that no faulty instrumentation can exhaust the available memory by setting certain limits on the number of span attributes, events, links, or attribute length. Although there's a default on the number of attributes, events, and links, the attribute length is not limited by default.

- **Sampler**: Method used to decide if a span should be sampled or not. We will cover samplers in detail, along with sampling on OpenTelemetry Collectors and how to configure the Java agent, in Chapter 10. The default behavior is to use a composite sampler that makes the same decision as the parent span. If no parent is available, it decides to sample any span created.

- **Resource**: Configures the Resource to be associated with the processed spans. The configuration of a Resource programmatically or via system properties is detailed in Chapter 4.

Assuming we have the opentelemetry-api and opentelemetry-sdk Maven artifacts as configured dependencies, we can create a new TracerProvider and use it to create a new OpenTelemetry instance as follows:

```
// Default values, equivalent to calling build() directly
SdkTracerProvider tracerProvider = SdkTracerProvider.builder()
  .setIdGenerator(IdGenerator.random())
  .setSampler(Sampler.parentBased(Sampler.alwaysOn()))
  .setSpanLimits(SpanLimits.getDefault())
  .setResource(Resource.getDefault())
  .build();

OpenTelemetry openTelemetry = OpenTelemetrySdk.builder()
  .setTracerProvider(tracerProvider)
  .setPropagators(ContextPropagators.create(
    W3CTraceContextPropagator.getInstance()))
  .buildAndRegisterGlobal();
```

Although this tracing configuration would generate spans, it would immediately discard them when finished, as no processor is configured. In the next subsection, we explain how to add a processor that can batch and export spans and how to configure this default processor when using the Java agent.

If using the Java agent, span limits can be controlled via the following properties:

- otel.span.attribute.value.length.limit

- otel.span.attribute.count.limit

- otel.span.event.count.limit

- otel.span.link.count.limit

These properties will all default to 128 if not specifically configured. There is also a way to limit attribute length and attribute count for all signals with the following properties, which will be used if no specific `otel.span.attribute` values are used:

- `otel.attribute.value.length.limit`

- `otel.attribute.count.limit`

In addition to configuration and to creation of tracers, the `TracerProvider` also provides methods to clean up spans in memory:

- `shutdown()`: Stops all tracers created by this provider so that newly created spans are returned as no-op spans and calls the `shutdown()` method on any registered processor to stop accepting new spans and flush any spans in memory

- `forceFlush()`: Calls the `forceFlush()` method on all registered processors to immediately export all spans in memory

Span Processors and Exporters

A `TracerProvider` is normally configured with one or more processors that get invoked when a span is started or finished (unless the `isRecording` property is set to false, as we'll see when we examine sampling in detail). These processors implement the `SpanProcessor` interface and provide implementations for `onStart()`, `onEnd()`, `shutdown()`, and `forceFlush()` methods.

The responsibility of span processors is to handle spans in memory in some way, like batching or modifying attributes, and optionally export them to a telemetry backend. The OpenTelemetry SDK provides two built-in span processors:

- `SimpleSpanProcessor`: Passes spans to a configured `exporter` as soon as they are finished

- `BatchSpanProcessor`: Groups spans in batches before calling a configured `exporter`

As we saw in Chapter 4 when we demonstrated the use of a span processor to modify the span error status under certain conditions, custom processors can also be implemented and added as extensions to the Java agent or configured when creating the tracer provider. The Java agent configures a `BatchSpanProcessor` with some default properties and an exporter that uses OTLP over gRPC to send spans to a backend. Having the `opentelemetry-exporter-otlp` Maven dependency in our build file, we could achieve the same programmatically (assuming we have a `resource` already created):

```
SdkTracerProvider tracerProvider = SdkTracerProvider.builder()
  .addSpanProcessor(BatchSpanProcessor
    .builder(OtlpGrpcSpanExporter.builder().build())
    .build())
  .setResource(resource)
  .build();
```

The processor builder accepts an exporter as a parameter, and it can configure a set of properties to control batching and buffering, available in all implementations. When using the Java agent, these properties can also be configured via system properties (or their equivalent environment variables):

- `otel.bsp.schedule.delay`: The maximum time interval, in milliseconds, that the processor will wait before exporting a batch. The processor may export batches earlier if the number of spans in the queue is larger than the maximum batch size.

- `otel.bsp.max.queue.size`: The maximum size of the queue of spans to export. If the queue is full, the processor will start to drop spans.

- `otel.bsp.max.export.batch.size`: The maximum number of spans per batch sent to the exporter. An export will be triggered if there are enough spans in the export queue to fill one batch of this size.

- `otel.bsp.export.timeout`: Maximum time to wait for a result after calling the exporter before an export is cancelled.

The `BatchSpanProcessor` implementation in Java generates a set of metrics using the Metrics API from within the processor, which can be monitored by application owners to optimize the preceding settings. These are `queueSize`, a gauge-type metric measuring the size of the queue at a given time, and a `processedSpans` counter, measuring the number of spans processed. The latter is split by a boolean attribute called `dropped`, which indicates if the counter represents spans dropped or not. If the count of `processedSpans` with `dropped: true` is greater than 0, it means the processor is not able to export spans fast enough at the current throughput.

> **Tip**   The OpenTelemetry SDK defaults to a relatively short queue on the
> `BatchSpanProcessor` to minimize overhead. In high-throughput systems, it
> may be necessary to increase the queue size or to tune other batch and exporting
> options, like the batch size.

The exporter used by default by the OpenTelemetry Java agent, and most other implementations, is the `OtlpGrpcSpanExporter`. Other exporters are maintained as part of the core libraries, like `opentelemetry-exporter-jaeger` or `opentelemetry-exporter-zipkin`, each one with different configuration options.

The exporter the Java agent uses along with the `BatchSpanProcessor` can be configured using the `otel.traces.exporter` property (e.g., `otel.traces.exporter=jaeger`). The configuration for exporters is extensive, including options to control endpoints, certificates, timeouts, headers, etc. This is documented under *https://opentelemetry.io/docs/instrumentation/java/automatic/agent-config*.

Although application owners are ultimately free to choose the exporter that is better suited for their needs, using OTLP exporters has certain advantages. The communication with OpenTelemetry Collectors via OTLP is the most widely used and thus the better supported path. Many observability vendors can also accept OTLP natively, making the decision easier. Additionally, OTLP supports mechanisms like backpressure and retries, which increase the reliability of exports. The OTLP exporter in Java is configured to retry exports for up to five times, with an exponential backoff from one to five seconds.

Trace Context Propagation

When we call `span.makeCurrent()` to mark a span as active in the current context, or manually use the Context API if handled explicitly, its `SpanContext` is stored as any other context value. This `SpanContext` is represented with a data structure that conforms to W3C TraceContext standards. It contains the following:

- **Trace ID**: A 16-byte trace identifier.

- **Span ID**: An 8-byte span identifier.

- **Trace flags**: A set of flags detailing aspects of a trace. The only flag currently defined is `sampled`, which indicates if the trace should be stored.

- **Trace state**: A list of key-value pairs containing vendor-specific information. For example, r and p values related to probability-based sampling as documented in *https://opentelemetry.io/docs/reference/specification/trace/tracestate-probability-sampling*, which will be covered in Chapter 10.

As any context value, the Propagators API must be used for SpanContext to be propagated between services, normally as HTTP headers, so that traces can be continued. As we saw in Chapter 5, the OpenTelemetry API provides TextMapPropagator implementations for W3C Baggage and W3C TraceContext. A set of propagators for other commonly used formats like B3, Jaeger, or OT are available in extension packages. Propagators, including trace propagators, can be configured via the otel.propagators property in the Java agent or using the appropriate builder if configured programmatically.

W3C TraceContext

One of the main goals of OpenTelemetry is interoperability. In past solutions, like OpenTracing, trace context propagation had been a pain point for large organizations, or systems undergoing migrations between vendors or tracer implementations. Tracers would normally only allow one propagator, and it would often be tied to a tracing framework (e.g., a tracer using uber-* headers would not be able to inject or extract context propagated with ot-* headers). This resulted in broken traces, or orphaned spans. To tackle this issue, apart from providing a way to propagate context with multiple propagators via the Propagators API, the OpenTelemetry project submitted a proposal to W3C to standardize an HTTP header format for trace context propagation, now available as a W3C Recommendation at *www.w3.org/TR/trace-context*. This format has now been adopted by many vendors and open-source tooling as the default trace context propagation format. It has enabled scenarios where vendor-specific agents can seamlessly participate in traces along with OpenTelemetry-instrumented services.

The W3C specification describes all aspects related to trace context propagation via HTTP request headers in detail, including header format, processing model for propagators, ID generation, privacy, and security considerations. As an overview, the request headers that are part of W3C TraceContext are as follows:

- traceparent: It describes the last active span in a trace, which will become the current span in the context extracted from the request, and consequently the parent of any span created under the same active context. Although not a requirement – as any span can be represented in this header – the parent span will normally be a CLIENT span and the child span a SERVER span. The value of this header follows a version-traceId-parentId-traceFlags format, where version is 1 byte representing an 8-bit unsigned integer describing the current version of the TraceContext specification (currently 00), traceId and parentId are nonzero 16-byte and 8-byte unique identifiers, and traceFlags is an 8-bit field, currently only using the rightmost bit to represent the sampled flag. All values are lowercase hex-encoded.

- tracestate: A header representing vendor-specific information related to the trace being propagated, encoded as a list of key-value pairs using a format similar to the W3C Baggage representation detailed in the last chapter. Vendors should not delete or update any keys not generated by themselves and should always add new or updated keys to the left of the header values.

The following is an example of valid headers propagating trace context:

```
traceparent: 00-8909f23beb409e44011074c591d7350e-d5d7d3b3a7d196ac-01
tracestate: vendor1=foo,vendor2=bar
```

Figure 6-5 illustrates how a trace context like this could make its way through a service. In this case, Service A made a sampling decision to keep the trace and propagated this value along with a new parent span ID to Service B. Also, Service A uses vendor2, which updates its value on the trace state and shifts its key to the beginning of the list as per W3C TraceContext specification.

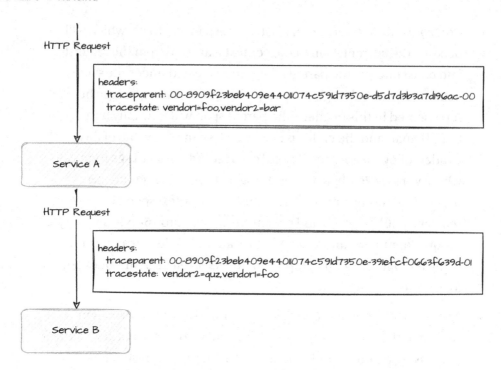

Figure 6-5. *W3C TraceContext propagated through a service*

Summary

Tracing gives structure to the contextualized telemetry produced from distributed systems. It allows engineers to gather information derived from relationships between operations executed on different services that are part of the same originating transaction. This is a lengthy topic, and there are certainly more details to cover, including trace sampling, which will be reviewed in more detail in Chapter 10. This chapter covered some of the most important concepts to understand the purpose of tracing, how to manually instrument a service to represent custom workflows, and how to configure the OpenTelemetry SDK to process and propagate trace context.

Albeit powerful, tracing alone is not the answer to all telemetry. Different signals have different constraints and requirements, and each is best suited to a particular use case. In the next chapter, we'll explore the Metrics API and SDK, and we'll see how OpenTelemetry can empower service owners to use the right signal for the right purpose. Using the same underlying context mechanisms, we'll start to see how telemetry can be linked between signals as well as between services.

## CHAPTER 7

Metrics

One of the basic requirements of operational monitoring is being able to track the state of services and resources over time. To effectively monitor key performance indicators, we need both real-time and historic views of stable signals that allow us to evaluate conditions against certain targets or thresholds. This is the purpose of metrics.

Metrics are one of the most widely known telemetry signals. They have been used in software systems for decades, although the popularity of microservice architectures and large-scale deployments, containing thousands of replicas per service, has stretched the technical requirements of metrics backends, which sometimes can struggle to handle the volume of data ingested, resulting in higher costs and degraded user experience. With OpenTelemetry, service owners are provided with the tools to choose the right signal (e.g., spans, metrics or logs) to instrument a given concept and to select the right level of aggregation in the metrics exported from a service. Using a common underlying context propagation system and semantic conventions allows metrics to form part of an integrated observability solution, rather than a series of events evaluated in isolation.

In this chapter, we'll explore the OpenTelemetry Metrics API and its design principles, different metric types, how context can help connect metrics with other signals, and how the Metrics SDK can be configured to aggregate and export data to telemetry backends.

Measurements, Metrics, and Time Series

When we think about metrics, the first image that comes to mind is normally a graph plotting a succession of values sorted in time order. Each of these values can either be backed by a single data point or aggregated across time intervals and dimensions. For example, if we have a collection of hosts where each host produces a data point per minute measuring its memory utilization, we may be interested in plotting the data coming from a single host or the mean value across all hosts. To do this, each data point

111

© Daniel Gomez Blanco 2023
D. Gomez Blanco, *Practical OpenTelemetry*, https://doi.org/10.1007/978-1-4842-9075-0_7

is normally decorated with a set of attributes (e.g., hostname, IP address, region). A succession of data points in time order, with a unique combination of name, attributes, and attribute values, is what defines a *time series*.

A time series alone does not define the meaning of its data or the relationship between successive points. Consider the following time series with three data points at different instants (t_0 to t_2):

```
t0 -> 5
t1 -> 8
t2 -> 12
```

How would we know if it's measuring a monotonically increasing sum, like the total number of customers that has visited a shop, or an independent measurement (i.e., a gauge), like the temperature of a fridge? The answer is: we can't. This is important, because although it would make sense to sum the number of customers across all shops, it probably wouldn't make much sense to sum the temperature across all fridges.

To get around semantics, most metrics backends defer that decision until the data is queried, although some backends like Prometheus propose some naming conventions using suffixes to hint at the type of data stored to help the user decide (see *https://prometheus.io/docs/practices/naming*). Ultimately, it is the responsibility of the user to give meaning to data by using appropriate query functions. In any case, the underlying semantics for a given group of time series must be common; otherwise the results would be inconsistent (e.g., it wouldn't make sense to obtain a sum of customers and temperature together). This notion of a group of time series with the same properties is usually referred to as a *metric*, which is identified with a name but may have other common properties like description or unit of measurement. Some backends require the aggregation type to be part of a metric definition (e.g., a sum or a gauge) to facilitate storage and querying, and they all normally have some expectations on the time interval considered for each data point, as we'll see later in this chapter. These are also intrinsic properties of a metric.

When read carefully, the last paragraph starts to display signs of one of the major challenges for metrics clients: the coupling of aggregations with their backend representation. Metrics are considered stable signals because they produce aggregated data points at regular intervals. Consider a service receiving 100,000 requests per minute on which we want to monitor response time. If we were to export every single request duration, the amount of out-of-band telemetry data (i.e., data transferred separately from service requests/responses) would potentially be larger than the in-band data, expensive to store, slow to query, and prompt to dropped or delayed events. To monitor service health, we're not normally interested in timings for very single request, so we can calculate some response time aggregates (e.g., min, max, mean, sum, etc.) every minute per service replica and query it at a service or replica level. Different metrics backends expect these aggregates in a given format, and as metrics clients are normally built for a specific backend, this results in instrumentation being locked to a specific framework, presenting difficulties already discussed in previous chapters.

In its mission to provide interoperability between telemetry backends, OpenTelemetry tackles this challenge by splitting the responsibilities of measuring from aggregating measurements. A *measurement* represents a single observation of a given concept, for instance, the duration of a request, along with a set of attributes. These measurements can then be aggregated according to a metric definition and exported in regular intervals to the telemetry backend of choice. Concepts like measurements, aggregations, views, and exporters may be familiar to OpenCensus users, as the OpenTelemetry specification is heavily influenced by the now superseded project.

Figure 7-1 gives a very general view of the metrics collection data flow when using the OpenTelemetry Metrics API and SDK. Individual measurements are aggregated in memory and then exported as metrics data in regular intervals to one or multiple backends.

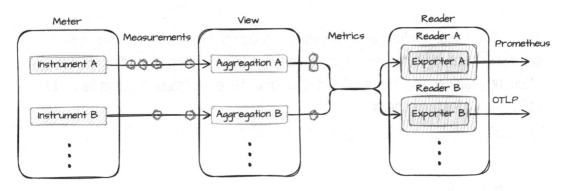

Figure 7-1. *General OpenTelemetry Metrics data flow*

Measurements are aggregated into metric data points according to an aggregation function and a set of attributes. For instance, let's assume that Instrument A in Figure 7-1 is tracking the duration of HTTP requests in a measurement named `http.server. duration` that gets reported with a single attribute called `http.status_code` for each request that goes through the server. Regardless of how many requests are served, this metric will report a single data point per status code (e.g., one data point for status code 200 and one for status code 503) with the configured aggregation (e.g., a histogram), at each collection interval.

Metric cardinality can be defined as the number of unique attribute combinations for a given metric, which directly correlates to the number of data points exported from a service. This is often a limiting factor for metrics backends and normally results in higher operational costs. Let's imagine that a developer adds a new `http.url` attribute to the measurement mentioned in the previous paragraph, containing the raw request URL processed by our server. If the URL contains unbounded values (e.g., a session ID), instead of producing two datapoints, we could be producing thousands at each collection interval, potentially even one data point per measurement! This is commonly referred to as a cardinality explosion. In this case, the resulting aggregation is no longer significant, as plotting a single time series may only show one data point (defeating the purpose of a time series) and alerting on a single session ID would be a very unusual requirement. The metric would normally need to be re-aggregated at query time to be useful. All the data transfer and computational costs necessary to collect and query this metric could have been avoided if the right attributes were used when producing the measurement. Although being able to see the duration of a single request may be useful for debugging, other telemetry signals, like tracing, would be better suited, providing added value like transactional context.

Tip   Metric aggregations should produce meaningful time series. If a unique combination of attributes is not generic enough to be plotted or alerted on, it is often too granular, and the developer may consider other telemetry signals that are better suited for their use case.

Metrics API

The OpenTelemetry Metrics API defines public interfaces to report measurements in a standard manner. Its responsibilities end there, delegating the processing of these measurements to the implementing SDK. In the absence of an SDK, the Metrics API behaves as a no-op API, allowing instrumentation authors to focus on providing the measurements and application owners to configure the desired aggregations and export format.

Meters and Meter Providers

Following a similar pattern to the Tracing API, the Metrics API defines a `MeterProvider` interface, which must be implemented by an SDK in order to provide working `Meter` instances. Although it is a common practice to have a single `MetricProvider` per application, initialized when building and registering a new global `OpenTelemetry` instance, multiple instances can coexist, each with different configurations.

Meters are responsible for creating `Instrument` instances, which are in turn used to report measurements. A `Meter` instance can be obtained from a `MeterProvider` by using the following parameters:

- **Name**: The name of the meter. This can be the name of an instrumentation library, or, for custom instrumentation or instrumentation built natively into libraries, it can be the library name, a class, a package, etc. This is a mandatory parameter. If none is passed, it will default to an empty string.

- **Version**: The version of the instrumentation or instrumented library. This is an optional parameter.

- **Schema URL**: Optional parameter to specify the `schema_url` for all events produced by this meter.

- **Attributes**: An optional set of attributes to associate with the instrumentation scope for any metrics emitted.

Together, name, version, and schema URL uniquely identify the *instrumentation scope* of a `Meter`. As we'll see in the "Duplicate Instrument Registration" section later, the instrumentation scope namespaces the metrics produced by an application. It should define the level at which a given concept is observed. For instance, if we are interested in measuring the total number of requests served by application, the instrumentation scope should either identify the server library or the application itself. However, if we want to independently consider each package or class, we may use a different scope for each.

The OpenTelemetry specification does not dictate if the same or different `Meter` instances are returned when obtaining a meter from a `MeterProvider` using the same parameters. Individual languages may implement this behavior differently. For example, in Java, instances are returned from a component registry in a thread-safe way, so two calls to get a meter with the same parameters will result in the same `Meter` instance being returned.

We can obtain a new `Meter` from a `MeterProvider` using the centrally configured `OpenTelemetry` instance as follows:

```
Meter meter = openTelemetry.meterBuilder("my-meter")
  .setInstrumentationVersion("0.1.0")
  .build();
```

Alternatively, a meter can be acquired directly from a standalone `MeterProvider`, without accessing it through an `OpenTelemetry` instance. We'll explain how to create a `MeterProvider` in the "Metrics SDK" section.

Instrument Registration

The responsibility of a meter is to create `Instrument` instances. These can be identified using the following properties:

- **Name**: The name of the instrument, which forms the name of the resulting metric after aggregation (some exporters, like Prometheus, may transform this name to meet naming conventions). Names must have a maximum length of 63 case-insensitive ASCII characters. They must start with an alphanumeric character, followed by zero or more alphanumeric characters, ".", "_", or "-".

- **Kind**: The type of instrument (e.g., a counter or an asynchronous counter).

- **Unit**: The unit of measurement (e.g., second). It must have a maximum of 63 ASCII characters and be case sensitive (i.e., kb is different to kB).

- **Description**: A short explanation of the type of measurements represented by this instrument. The maximum length and encoding depend on the implementation, but it must support at least 1024 characters and Basic Multilingual Plane (BMP) encoding (i.e., the first plane of UTF-8).

Instruments are uniquely identified by these fields, optionally including language-level features like the number type (i.e., floating point vs integer). The OpenTelemetry specification does not dictate under which conditions the same or different Instrument instances will be returned when requesting more than one instrument with the same identifying fields under the same instrumentation scope (i.e., meter properties). For instance, the Java implementation will return different instances of an Instrument on each call, sharing the same underlying storage and aggregation so that all measurements are collected under the same metric data points.

Duplicate Instrument Registration

If multiple distinct instruments are registered under the same name and instrumentation scope, the SDK should output "duplicate instrument registration" warnings. A working instrument will be returned, but this type of conflict may result in metrics containing semantic errors.

The implementation may try to remediate these conflicts. For example, if two counters are registered under the same name, but with different description or unit, the implementation may aggregate both metrics, choosing the longer description or converting between units (e.g., from MB to KB). However, this is not a requirement. In Java, these would be treated as different counters and not aggregated, resulting in two metrics emitted with the same name.

Caution   To avoid semantic errors, ensure that the same instrument properties are used to measure a specific concept under the same instrumentation scope. Pay attention to any duplicate registration warnings produced by the SDK.

Although the SDK will output warnings when instruments with the same name are registered, meters with distinct instrumentation scopes are treated as separate namespaces. This means that two instruments registered with the same name under distinct meters will not be considered a conflict. For instance, registering the following two instruments will not generate any warnings, as the version property of the my-meter is different, and they will be aggregated independently under different metrics:

```
Instrument={
  InstrumentationScope={name=my-meter, version=1.0.0},
  name=my-counter,
```

```
  description=random counter,
  type=LONG_SUM
}

Instrument={
  InstrumentationScope={name=my-meter, version=2.0.0},
  name=my-counter,
  description=random counter,
  type=LONG_SUM
}
```

Individual exporters may handle this situation differently. For instance, OTLP is built around the concept of `Metric` streams, with separate streams for different instrumentation scopes, while the Prometheus exporter would represent them as different labels:

```
my_counter_total{otel_scope_name="my-meter", otel_scope_version="1.0.0"}
1707.0 1665253818117

my_counter_total otel_scope_name="my-meter", otel_scope_version="2.0.0"}
345.0 1665253818117
```

Synchronous and Asynchronous Instruments

Measurements can either be reported as part of application logic, like the number of items processed, incremented on each request, or asynchronously, invoked on demand when the configured metric reader periodically collects metrics, like the temperature of a CPU at a given point in time.

When measurements are reported asynchronously, the `Instrument` is created with a callback function responsible for reporting individual measurements. Depending on the language, this function may return a collection of `Measurement` values or have access to an `ObservableMeasurement` passed as a parameter that can be used to report values. In any case, to avoid semantic errors, no duplicate measurements (i.e., measurements with the same attributes) should be reported on a single execution.

As synchronous instruments report measurements as part of application logic, they can use features that rely on `Context` that allow to link different types of signals. Due to their asynchronous nature, this is not available to asynchronous instruments.

Monotonicity

In mathematics, monotonicity refers to the relation between successive values in an ordered set. A function is set to be monotonically increasing, or non-decreasing, if a given value is always greater or equal than the previous value (i.e., it never decreases). As illustrated in Figure 7-2, for all x and y, if x <= y, then f(x) <= f(y).

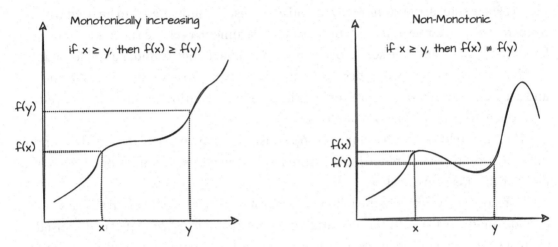

Figure 7-2. *Monotonic vs. non-monotonic functions*

Within the frame of metrics data, monotonically increasing measurements and non-monotonic measurements are designed to answer different questions. The former are normally recommended to measure total counts, while the latter usually represent the state of a system at a specific instant. For instance, if we increase a counter with each request handled by a service, when we aggregate and collect these measurements in periodic intervals, we can tell the total number of requests served in each interval. In contrast, if we increase a counter when a request is accepted and we decrease it when it's processed, at a given point in time, we can only know the number of requests in-flight, but not the total number of requests served.

Note   The monotonicity of measurements does not imply that the reported metric values never decrease. As we will see in the "Metrics SDK" section, data points exported for monotonically increasing measurements can be represented as deltas between two consecutive collection intervals (i.e., delta temporality), so the resulting metric values could go up or down.

Instrument Types

Choosing the right instrument type when instrumenting metrics in an application has many advantages. Although OpenTelemetry allows custom configuration, every instrument has a default aggregation and some intrinsic properties that give it meaning. This informs users about the instrumentation author's intended treatment for a given metric. For instance, the author may intend a request duration metric to be used with histogram or percentile functions, or they may instrument a vehicle speed metric knowing that it makes little sense to sum multiple vehicle speeds under a single value. In addition to providing semantics, each instrument type provides the most efficient and accurate way to report measurements in different scenarios, resulting in reduced performance overhead to report metrics.

The OpenTelemetry API defines multiple instrument types, each designed to support different use cases when reporting measurements. The next subsections detail each of the available instrument types.

As readers may notice in the following examples, in Java, the `Attributes` class provides methods like `Attributes.builder()` and `Attributes.of()` that can be used to create measurement attributes. Measurements are aggregated into metric data points according to each unique combination of attributes. Although it is possible to drop attributes in a metric `View`, as detailed in the "Metrics SDK" section, developers should consider metric cardinality when creating attribute values.

Counter

A `Counter` is a type of instrument that allows to report monotonically increasing values. It is intended to be used within application logic to report individual measurements, for instance, the number of tickets sold or the amount of data processed by a service. A `Counter` can be registered as follows:

```
LongCounter counter = meter
  .counterBuilder("tickets.sold")
  .setDescription("number of tickets sold")
  .build();
```

In Java, the default value type of the counter is Long. To obtain a counter for Double values, we can call the `ofDoubles()` method that informs the builder to return a `DoubleCounter` instead of a `LongCounter`:

```
DoubleCounter counter = meter
  .counterBuilder("data.processed")
  .setUnit("kB")
  .ofDoubles()
  .build();
```

Counters can only be incremented with positive or zero values. Incrementing a counter with a negative value should log a warning, and the measurement will be omitted. To increment a counter (with or without attributes):

```
counter.add(12);
```

```
counter.add(8,
  Attributes.of(stringKey("myKey"), "myValue"));
```

Asynchronous Counter

This type of instrument, normally named `ObservableCounter` (or idiomatic equivalent), can be used to report monotonically increasing values in an asynchronous manner. It is normally used to report precalculated values, like the number of garbage collections or the CPU time per process. At each collection interval, which may be configured via a periodic reader or on-demand, the registered callback function is invoked to report measurements. It is recommended to avoid duplicate measurements (with the same attributes) in a single callback execution, as the SDK may not process them as expected, or drop them entirely.

Note   Contrary to `Counter.add()`, each callback execution should report the total value of a counter, not the delta or increment, so that aggregations can find the delta between two reporting intervals by subtracting a value from its previous value. To report a non-monotonic measurement of a precomputed value, an asynchronous Gauge or UpDownCounter can be used.

In Java, an `ObservableMeasurement` instance is passed as a parameter to the function in order to report individual measurements:

```
ObservableLongCounter counter = meter
  .counterBuilder("mycounter")
```

```
.buildWithCallback(measurement -> {
  measurement.record(2, Attributes.of(
    AttributeKey.stringKey("myKey"), "foo"));
  measurement.record(5, Attributes.of(
    AttributeKey.stringKey("myKey"), "bar"));
});
```

The builder also provides an ofDoubles() method to generate an asynchronous counter that can measure Double values.

The ObservableLongCounter object returned is an auto-closable object. Calling close() will de-register the counter so that the callback function is no longer invoked. Other implementations support different ways of de-registering asynchronous counters.

Histogram

A Histogram is a type of synchronous instrument that is normally used to report measurements that exhibit meaningful statical distributions, like request duration, or payload size. The measurements are aggregated into metric types that support query functions such as percentiles, histograms, or distributions. For example, by using a histogram representation, we can obtain the 95th percentile (i.e., the value below which 95% of all values are found) of a request duration distribution across time, without having to store every single request timing. As we'll see in the "Metrics SDK" section, different histogram aggregations provide different levels of accuracy, normally at the expense of the number of data points produced.

Due to its statistical intended usage, the default type in Java is a histogram that measures Double values:

```
DoubleHistogram histogram = meter
  .histogramBuilder("http.client.duration")
  .setUnit("milliseconds")
  .build();
```

To create a histogram measuring Long values, the ofLongs() method can be invoked on the builder, analogous to the example on Counter previously. Histogram measurements must be zero or greater than zero, as histogram representations normally rely on the monotonicity of the reported values to provide accurate data representations. Measurements can be recorded as follows:

```
histogram.record(121.3);
histogram.record(332.1 ,
  Attributes.builder().put("myKey", "myValue").build());
```

UpDownCounter

An UpDownCounter helps to track the value of measurements that can increase or decrease. As it is non-monotonic, its value does not represent the total value of recorded measurements in a given interval, but rather the current value at the time of metric collection. For example, we can measure the number of items in a queue by increasing the counter when an item is added to the queue and decreasing it when it is removed. When metrics are collected, the counter will represent the number of items in the queue at that moment in time, rather than the total number of items that were added or removed.

An UpDownCounter is intended to be used when obtaining the current value of a measured concept is not trivial, or it is an expensive operation, so keeping track of increments and decrements is preferred. In other cases (e.g., obtaining the size of an array), an asynchronous UpDownCounter is recommended, as it is less computationally expensive.

The operations of an UpDownCounter are very similar to a Counter, with the difference that it accepts negative values on the add() operation:

```
LongUpDownCounter counter = meter
  .upDownCounterBuilder("queue.size")
  .setUnit("items")
  .build();

# After adding 4 items to the queue
counter.add(4,
  Attributes.of(AttributeKey.stringKey("name"), "myqueue"));
# After removing 2 items from the queue
counter.add(-2,
  Attributes.of(AttributeKey.stringKey("name"), "myqueue"));
```

As with Counter, UpDownCounter supports Double values by calling the ofDoubles() method when using the builder.

Asynchronous UpDownCounter

To report non-monotonic measurements with values that are already precomputed at the time of metric collection, an asynchronous UpDownCounter is recommended. This type of asynchronous instrument is meant to be used when sums of data points are meaningful across time series (e.g., memory usage across replicas). If summing values across individual time series does not make sense (e.g., the current fridge temperature across all fridges), an asynchronous Gauge provides a more semantically correct alternative.

Normally named ObservableUpDownCounter (or idiomatic equivalent), it behaves in a similar way to an ObservableCounter. Consequently, all concepts explained previously related to registering or deregistering callbacks, or how duplicate measurements are handled, apply here too. The difference between these two instruments is that an ObservableUpDownCounter should report the current value of non-monotonic measurements (e.g., memory usage in bytes, which can go up or down). For monotonically increasing measures (e.g., disk operations), an ObservableCounter should be used.

The default measurement value type for this instrument is a Long. To register an ObservableUpDownCounter that measures Double values, we can use the following Java instruction, calling the ofDoubles() method on the builder:

```
ObservableDoubleUpDownCounter counter = meter
  .upDownCounterBuilder("mycounter")
  .ofDoubles()
  .buildWithCallback(measurement -> {
    measurement.record(2.3, Attributes.of(
      AttributeKey.stringKey("myKey"), "foo"));
    measurement.record(5.4, Attributes.of(
      AttributeKey.stringKey("myKey"), "bar"));
});
```

Asynchronous Gauge

An asynchronous Gauge, normally called an ObservableGauge (or idiomatic equivalent) in language implementations, is intended to be used to report the current value of non-monotonic nonadditive measurements at metric collection time. While almost identical in operation to an ObservableUpDownCounter, its semantics are different. The values reported by gauges represent concepts that are not meant to be added across time series, like memory utilization (as a percentage) or CPU temperature.

As an asynchronous instrument, all previous concepts discussed in `ObservableCounter` apply to `ObservableGauge`. The default value type of this type of instrument is a `Double`. It can be registered with the following code:

```
ObservableDoubleGauge gauge = meter
  .gaugeBuilder("mygauge")
  .buildWithCallback(measurement -> {
    measurement.record(2.3);
  });
```

Metrics SDK

The responsibility of the Metrics SDK is to provide implementations for `MeterProvider`, `Meter`, `Instrument`, and all other public interfaces that allow to report measurements. Additionally, it provides mechanisms to aggregate measurements into metric data points, collect metrics, and export them to suitable backends.

In addition to providing a way to create `Meter` instances, a `MeterProvider` holds all the configuration related to metric collection, aggregation, and exporting. It configures the following:

- **Meter readers**: Responsible for collecting metrics reported by instruments and optionally exporting them to configured metrics backends. Multiple meter readers can be configured on a single provider.

- **Views**: They dynamically define the aggregations and attributes to process measurements from individual instruments into metrics. A single provider can register multiple views.

- **Resource**: The `Resource` to be associated with every metric produced. Depending on the metric reader and exporter configuration, this may not result in attributes directly added to metric data points.

Assuming we have the `opentelemetry-api` and `opentelemetry-sdk` Maven artifacts declared as dependencies, we can create a `MeterProvider` and assign it to a globally available `OpenTelemetry` instance as follows:

```
# Empty provider, equivalent to calling build() directly
SdkMeterProvider meterProvider = SdkMeterProvider.builder()
  .setResource(Resource.getDefault())
  .setClock(Clock.getDefault())
  .build();

OpenTelemetry openTelemetry = OpenTelemetrySdk.builder()
  .setMeterProvider(meterProvider)
  .buildAndRegisterGlobal();
```

In Java, it is possible to set a specific `Clock` implementation used to obtaining current and elapsed time. By default, it uses `System.currentTimeMillis()` and `System.nanoTime()`, so calling `setClock()` is not usually required.

Although the previous configuration is valid, it would not collect any metrics from any instruments. Later in this section, we'll examine how to create `View` and `MetricReader` instances and register them against a `MeterProvider` and how to configure the Java agent for the same purpose.

The `MeterProvider` also provides two functions that may be used to clean up any remaining measurements or metrics in memory:

- `shutdown()`: Stops all registered meter readers. For readers with pull-based exporters, like Prometheus, this stops the server endpoint to export metrics. In the case of push-based exporters, metrics are flushed before shutting down. Any future calls to obtain a meter after calling this method return a no-op `Meter` instance.

- `forceFlush()`: It flushes metrics on all registered meter readers, exporting the current values for all aggregated metrics. Therefore, this only makes sense on readers using push-based metrics exporters.

Aggregation

When measurements are reported by instruments, they need to be aggregated in memory according to a given function and a set of unique attributes. These aggregates are extracted by metric readers at regular intervals in the form of metric data points, which are then exported to metrics backends in the appropriate format. This is not to be confused with aggregation temporality, which defines the interval considered for the aggregation, discussed along with metric readers further into this chapter.

The aggregation functions described in this section have one thing in common: they're all *decomposable aggregation functions*. This allows values generated by these functions to be combined across measurements and re-aggregated across different dimensions if required, without having access to every individual measurement at aggregation time. More information on this type of functions is available at *https:// en.wikipedia.org/wiki/Aggregate_function#Decomposable_aggregate_functions*.

Each instrument type has a default aggregation associated with it that represents its meaning in the most accurate possible way:

Instrument kind	Default aggregation
Counter	Sum
Asynchronous Counter	Sum
UpDownCounter	Sum
Asynchronous UpDownCounter	Sum
Asynchronous Gauge	Last value
Histogram	Explicit bucket histogram

Figure 3-3, in Chapter 3, showed us how applying different aggregations to the same measurements results in different reported values. The details of each of the aggregations supported by OpenTelemetry is discussed in the following sections.

Sum

A sum represents the addition of *all* measurements recorded by an instrument for a given interval across a set of unique attributes. It is compatible with histograms and counters of any type. As gauges are, by definition, not additive, individual implementations may not support sum aggregations for Gauge instruments (e.g., Java).

The monotonicity of the resulting aggregation will depend on the originating instrument. Monotonically increasing instruments like Counter, asynchronous Counter, or Histogram will result in monotonic sums, while UpDownCounter and asynchronous UpDownCounter will not.

Last Value

A last value aggregation uses the last value reported by a Gauge instrument for a given interval across a set of unique attributes. For instance, if we record temperature measurements via a Gauge instrument using a room attribute, if we apply a last value aggregation dropping that attribute, the resulting value will represent the last recorded temperature on *any* room. This aggregation type is intended to be used with gauges, and using it on any other instrument kind may not be supported by the implementing SDK (e.g., Java).

Explicit Bucket Histogram

A histogram is an approximate representation of the distribution of a set of values. It allows to obtain statistics (e.g., arbitrary percentiles) from a collection of measurements without having to store every single value. In order to do so, histograms divide the range of values in buckets, or bins. This is illustrated in Figure 7-3, which represents the response times for requests divided into 11 buckets. When a given value is recorded with a histogram aggregation, first the bucket corresponding to the value is found, and then its corresponding bucket counter is increased by one. This means that each of the buckets can be thought of as a monotonically increasing counter.

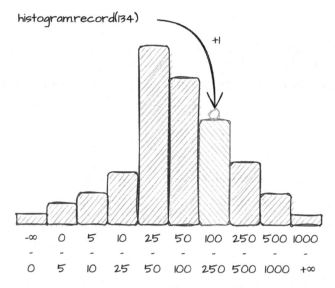

Figure 7-3. *A simple histogram representation recording a value into a bucket*

Histograms require individual measurements with monotonically increasing values in order to find the appropriate bucket to increment. For this reason, the only supported instruments for a histogram aggregation are Counter and Histogram.

Metrics backends normally need to do some type of interpolation within bucket boundaries to be able to answer certain queries. For example, if we want to know the 90th percentile of a distribution with 200 reported measurements, we could add all bucket counters starting from 0 until we reach 180 (90% of 200). This process, however, does not normally end at an exact bucket boundary (e.g., we could have added bucket counters up to 170, and the next bucket adds 20), so the query function needs to interpolate the result, normally using linear interpolation, and give an approximation of where 180 would lie within that last bucket. In this case, it'd be the middle of the bucket, as 180 lies in the middle between 170 and 170+20. This makes the selection of bucket boundaries crucial to accurately represent a distribution. The more buckets, the more accurate the representation will be. However, a higher number of buckets normally results in higher memory and data transfer costs, so it must be done carefully.

Bucket boundaries are configurable when defining explicit bucket histogram aggregations. The default boundaries are spread into incrementally wider boundaries in order to represent lower values more accurately than higher values:

[0, 5, 10, 25, 50, 75, 100, 250, 500, 1000, 2500, 5000, 7500, 10000]

which correspond to the following buckets:

(-∞, 0],
(0, 5.0],
(5.0, 10.0],
(10.0, 25.0],
(25.0, 50.0],
(50.0, 75.0],
(75.0, 100.0],
(100.0, 250.0],
(250.0, 500.0],
(500.0, 1000.0],
(1000.0, 2500.0],
(2500.0, 5000.0],
(5000.0, 10000.0],
(10000.0 +∞)

In addition to bucket counts, the histogram aggregation in OpenTelemetry can also calculate minimum, maximum, and sum of all values (which, along with total count, allows to easily compute the mean), to give a more complete view of a distribution.

Histogram aggregations may be exported as a single data point or as multiple data points depending on the exporter (e.g., Prometheus represents histogram buckets and min/max as individual data points, while OTLP represents them as a single data point with multiple values).

Exponential Histogram

As we've seen, the selection of histogram bucket boundaries is key to accurately represent a distribution. In computing, we are normally interested in higher accuracy for lower values. For instance, if we have a service that serves most requests under 100 ms, having the first bucket boundary as (0, 100.0] would not be very informative. All requests would fall into the same bucket, and linear interpolation would not help us (e.g., the 80th percentile would most likely be 80).

Software systems normally expose distributions with a long tail. The vast majority of response times from HTTP servers usually fall within a small area toward the lower end of a distribution, and long response times, representing unusual responses affected by external factors like garbage collection, CPU throttling, or network hiccups, are less common and more widely spread all the way toward the higher end of the distribution.

To support these types of distributions more dynamically, OTEP-149 (detailed in *https://github.com/open-telemetry/oteps/blob/main/text/0149-exponential-histogram.md*) added support for exponential histograms. This OTEP explains the mathematical rationale for this type of aggregation in more detail than we could reasonably cover in this section. For our purposes, it is sufficient to understand that exponential histogram aggregations use an exponential formula to control bucket boundaries and a scale parameter to control the resolution. This parameter is not configurable on OpenTelemetry SDKs and is calculated by the implementation according to the range of values reported. The use of exponential buckets defined this way results in more accurate distribution representations, normally with fewer bucket boundaries that explicit buckets, while tackling a challenge with histograms, which is the merging of buckets with overlapping buckets (e.g., merging a histogram of [0, 5, 10] boundaries with one of [0, 3, 9] boundaries).

Exponential histograms are not a requirement for an OpenTelemetry implementation to be compliant with the specification. Those that do implement it (e.g., Java) accept certain parameters to configure them, like the maximum number of buckets for a given histogram. Exponential bucket histograms, like explicit bucket histograms, are only supported for `Counter` or `Histogram` instruments.

Drop

When configuring views, it is possible to define this aggregation to drop measurements from any instrument matching a given condition. Any measurements reported to an instrument with this type of aggregation are immediately discarded. The drop aggregation is supported on any instrument kind.

Views

Default aggregations are normally the best fit to represent a metric. After all, the instrumentation author originally intended metrics to represent a certain concept. Nevertheless, when configuring the OpenTelemetry SDK, application owners may decide to dynamically specify the aggregation for individual instruments or change metric properties like name, description, or attributes. This can be beneficial when rolling out OpenTelemetry within an existing system at a certain scale, as it can help reduce the cardinality of auto-instrumented metrics or remove unnecessary attributes. Ultimately, metric views should represent meaningful aggregations for service owners.

A `MeterProvider` can register one or multiple `View` definitions. They consist of the following properties:

- **Instrument selection criteria**: Instruments must match *all* the specified properties in the given criteria for the `View` to apply to them. These can include one or many of instrument name, instrument kind, meter name, meter version, or meter schema URL. For instrument name matching, SDKs support a single * character to match all instrument names, and they may also support individual wildcard characters like ? or * to match zero or more characters.

- **Metric configuration**: Allows to configure how metrics from matched instruments are produced:

- **Name**: If provided, it overwrites the instrument name in the resulting metrics.

- **Description**: If provided, it overwrites the instrument description in the resulting metrics.

- **Attribute keys**: If provided, the configured aggregation will be applied across the given attribute key list. Attributes that are not in the list will be ignored.

- **Aggregation**: If provided, it overrides the default aggregation for an instrument. The instrument must support the specified aggregation type.

Registering multiple views with the same name under the same `MeterProvider` may result in duplicate metrics or semantic errors, as mentioned previously when discussing instrument registration.

The following Java example registers two metric views when building a `MeterProvider` – one that uses histograms to aggregate all `Counter` instruments matching a given criteria and another one that renames a histogram metric while dropping any attributes except `foo` or `bar`:

```
SdkMeterProvider sdkMeterProvider = SdkMeterProvider.builder()
  .registerView(
    InstrumentSelector.builder()
      .setType(InstrumentType.COUNTER)
      .setName("*-counter")
      .setMeterName("my-meter")
      .setMeterVersion("1.0.0")
      .setMeterSchemaUrl("http://example.com")
      .build(),
    View.builder()
      .setAggregation(
        Aggregation.explicitBucketHistogram(
          Arrays.asList(1.0, 3.0, 9.0)))
      .build())
  .registerView(
    InstrumentSelector.builder()
```

```
    .setName("my-histogram")
    .build(),
  View.builder()
    .setName("a-histogram")
    .setAttributeFilter(
      key -> key.equals("foo") || key.equals("bar"))
    .build())
.build();
```

Configuring metric views via auto-configuration when using the Java agent is still a feature in incubation at the time of writing. Nevertheless, it can be used by passing an `otel.experimental.metrics.view-config` system property (or equivalent environment variable) containing a YAML file. The equivalent views registered previously would be as follows:

```
- selector:
    instrument_type: COUNTER
    instrument_name: *-counter
    meter_name: my-meter
    meter_version: 1.0.0
    meter_schema_url: http://example.com
  view:
    aggregation: explicit_bucket_histogram
    aggregation_args:
      bucket_boundaries: [1.0, 3.0, 9.0]
- selector:
    instrument_name: my-histogram
  view:
    name: a-histogram
    attribute_keys:
      - foo
      - bar
```

Exemplars

When measurements are recorded using synchronous instruments, like counters or histograms, each measurement represents an individual action or event. Although measurement values are aggregated into lower-granularity metrics, data points can be decorated with higher-granularity data captured at some point during an aggregation interval. This high-granularity data is called an *exemplar*. Exemplars provide two major features:

- Recording sample data that was grouped into a metric, for instance, a single value recorded in a specific histogram bucket, potentially containing measurement attributes not aggregated in the active view

- Linking telemetry signals, like metrics and traces, allowing to navigate from a specific metric point (e.g., a slow request counted in a histogram bucket) to an individual trace, providing the necessary telemetry context to debug meaningful operations

To achieve this, exemplars record the following information:

- The value of an individual measurement

- The timestamp of an individual measurement

- The set of attributes associated with an individual measurement that were not included in the active *View* for its instrument

- The trace and span IDs if there is an active `SpanContext` in the current `Context` when the measurement is recorded

The behavior that controls when to record an exemplar is controlled by two extensible hooks:

- **Filter**: Applies a function on a measurement to decide if a given measurement should record an exemplar. This function has access to the measurement properties and the current `Context`. Some built-in filters are provided, such as filter to always sample, a filter to never sample, and a filter to sample if the active trace is being sampled.

- **Reservoir**: Defines a function to "offer" an exemplar to be stored in a reservoir of exemplars and another one to "collect" exemplars in the reservoir, called by a metric reader for a given collection period.

At the time of writing, although exemplars are in feature-freeze state in the specification, they are still in experimental state in implementations. Exemplar filters and reservoirs can be configured when building a MeterProvider. In Java, ExemplarFilter configuration is not yet part of the MeterProviderBuilder, but it can be configured using SdkMeterProviderUtil on a MeterProviderBuilder:

```
SdkMeterProviderUtil
  .setExemplarFilter(builder, ExemplarFilter.alwaysSample());
```

Alternatively, if using auto-configuration with the Java agent, the pre-built filter to use can be configured using the otel.metrics.exemplar.filter system property (or equivalent environment variable) with the following supported values: NONE, ALL, WITH_SAMPLED_TRACE (the default).

Custom ExemplarReservoir configuration is not yet available in Java, although it will be implemented as a property of a View, being able to specify different reservoirs for individual instruments. The current implementation configures default fixed size reservoirs, with reservoir sizes depending on the number of available processors to the application.

Figure 7-4 shows the results of configuring the Prometheus instance in Chapter 4 adding the --enable-feature=exemplar-storage flag and querying for the 90th percentile of request durations. We can see exemplars of individual measurements, along with trace and span IDs. An integrated observability platform can use this data to allow easy navigation between metrics and traces.

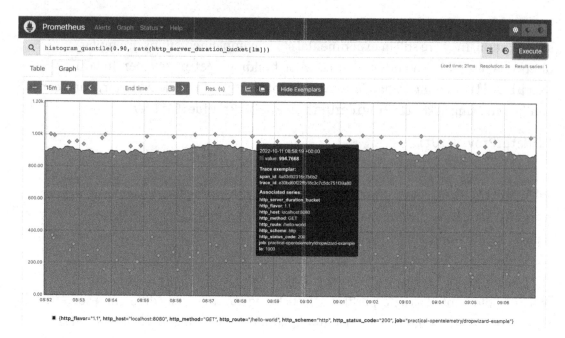

Figure 7-4. *Exemplar support in Prometheus*

Metric Readers and Exporters

So far, we've explored how metrics are aggregated in memory within an application. This would not be very useful if those metrics were not collected and exported to appropriate metrics backends. For this purpose, the OpenTelemetry SDK provides a `MetricReader` interface and built-in implementations that provide the following features:

- Collect metrics (and exemplars) from in-memory aggregations. This can happen in scheduled intervals for push-based exporters like OTLP or on-demand for pull-based exporters like Prometheus.

- Handing `forceFlush()` and `shutdown()` operations to make sure all in-memory metrics are cleaned up and exported.

The following properties can be used to initialize a `MetricReader`:

- **Exporter**: An instance of `MetricExporter` to use. Built-in implementations are normally provided by the SDK for OTLP and Prometheus, plus a logging exporter that outputs metrics in text format for debugging purposes.

- **Default aggregation**: The default aggregation to use per instrument type. This is not a required parameter. The default aggregation per instrument type will be used if not provided. In any case, registered metric views can configure aggregations a posteriori.

- **Default temporality**: By default, exporters will use cumulative temporality (see the following text for an explanation of aggregation temporality). When configured, delta temporality can be used for aggregations that support it.

MetricReader instances can be registered when building a MetricProvider. It is possible to register multiple metric readers with their own exporter configuration. For example, the following example will register three MetricReader instances on a single MetricProvider:

```
SdkMeterProvider sdkMeterProvider = SdkMeterProvider.builder()
  .registerMetricReader(PeriodicMetricReader
    .builder(LoggingMetricExporter.create())
    .setInterval(Duration.ofMillis(30_000L))
    .build())
  .registerMetricReader(PrometheusHttpServer
    .builder()
    .setPort(9464)
    .build())
  .registerMetricReader(PeriodicMetricReader
    .builder(OtlpGrpcMetricExporter
      .builder()
      .setDefaultAggregationSelector(
        DefaultAggregationSelector.getDefault()
          .with(InstrumentType.HISTOGRAM, Aggregation.sum()))
      .setAggregationTemporalitySelector(
        AggregationTemporalitySelector.deltaPreferred())
      .setEndpoint("http://otel-collector:4317")
      .build())
    .build())
  .build();
```

A `PeriodicMetricReader` is registered to collect metrics every 30 seconds and use a `LoggingMetricExporter` to output metrics as `INFO` level log messages. The `PrometheusHttpServer` will serve metrics on the default *metrics* path in port 9464. Each time that endpoint is called, the `MetricReader` will collect all in-memory metrics and export any monotonically increasing values with cumulative temporality (the only supported aggregation temporality in Prometheus). Finally, the `OtlpGrpcMetricExporter` will be used by a default `PeriodicMetricReader` (1-minute intervals) to push metrics in OTLP format to *http://otel-collector:4317*. It will default to sum aggregations for `Histogram` instruments unless a `View` is configured, and it will use delta temporality to aggregate monotonically increasing values.

Each `MetricReader` instance will register against instruments and metric views and have access to in-memory aggregations to keep some internal state. This allows readers to operate independently, allowing for individual export intervals and different temporality aggregations.

When using auto-configuration with the Java agent, the list of exporters to use can be configured with the `otel.metrics.exporter` property (or equivalent environment variable). It accepts a comma-separated list with the following possible values:

- `otlp`: This is the default exporter. When this exporter is used, properties under `otel.exporter.otlp.metrics.*` allow to control endpoint, certificate, authentication, etc. These can also be controlled globally for all OTLP exporters (traces, metrics, logs) under the `otel.exporter.otlp.*` prefix. Within the OTLP metrics exporter prefix, two properties can control temporality and aggregation:

  - `temporality.preference`: Can be `CUMULATIVE` or `DELTA`.

  - `default.histogram.aggregation`: Can be `EXPONENTIAL_BUCKET_HISTOGRAM` or `EXPLICIT_BUCKET_HISTOGRAM`.

- `prometheus`: Opens up a Prometheus server bound to the configured `otel.exporter.prometheus.port` and `otel.exporter.prometheus.host`, which Prometheus can use to scrape metrics on the /*metrics* path.

- `logging`: Outputs metrics as `INFO` level log messages. It exposes no other configuration.

Finally, the `otel.metric.export.interval` property allows to define the collection interval, in milliseconds, to be used by periodic metric readers. It defaults to 60,000 (1 minute).

Aggregation Temporality

When metrics are collected for a Gauge, which reports the last value of a measurement in each collection period, each data point represents a single point in time. There are no past measurements aggregated into a single data point. In contrast, the data points for sums or histograms represent a collection of individual data points across time. The time period considered for each data point is called the *aggregation temporality*.

There are two main types of aggregation temporality:

- **Cumulative**: Each metric data point contains the sum of all recorded measurements, from the moment the instrument was initialized until the data point timestamp.

- **Delta**: Each metric data point contains the sum corresponding to a particular collection interval. It'd be similar to resetting the sum to zero every time it's reported.

Figure 7-5 illustrates the difference between cumulative and delta temporality in a monotonically increasing counter.

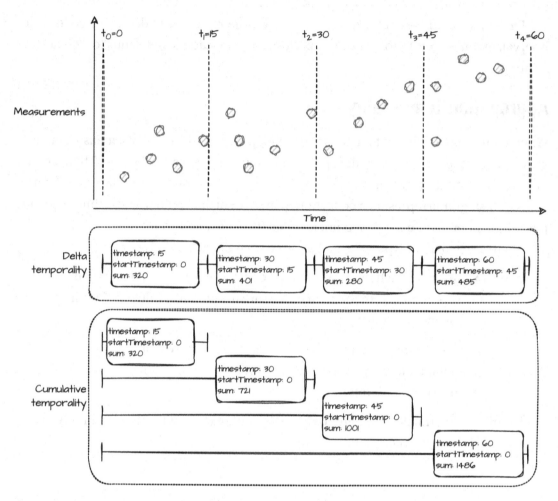

Figure 7-5. *Cumulative vs. delta temporality for a sum aggregation*

The choice of aggregation temporality is normally conditioned by the metrics backend where data is exported to, which usually supports a single type. For instance, *cumulative temporality* was popularized by backends like Prometheus or OpenTSDB. Although Figure 7-5 displays all data points with start and current timestamps, this is optional in OpenTelemetry, as backends that require cumulative temporality may not need them. Instead, they implement mechanisms that rely on the monotonicity of a time series to identify counter/histogram resets (i.e., when a value is lower than the previous value due to process restarts or aggregation overflow). These are normally implemented as rate or increment query functions, which calculate the delta between two data points given a time interval. Therefore, it is important that the underlying metrics uniquely identify the producer; otherwise it'd be impossible to tell if data points for a monotonically increasing time series have gone from 120 to 10 because a process restarted or because it is a measurement from a different process altogether.

There are some advantages to using cumulative temporality. For pull-based systems like Prometheus, for instance, the failure of an individual scrape, and thus a missing data point, can be remediated at query time. If we consider the following data points being scraped every 15 seconds:

```
t0  -> 4
t15 -> 8
t30 -> 12
t45 -> 13
t60 -> 15
```

If we want to get the 1-minute increase for this counter, we only need the values for t0 and t60. We could afford to have a gap of three data points and our result would still be correct. This often results in some memory cost on the producer side, which is directly related to the cardinality of a given metric. For each combination of attributes, the sender must "remember" the previous value in order to aggregate a new measurement.

Delta temporality, on the other hand, only needs to aggregate values during a given collection interval, potentially reducing memory usage on the sender. It does so at the expense of having to handle intermittent failures in other ways. For example, push-based exporters like the OTLP exporter implement queuing and retrying to minimize potential gaps in metrics points. As sums only represent a single collection interval, the start timestamp is required when using this type of aggregation temporality. This also allows this type of exporters to be able to report metrics in batches, rather than as separate requests per interval.

Reasoning about delta temporality metrics may be easier for end users as backends do not need to account for counter resets, and individual data points can be considered independently. Additionally, metrics backends may support sums produced by different producers using the same identifying attributes, as their decomposable additive properties remain intact. This is not usually recommended, as we're normally interested in identifying the unique producer of a time series exported at regular intervals, but it may be helpful in specific circumstances to reduce the cardinality of system-wide metrics. For instance, OpenTelemetry collectors could report sums of metrics generated from spans across all services, without the need to add the individual collector instance ID.

The OTLP format supports both types of aggregation temporality. As demonstrated previously, the OTLP exporter can be configured to use delta temporality as a preferred aggregation. The reason it is "preferred" and not "explicit" is that non-monotonic instruments, like `UpDownCounter` or its asynchronous version, should always use cumulative temporality. The semantics of a non-monotonic sum mean that the time interval considered for the aggregation is conditioned to include all measurements since the first measurement. This means that delta temporality can only apply to `Histogram`, `Counter`, and asynchronous `Counter` instruments.

Processors in OpenTelemetry Collectors can help to transform cumulative into delta temporality. However, there are some caveats in this approach, for example, it is not possible to reliably transform min and max values reported in histograms with cumulative temporality, as these will refer to min and max since the process started, not for a particular interval. Conversely, some exporters in OpenTelemetry Collectors, like the Prometheus exporter, can aggregate delta temporality sums into cumulative temporality to be compatible with Prometheus backends.

Summary

Metrics are a wide topic, with many years of accumulated knowledge and countless use cases to be catered for. In this chapter, we've covered the basic purposes of metrics in modern observability systems, and we've explored how OpenTelemetry signals can help provide a more integrated and contextual view of a system by correlation metrics with other telemetry signals. We have also examined the different types of instruments that can be used to report measurements via the OpenTelemetry API and how to configure the SDK to aggregate and export these measurements as metrics.

In our mission to provide a unified solution to export and correlate observability data from multiple telemetry signals, in the next chapter, we'll be looking at logging – another one of the traditional forms of telemetry for which OpenTelemetry offers a slightly different approach.

CHAPTER 8

Logging

Logs are one of the earliest forms of telemetry. As such, this signal benefits from native support in many languages and from well-supported frameworks that allow to produce them as structured or unstructured events. At the time of writing, the OpenTelemetry Logs specification is still under development, in the experimental stage. Therefore, the concepts and examples used in this chapter are subject to change. Nonetheless, even at this early stage, the specification contemplates that in order to support this long legacy of logging solutions, the OpenTelemetry Logs API and SDK must integrate with existing frameworks and protocols, rather than start from a clean slate. In this chapter, we'll cover how OpenTelemetry can integrate with existing solutions and the purpose of application logging in modern observability.

The Purpose of Logs for Observability

In previous chapters, we've seen how metrics and tracing can satisfy some of the main purposes of observability: gathering key performance indicators, asserting the status of a system, detecting anomalies, and finding the root cause of regressions. Metrics offer steady and complete signals, which can then link to sampled traces to provide high-granularity context around individual operations. This poses the question: What is the role of logs in modern observability?

A good way to start exploring the purpose of application logs is to analyze what use cases traditionally fulfilled by logs can now be better suited to other telemetry signals. Before the popularization of distributed tracing, applications would normally

143

© Daniel Gomez Blanco 2023
D. Gomez Blanco, *Practical OpenTelemetry*, https://doi.org/10.1007/978-1-4842-9075-0_8

be instrumented using logs for high-granularity data related to individual transactions, like access logs, exceptions, and other internal messages describing the internal state of services handling requests. This presents a few challenges:

- Even with access to the Context API, logs lack the predefined structure of distributed tracing. Correlating logs across services and operations without a tracing backdrop cannot be easily done by observability platforms.

- Without trace context, log sampling becomes difficult and less meaningful. When an operation fails, or its duration is longer than expected, we're normally interested in looking at telemetry from other services within the same transaction to give us more debugging context. Log events can only be considered individually, so even though it would be possible to store all ERROR level logs and only a percentage of INFO or DEBUG logs, the status of other services or operations that are part of the same transaction cannot be reflected in the sampling decision. This ultimately means logs are rarely sampled within organizations. At large scale, this can incur high costs for very little debugging value, as most of these logs do not correspond to "interesting" operations (i.e., those worth debugging).

In most situations, tracing is a better signal than logs to instrument operations happening within distributed transactions for observability purposes. This does not mean that standard, unsampled, access logging is not useful. This type of logging, which can be considered a form of audit logging, is crucial in areas like security or threat detection. In these cases, sampling is not an option. However, the data requirements for these purposes are orthogonal to those of observability systems. They favor completeness of the dataset and lower storage costs and can accept slightly longer data delivery delays or no cross-signal correlation, as they're ultimately not used to identify if systems are working as expected for the majority, but rather if they're not being used as intended by the minority. Storing unsampled audit logs in platforms designed for observability normally incurs high costs for no added debugging value. For these cases, cheaper forms of storage, or pipelines built for a more reliable delivery of events at the expense of data delay (e.g., including backfills or replays), can provide better value. OpenTelemetry SDKs and Collectors (or preexisting solutions like FluentBit) can still help in this case, by providing ways to standardize the production of logs and then filtering and distributing them to appropriate backends according to the usage type.

> **Tip**   Not all logging is useful for observability purposes. When instrumenting a system, different types of logs can be routed to the most appropriate backends for their use case (e.g., auditing), maximizing their value.

Some logging backends allow to execute queries using aggregate functions, like querying the count of logs matching a given condition, and then plot or alert on them. Some even allow to treat log attributes as numerical fields, able to calculate statistics from individual events. In some cases, this has led to using logs as a substitute for metrics. For example, operators may monitor the number of errors on a service by counting the number of ERROR level logs and alerting when it goes over a certain threshold. As we've seen in Chapter 7, metrics provide accurate representations of the same measurements. By aggregating measurements at source, metrics reduce the transfer, storage, and querying cost requirements while maximizing signal stability. For these reasons, metrics, rather than logs, should be used to instrument concepts that can be computed into aggregates at the producer level.

Logs do support key use cases in observability. After what's been discussed so far, the most obvious one is probably monitoring operations that are not part of user transactions, for instance, startup or shutdown routines, background tasks, or operations that relate to the internal state of a service replica. Although these logs may not be part of a request context (i.e., a trace), producing them in a standard way via OpenTelemetry APIs and SDKs enhances observability. Resource information, used to enrich logs produced from a service replica, helps to easily correlate them with signals, like metrics, collected around the same time period.

Another important log use case comes from logs that are produced by third-party libraries, or internal legacy applications that are difficult to update, and that were originally instrumented using standard logging frameworks. In these cases, logs are often part of a request context and can be correlated to spans and traces. OpenTelemetry instrumentation can enrich these logs with trace and span IDs, present in the active *context* at the time logs are generated. As Figure 8-1 illustrates, observability platforms can display logs along with traces and other signals to enhance their observability value, allowing to traverse from an aggregated view to a high-granularity view, useful for debugging, even if services were not originally instrumented using tracing libraries.

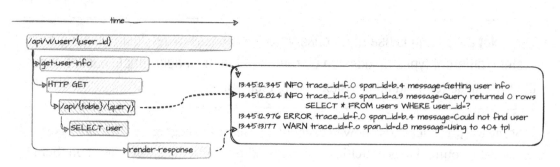

Figure 8-1. *Correlation between spans and logs on a single trace*

Although metrics should be the preferred signal to instrument measurements that can be aggregated at source, this is not always feasible. For example, browsers generate some of the most valuable operational data, as they come straight from user devices. They can ultimately tell us what the system looks like from an external perspective. This is what is commonly referred to as Real User Monitoring (RUM), and it includes key indicators like page or document load timers, JavaScript errors, and other markers that are critical to Search Engine Optimization (SEO) like Google's Core Web Vitals, which reflect the overall end-user experience and affect search ranking. The same applies to mobile applications. The number of individual producers (i.e., user devices) for these events means aggregations at the producer level are futile, so raw events need to be exported and then aggregated at a common destination, rather than at source.

Finally, logs are the main form of event monitoring for operating systems and infrastructure components. In these cases, operators don't normally have access to modify the logs content, and they don't normally form part of an execution context. They are produced in a variety of different formats and frameworks (e.g., log files, Kubernetes Events, Syslog, Windows Event Logs). Although it is not possible to correlate execution context in these cases, as mentioned previously for certain cases in application logs, they can be enriched with standardized attributes to provide resource-level correlation and extract valuable debugging insights. Logs can be enriched with resource information by OpenTelemetry Collectors, for instance, providing functionality to automatically enrich processed logs with resource information.

Logging API

When it comes to logging, OpenTelemetry takes a slightly different approach to other signals. The Logging API defines a set of public interfaces that follow a similar pattern to the Metrics and Tracing APIs. However, application owners should only need to use the Events API interface directly and are normally discouraged from using the Logs API interface, which can be treated as a backend API. Instead, as shown in Figure 8-2, these APIs are used within logging handlers or *appenders*, maintained by OpenTelemetry maintainers or third-party libraries, that can integrate with existing logging frameworks. Later in this chapter, we'll see an example of this.

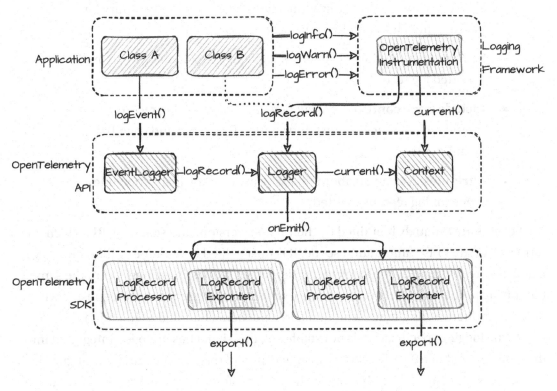

Figure 8-2. *Integrating OpenTelemetry logging within a logging framework*

The Logging API defines a `LoggerProvider` interface, which must be implemented by the underlying SDK to hold any log processing or export configuration and to provide `Logger` instances that are, in turn, responsible for emitting logs and events (via an `EventLogger`). `LoggerProvider` instances can be configured as part of a central OpenTelemetry instance, and they can also be independently initialized and used in isolation, following a similar pattern to `TracerProvider` and `MeterProvider`. Like other OpenTelemetry APIs, the Logging API behaves as a no-op implementation if no SDK is configured.

A `Logger` can be obtained from a `LoggerProvider` by providing the following properties:

- **Name:** The name for the `Logger` instance, which can refer to the instrumentation library, or to an application, library, package, or class for applications and libraries natively instrumented with OpenTelemetry. This is a required property.

- **Version:** The version of the application, instrumentation library, or instrumented library. This is an optional parameter.

- **Schema URL:** Optional property specifying the schema URL to use in exported log records.

- **Include trace context:** Boolean flag that controls if log records should include trace context information (i.e., trace and span ID). It defaults to true.

- **Attributes:** A set of attributes to associate with the instrumentation scope for log records emitted.

Loggers are uniquely identified by their name, version, and schema URL, which form part of their instrumentation scope. It is unspecified if the same or different `Logger` instances are returned by the implementation when requesting a logger with the same identifying properties. Users must ensure that identical loggers are not requested with different properties, as it may result in records not being handled as intended.

As the logging specification is not stable yet, this signal has not been integrated into the globally available `OpenTelemetry` instance, part of the API. A centrally configured `LoggerProvider` can still be obtained by holding a reference to an individual instance, or managing it via `GlobalLoggerProvider`:

```
Logger logger = GlobalLoggerProvider.get()
  .loggerBuilder("my-browser-logger")
  .setInstrumentationVersion("1.0.0")
  .setSchemaUrl("http://example.com")
  .build();
```

Logs API Interface

A `Logger` is responsible for emitting log records. A `LogRecord` is a structured data type. Although the API and SDK are not stable yet, the log data model is stable under the OpenTelemetry specification, available at *https://opentelemetry.io/docs/reference/specification/logs/data-model*. This describes the different field types and pays special importance to providing mappings for existing logging frameworks and formats like Windows Event Log, Syslog, Log4j, Zap, CloudTrail, Apache HTTP access log, etc. It also defines standard severity levels that can support existing solutions.

The API allows to produce `LogRecords` with the following fields:

- **Timestamp**: Unix epoch (nanoseconds) when the event occurred, measured by the local clock. If not provided, the current timestamp is used.

- **Observed timestamp**: Unix epoch (nanoseconds) when the event was observed by an OpenTelemetry collection process, like an OpenTelemetry Collector, when events are not produced by an OpenTelemetry SDK.

- **Context**: A valid `Context` from which `TraceContext` information can be obtained.

- **Severity number**: A number defining the severity of the event (e.g., numbers 17–20 represent `ERROR` events).

- **Severity text**: The description of the severity (i.e., the human-readable log level).

- **Body**: The human-readable log message.

- **Attributes**: A set of key value pairs containing attributes to be associated with the event.

In Java, we can emit a `LogRecord` using a `Logger` instance as follows:

```
logger.logRecordBuilder()
  .setBody("something bad happened")
  .setSeverity(Severity.ERROR)
  .setAttribute(AttributeKey.stringKey("myKey"), "myvalue")
  .emit();
```

Note   OpenTelemetry provides integration with standard logging frameworks in the form of logging handlers or appenders, so using the API to emit logs is not recommended. See below for a section integration with logging frameworks.

Events API Interface

Having access to a Logging API that allows the creation of structured log records means there's effectively no distinction between the data modelling of logs or events for the purpose of observability. Both can be represented as LogRecord objects with a specific set of fields. However, end users may assign different meanings to each, and observability platforms may provide different features between what's traditionally considered logging and other types of events. For instance, browser events may include a collection of attributes representing a page view and have no message body, but one would expect logs to always have a message body.

Note   The Events API interface contained in version 1.16.0 of the OpenTelemetry Specification is still under early development and will most likely change in future versions. For this reason, no Java examples are provided in this section, and any definitions must be considered experimental.

As opposed to logs, the creation of events is normally not tied to logging frameworks. Depending on the environment, it may not even be possible to use a logging framework. To cater for this use case and to segment logs, which should integrate with existing frameworks, from events, which require an API, OpenTelemetry proposes the creation of an EventLogger interface. This interface sits on top of the Logging API and exposes functionality to emit events following OpenTelemetry standards and naming conventions.

An EventLogger can be created with the following properties:

- **Logger**: An instance of a Logger used to emit events as LogRecords.

- **Event domain**: Specifies the event.domain attribute, which acts
  as a namespace for the event records produced. According to
  OpenTelemetry semantic conventions, this value must be browser,
  device, or k8s if applicable. Otherwise, custom values are allowed.

Having access to an EventLogger instance, events can be emitted using the following
arguments:

- **Event name**: The event.name attribute for the emitted LogRecord.
  This identifies a given event type within an event domain.

- **Log record**: A LogRecord instance representing the event attributes
  (see the LogRecord definition in the previous section).

Logging SDK

Following the same design patterns from Tracing and Metrics SDKs, the Logging SDK
provides LoggerProvider and Logger implementations for the public interfaces detailed
in the previous section. A LoggerProvider holds all configuration related to handling
logs and events, which includes the following:

- **Resource**: The OpenTelemetry Resource to associate with all logs or
  events produced by the loggers under this provider

- **Log record processors**: A collection of LogRecordProcessor
  instances that can be registered when creating the provider and that
  take care of processing and exporting log records

Individual implementations may provide other configuration options. For example,
the Java implementation allows to specify the clock implementation (equivalent to
Metrics or Tracing SDKs), or limits associated with log attributes (e.g., max attribute
length).

The LoggerProvider is also responsible for implementing forceFlush() and
shutdown(), which execute its namesake methods on every registered LoggerProcessor
to ensure that in-memory logs and events are processed when required.

Having the opentelemetry-api and opentelemetry-sdk Maven artifacts declared as dependencies, we can use the following Java example to register a LoggerProvider with the globally available OpenTelemetry instance (please note it will not be available to be retrieved via the OpenTelemetry API instance until the API is declared stable).

```
# Empty provider, equivalent to calling build() directly
SdkLoggerProvider loggerProvider = SdkLoggerProvider.builder()
  .setResource(Resource.getDefault())
  .setClock(Clock.getDefault())
  .setLogLimits(LogLimits::getDefault)
  .build();

OpenTelemetry openTelemetry = OpenTelemetrySdk.builder()
 .setLoggerProvider(loggerProvider)
 .buildAndRegisterGlobal();
```

The Java agent exposes logging configuration for exporters (detailed in the next subsection) and log attribute limits via auto-configuration. Attribute limits can be configured via the otel.attribute.value.length.limit and otel.attribute.count.limit system properties (or equivalent environment variables). These apply globally across spans, span events, span links, and logs, although span-related configuration can be specifically configured as explained in Chapter 6.

Log Processors and Exporters

Figure 8-2 showed an example of how a log appender may interact with the Logging API. When log records are emitted via a logger, the onEmit() method is invoked on one or many registered processors that implement the LogRecordProcessor interface. These can then optionally use a LogRecordExporter to transform and export log records into the desired transport format.

Similar to the Tracing API, the Logging API provides two built-in processors:

- SimpleLogRecordProcessor: Exports individual logs and events as soon as they arrive. Due to the throughput of logging systems, this should not be used in production systems.

- BatchLogRecordProcessor: Processes logs and events in batches, adding them to a queue that serves as a buffer in case of export failures. In the event of the queue getting full due to continued export failures (or high throughput), logs will start to get dropped from the queue. The configuration is equivalent to that of a BatchSpanProcessor (detailed in Chapter 6). It uses the same defaults, except the default export delay, which is configured to be 200 milliseconds. At the time of writing, this configuration is not available via system properties in the Java agent, although it can be configured via an SPI. When a batch processor is configured, a MeterProvider instance can be passed to be able to produce metrics like queue size or processed events size, which can help tune this processor's properties.

Both these processors require a LogRecordExporter to export logs. In Java, these exporters are provided under the relevant opentelemetry-exporter-{exporter} Maven artifacts. The following example uses a simple processor with a standard out exporter (it does not use java.util.logging to avoid logging loops if an appender is configured), provided by the opentelemetry-exporter-logging package, and a batch processor with an OTLP gRPC exporter, provided by the opentelemetry-exporter-otlp package:

```
SdkLoggerProvider loggerProvider = SdkLoggerProvider
  .builder()
  .setResource(resource)
  .addLogRecordProcessor(BatchLogRecordProcessor
    .builder(OtlpGrpcLogRecordExporter
      .builder()
      .setEndpoint("http://otel-collector:4317")
      .build())
    .setMeterProvider(meterProvider)
    .setMaxQueueSize(10240)
    .build())
  .addLogRecordProcessor(SimpleLogRecordProcessor
    .create(SystemOutLogRecordExporter.create()))
  .build();
```

The Java agent allows to configure these two exporters using auto-configuration via the otel.logs.exporter property. This property has a default value of none, so no logs are exported, and it accepts the following:

- logging: It configures a simple log record processor and a standard out exporter as per the previous example.

- otlp: It configures a batch processor with an OTLP gRPC exporter. Individual exporter properties can be configured via the otel. exporter.otlp.logs.* prefixed keys (e.g., endpoint, TLS, etc.) or via the global otel.exporter.otlp.* prefixed keys affecting all OTLP exporters. This generates metrics using the auto-configured MeterProvider.

Integration with Logging Frameworks

OpenTelemetry provides instrumentation for logging frameworks in two ways:

- **Appenders**: Logging handlers and appenders that can integrate with frameworks like Logback, Log4j, or JBoss Logging in Java. After the Logging signal becomes stable, more handlers and appenders will be available for other languages and frameworks. These use the OpenTelemetry API to emit logs, which are the handled by the configured LoggerProvider.

- **Context injectors**: Instrumentation libraries that can use the active context to inject SpanContext information into standard logging frameworks like MDC in Java, Winston hooks in Node, or log records factories in Python. This allows to correlate traces to legacy logs as previously discussed in this chapter, with no other changes needed to logging configuration.

In our dropwizard-example from Chapter 4, the logback-appender and logback-mdc instrumentation packages were already enabled (as all instrumentations are, by default). The reason trace and span ID did not appear in the logs is that our example uses a log formatter that does not output MDC values. In Dropwizard, this can be configured as part of the bootstrapping process, in the example.yml file passed as parameter to the main process. In the logging section, we can use trace_id, span_id, and trace_flags fields in our log format:

```
logging:
  appenders:
    - type: console
      logFormat: "%-6level [%d{HH:mm:ss.SSS}]
        [%t] %logger{5} - %X{code} %msg
        trace_id=%X{trace_id} span_id=%X{span_id}
        trace_flags=%X{trace_flags}%n"
```

Having our Docker Compose stack running (containing OTLP and logs pipeline as defined in the example), we can navigate back to the application directory and start our application. In order to enable OTLP to export the logs emitted by this appender (disabled by default), we need to pass one extra property:

```
# Change directory to Dropwizard-example
cd dropwizard-example

# Start application
java -javaagent:opentelemetry-javaagent.jar \
 -Dotel.service.name=dropwizard-example \
 -Dotel.logs.exporter=otlp \
 -jar target/dropwizard-example-2.1.1.jar \
 server example.yml
```

As expected, the logs produced during initialization will not contain any span_id or trace_id, as there is no active span context when the logs are generated. To produce a log message that exposes those fields, we can open *http://localhost:8080/hello-world/date?date=2023-01-15* in our browser. This should return the date passed as parameter and output the following log line:

```
INFO   [18:09:00.888] [dw-65 - GET /hello-world/date?date=2023-01-15]
c.e.h.r.HelloWorldResource -  Received a date: 2023-01-15 trace_id=6e62f
4d5927df8bb790ad7990d9af516 span_id=2409065755502df3 trace_flags=01
```

Our collector had been configured to have a logs pipeline that would receive records in OTLP, batch them, and export them to console. By looking at its logs, we can see how the logs made it to the collector:

```
2023-01-16T16:09:01.031Z info ResourceLog #0
Resource SchemaURL: https://opentelemetry.io/schemas/1.16.0
```

```
Resource attributes:
     -> host.arch: STRING(x86_64)
     ...
     -> telemetry.sdk.version: STRING(1.21.0)
ScopeLogs #0
ScopeLogs SchemaURL:
InstrumentationScope com.example.helloworld.resources.HelloWorldResource
LogRecord #0
ObservedTimestamp: 1970-01-01 00:00:00 +0000 UTC
Timestamp: 2023-01-16 16:09:00.888 +0000 UTC
Severity: INFO
Body: Received a date: 2023-01-15
Trace ID: 6e62f4d5927df8bb790ad7990d9af516
Span ID: 2409065755502df3
Flags: 1
```

This OpenTelemetry Collector could now be configured to gather these logs and export them to logging backends in many supported formats.

Summary

In this chapter, we've covered the basics of OpenTelemetry Logging and the different approach taken for this signal to provide support for the vast amount of existing logging frameworks. We have seen how the Logging API allows to emit structured logs and events and how to configure the SDK and instrumentation packages to enrich legacy logs with trace context and to export them to OpenTelemetry Collectors. This is a signal currently undergoing development, and although most of the concepts in this chapter will not be changed in future releases, small breaking changes are still allowed until the signal is declared stable.

This is the last main OpenTelemetry signal to cover, along with baggage, tracing, and metrics, covered in previous chapters. In the next chapter, we'll explore OpenTelemetry Collectors, one of the most useful tools in OpenTelemetry to provide a central point to ingest, process, transform, and integrate with other observability frameworks and platforms.

## CHAPTER 9

Protocol and Collector

The previous four chapters focused on the OpenTelemetry API and its SDK implementation and how interoperability, as one of the core values of the project, is implemented by allowing application owners to choose between multiple telemetry exporters. Exporters that are specific to a backend tend to support only a single signal, and they normally support a subset of all OpenTelemetry features. In order to provide a standard data exchange format that can support all signals and features, the OpenTelemetry Protocol (OTLP) was proposed. The popularity of this protocol is steadily increasing, with multiple observability vendors and telemetry backends adding native support for it on their platforms. Along with individual contributions, this is making OTLP the best supported transport format in OpenTelemetry-instrumented ecosystems. In this chapter, we'll study the main characteristics of this protocol.

Although OTLP is usually the recommended exporter for applications using OpenTelemetry, not all systems are currently instrumented with OpenTelemetry and not all backends accept OTLP. We'll also introduce the OpenTelemetry Collector in this chapter, to assist in these scenarios and to provide advanced capabilities to ingest, transform, process, and forward telemetry data.

Protocol

OTLP, the OpenTelemetry Protocol, was created as a solution to provide a native data exchange protocol that could support all OpenTelemetry signals. The specification is currently stable for traces, metrics, and logs, and it was designed with the following features in mind:

- **Supported node and data types**: The protocol supports all OpenTelemetry signals (i.e., traces, metrics, and logs), and it can be used to transmit data between applications, agents, and telemetry backends.

© Daniel Gomez Blanco 2023
D. Gomez Blanco, *Practical OpenTelemetry*, https://doi.org/10.1007/978-1-4842-9075-0_9

- **Backward compatibility**: Following the general OpenTelemetry design guidelines, OTLP versions are backward compatible to facilitate the communication between multiple components running different versions.

- **Throughput**: Telemetry data can be very high throughput, especially between OpenTelemetry Collectors and observability backends, often in different data centers. The protocol is designed to support high-throughput data delivery in high-latency networks.

- **Batching, compression, and encryption**: OTLP allows to batch telemetry data into collections of events (e.g., data points, spans, log records) and to compress these using algorithms that can achieve high-compression ratios (e.g., Gzip). Data can then be transferred using industry standards for encryption (e.g., TLS/HTTPS).

- **Reliability, backpressure signaling, and throttling**: The protocol has been designed to ensure reliable data delivery between clients (e.g., applications or collectors) and servers (e.g., collectors or telemetry backends). This is accomplished via data acknowledgments, which are sent from server to client to guarantee that no data is lost in transit between a single client-server pair. The client may also react to other signals, like transient error codes that allow for retry strategies, or backpressure signals, which indicate to the client that the server cannot handle the current throughput and it must throttle itself to avoid impacting the health of the server.

- **Serialization and memory usage**: The protocol is aimed at minimizing memory usage and garbage collection requirements resulting from serialization or deserialization. It's also designed to support very fast pass-through mode (i.e., when no data modifications are needed), fast enrichment of telemetry data, and partial inspection, to support OpenTelemetry Collector use cases.

- **Layer 7 load balancing**: The protocol allows L7 load balancers to rebalance traffic between different batches of telemetry data. Not pinning traffic to one server for a long-lasting connection avoids imbalanced server loads behind a load balancer.

Note   Request acknowledgments may not always be received (e.g., in case of network interruptions). In this case, and due to the nature of telemetry data, OTLP favors the acknowledgment of data being delivered over a potential duplication on the server side, that is, requests with no response received may be retried.

In previous chapters, we used OTLP over gRPC as the exporter implementation in multiple examples. OTLP/gRPC exporters and receivers were the first to be introduced. Support for gRPC was originally included in OTEP 0035, the initial OTLP specification proposal, and it still remains the recommended transport if the implementation enables it, as some of the features listed above have native support in gRPC (e.g., flow control mechanisms like backpressure). More recently, the OTLP/HTTP specification was added to support use cases where gRPC is not feasible (e.g., browsers). Regardless of transport or encoding, payloads are defined in Protocol Buffers (Protobuf) schemas. These schemas, and their release status, are available at *https://github.com/ open-telemetry/opentelemetry-proto*.

OTLP/gRPC

When a client sends telemetry data to a server, they can do it sequentially, waiting for each export request to be acknowledged, or they may do it concurrently, managing multiple concurrent Unary calls in parallel. The former is only recommended in simple cases where latency between client and server is not seen as a concern, while the latter is used to enable high throughput in high-latency environments (e.g., export data between regions or data centers). The level of concurrency is normally configurable. For instance, the OpenTelemetry Collector uses a sending queue and a configurable number of consumers that read from that queue to process batches individually.

Each response sent from the server may contain information to inform the client of how the request was handled:

- **Full success**: All telemetry exported was accepted by the server.

- **Partial success**: Some of the telemetry in the request was not accepted by the server. In this case, the server informs the client of how many data points, spans, or logs were rejected and the reasons for doing so (e.g., no timestamp). This can then be surfaced by client/ server implementations in the form of metrics or other telemetry that can be used by application owners or operators to correct any data issues. Requests resulting in partial successes are not retried.

- **Failure**: None of the telemetry data was accepted by the server. This could be due to a transient error on the server (e.g., a timeout) or an error that indicates that the telemetry data is not processable (e.g., it cannot be deserialized) and must be dropped. The list of gRPC error codes that may be retried is as follows:

  - CANCELLED

  - DEADLINE_EXCEEDED

  - RESOURCE_EXHAUSTED (only if status contains RetryInfo)

  - ABORTED

  - OUT_OF_RANGE

  - UNAVAILABLE

  - DATA_LOSS

When failed requests can be retried, the gRPC client will normally implement an exponential backoff strategy. This type of strategy adds incremental waits between retries to let the server recover from a potential saturation state. In some cases, the server may signal backpressure by adding RetryInfo to an UNAVAILABLE or RESOURCE_EXHAUSTED response status. This includes a recommended retry delay that clients should observe before the next request.

OTLP/HTTP

Not all telemetry clients can implement gRPC or HTTP/2. For instance, web browser APIs do not have the necessary fine-grained control over requests to implement it natively, and they normally rely on HTTP-gRPC translation proxies to communicate with gRPC servers. Other clients or network components may also limit the use of gRPC. For such cases, OTEP 0099 was created to address support for HTTP/1.1 and HTTP/2 transports for OTLP.

OTLP/HTTP uses the same Protobuf schemas as its gRPC variant. These can be encoded either in binary format, using the proto3 encoding standard and denoted by the `Content-Type: application/x-protobuf` header in requests, or in JSON format, using the JSON Mapping defined in proto3 and denoted by the `Content-Type: application/json` request header.

Each signal has a separate default URL path on which `POST` requests are accepted with their respective binary/JSON encoded Protobuf:

- `/v1/traces`

- `/v1/metrics`

- `/v1/logs`

The concepts explained above for gRPC regarding full success, partial success, and failure responses still apply in the relevant Protobuf-encoded server responses. Clients should retry requests unless the response status code is `HTTP 400 Bad Request`, implementing the relevant exponential backoff strategies. To implement backpressure, the server may include a `Retry-After` response header along with a `HTTP 429 Too Many Requests` or `HTTP 503 Service Unavailable` response code. This includes the number of seconds to wait before the next retry.

Exporter Configuration

As we've seen in previous chapters, OTLP exporters provide options to configure their behavior. Some of these options are self-explanatory, like the file paths for certificates or client files, headers to include in requests, compression, or timeout options. There are, however, a few considerations worth exploring depending on the value of `OTEL_EXPORTER_OTLP_PROTOCOL` (or equivalent Java system property). The value of this configuration option may be (depending on implementation) `grpc`, `http/protobuf`, or `http/json`.

When the protocol is `grpc`, the endpoint configured via the `OTEL_EXPORTER_OTLP_ENDPOINT` config option (or its signal-specific overrides via `OTEL_EXPORTER_OTLP_<SIGNAL>_ENDPOINT` where signal can be `TRACES`, `METRICS`, or `LOGS`) has a special meaning. In some implementations, like Java, this is all that's required to indicate if the gRPC connection should be secure or not. If the endpoint URL scheme is `https`, a secure connection will be established, optionally using the certificates specified in the appropriate config options. If the scheme is `http`, an insecure connection will be

established. Some implementations, like Node, allow to specify an `OTEL_EXPORTER_`
`OTLP_INSECURE` boolean option (or signal-specific overrides) that applies when no
scheme is provided in the endpoint URL. If enabled, an insecure connection will be
established if the endpoint URL has no scheme (e.g., `otel-collector:4317`).

When the protocol is `http/protobuf` or `http/json`, the `OTEL_EXPORTER_OTLP_`
`ENDPOINT` config option is used to compose the final URLs for each signal. For instance,
if the OTLP endpoint is `http://otel-collector:4317`, this will result in the following
URLs being used:

- `http://otel-collector:4317/v1/traces`

- `http://otel-collector:4317/v1/metrics`

- `http://otel-collector:4317/v1/logs`

If signal-specific config is used (e.g., `OTEL_EXPORTER_OTLP_TRACES_ENDPOINT`), then
the full URL must be specified, including the path.

Collector

OTLP and the OpenTelemetry exporters that implement this protocol were designed
with performance and reliability in mind to be a standard for telemetry transport across
languages and frameworks. As part of the core SDK distribution in each language, they
benefit from a wide community of developers that maintain and develop new features,
including those from observability vendors and telemetry platforms that now support
OTLP as a protocol to ingest data. However, the reality of telemetry transport is much
more diverse, with services exporting each signal type using different clients and
formats, multiple agents and container sidecars to transform data, and backends that
only accept a certain telemetry format.

OpenTelemetry Collectors provide a *vendor agnostic* solution to receive, process,
and export data in a wide range of existing telemetry formats and protocols. They allow
to integrate systems instrumented with different clients under the same set of transport
pipelines. They also feature telemetry data processors that can filter, aggregate, or enrich
data before it is exported to other telemetry backends, which can be useful even in
environments with a single standard transport format.

Figure 9-1 illustrates the main components of an OpenTelemetry Collector – receivers, processors, and exporters – and how these can be arranged in telemetry pipelines to support different scenarios. A pipeline normally starts at one or more receivers, goes through a series of processors, and then can "fan out" to one or more exporters. The same receiver, processor, and exporter definitions can be used in multiple pipelines.

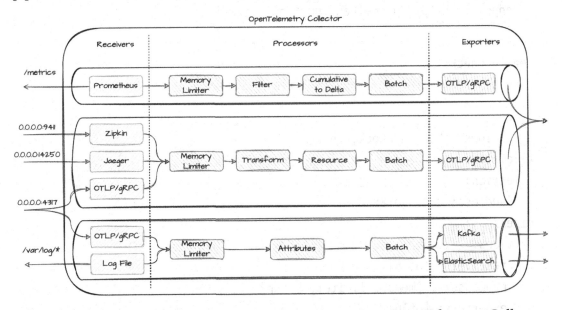

Figure 9-1. *Example of multiple telemetry pipelines in an OpenTelemetry Collector*

These components and pipelines are defined, along with extensions and other config detailed further in this chapter, in a single YAML configuration file. The following is an example of such configuration:

```yaml
receivers:
  otlp:
    protocols:
      grpc:

processors:
  batch:
  memory_limiter:
    check_interval: 1s
    limit_percentage: 75
    spike_limit_percentage: 10
```

```
exporters:
  otlp:
    endpoint: otel-collector:4386
    tls:
      insecure: true
  prometheusremotewrite:
    endpoint: http://prometheus:9090/api/v1/write

extensions:
  health_check:
  zpages:

service:
  extensions: [health_check, zpages]
  telemetry:
    metrics:
      address: 0.0.0.0:8888
  pipelines:
    traces:
      receivers: [otlp]
      processors: [memory_limiter, batch]
      exporters: [otlp]
    metrics:
      receivers: [otlp]
      processors: [memory_limiter, batch]
      exporters: [otlp, prometheusremotewrite]
```

It is possible to have more than one instance of a component for a given component type, normally configuring different properties. For example, the following configuration creates two otlp receivers in different ports and with different TLS configuration:

```
receivers:
  otlp:
    protocols:
      grpc:
        tls:
          cert_file: server.crt
          key_file: server.key
```

```
otlp/differentport:
  protocols:
    grpc:
      endpoint: 0.0.0.0:4319
```

These can later be referenced in pipelines by their unique name, in this case `otlp` and `otlp/differentport`:

```
service:
  pipelines:
    traces:
      receivers: [otlp]
      processors: [memory_limiter, batch]
      exporters: [otlp]
    metrics:
      receivers: [otlp/differentport]
      processors: [memory_limiter, batch]
      exporters: [otlp]
```

The same naming format applies to other components like processors, extensions, or exporters.

The OpenTelemetry project maintains two main repositories containing the codebase for the collector and its multiple components:

- *https://github.com/open-telemetry/opentelemetry-collector*: The core repository, containing general-purpose processors, and receivers and exporters to work with standard protocols like OTLP.

- *https://github.com/open-telemetry/opentelemetry-collector-contrib*: Hosts optional processors for multiple use cases and supports receiving and exporting telemetry for many popular open-source frameworks and vendor-specific formats. Releases of the contrib version of the collector also include core components.

The status of the OpenTelemetry Collector depends on the individual components and signals that are used within the configured pipelines. For instance, at the time of writing, the `otlp` receiver is considered stable for metrics and traces and beta for logs. The documentation of each component specifies the supported data types and the status of the component for each of them.

Deployment

The OpenTelemetry Collector is distributed as a small Go binary (or Docker image including the binary), designed to be highly performant and to provide an easy way to apply custom configuration in order to meet most common requirements out of the box. There are two main modes to run collectors:

- **Agent**: The collector runs on the same host or alongside the application (e.g., as a sidecar container or a daemon process), receiving data or scraping local targets to enrich telemetry and export it to other backends.

- **Gateway**: The collector runs as a standalone, horizontally scalable service, capable of having a centralized view of all data and providing a central configuration and authentication point against third-party providers for all telemetry within a cluster, region, or account.

We will explore these deployment models in detail in Chapter 10 along with sampling for distributed tracing.

Docker

In Chapter 4, we deployed our first OpenTelemetry Collector using Docker Compose. In order to do so, we used one of the publicly available images that can be pulled from:

- **DockerHub**: otel/opentelemetry-collector[-contrib]

- **ghrc.io**: ghcr.io/open-telemetry/opentelemetry-collector-releases/opentelemetry-collector[-contrib]

As we've seen, to load any custom configuration, we can pass the --config flag as an argument to start the collector, pointing to a mounted volume:

```
otel-collector:
  image: otel/opentelemetry-collector
  command: ["--config=/etc/otel-config.yaml"]
  volumes:
    - ./otel-config.yaml:/etc/otel-config.yaml
  ports:
    - "4317:4317" # OTLP gRPC
```

In Kubernetes, it is also possible to use these images within the official Helm Charts, with their repo hosted in *https://open-telemetry.github.io/opentelemetry-helm-charts* (source in *https://github.com/open-telemetry/opentelemetry-helm-charts*). This repository contains two charts:

- **opentelemetry-collector**: Provides a standard way to deploy the collector as a Kubernetes `deployment` or `statefulset` (gateway mode) or as a `daemonset` (agent mode), along with all necessary configuration (e.g., config map, volumes, HPA, cluster roles, service monitors, etc.).

- **opentelemetry-operator**: A Kubernetes Operator that can deploy collectors defined via a `OpenTelemetryCollector` Custom Resource Definition (CRD). In addition to the deployment modes of the `opentelemetry-collector` chart, the operator provides a mutating admission webhook that can automatically inject collectors as container sidecars when creating pods. This can be beneficial to offload telemetry export as quickly as possible to a container outside the main application container.

Linux, MacOS, and Windows Packaging

Standalone packages for the core and contrib distributions can also be found at *https://github.com/open-telemetry/opentelemetry-collector-releases/releases*. This includes the following:

- **Linux**: APK, DEB, and RPM packaging for Linux amd64/arm64/i386 systems. These install a config file at /etc/otelcol/config.yaml, which can be customized after installation. This is the default used by the `otelcol` systemd service automatically created, but these options can be configured by modifying the `OTELCOL_OPTIONS` variable in /etc/otelcol/otelcol.conf.

- **MacOS**: gzipped tarballs compatible with Intel and ARM-based systems. The resulting `otelcol` executable must be unpacked and placed in the desired installation directory.

- **Windows**: gzipped tarballs containing the `otelcol.exe` executable.

Receivers

Every telemetry pipeline in an OpenTelemetry Collector requires at least one receiver, responsible for ingesting data, potentially from multiple signal types, like metrics and traces, and transforming it into in-memory representations for further processing. Pipelines can have more than one receiver, and one receiver may be part of multiple pipelines, in which case the ingested telemetry data "fans out" to the next component in each of the pipelines. Receivers can be pull-based, requiring configuration of what targets to pull telemetry from (e.g., `prometheus`, `filelog`), or push-based, binding to a port and address on which they listen for incoming requests (e.g., `otlp`, `zipkin`). The full list of receivers, along with their status and configuration options, can be found in the `/receiver` path on the core and contrib GitHub repositories linked above.

Within the collector configuration file, receivers are defined under the `receivers` block (note they will not be enabled until they're included in at least one pipeline). Some receivers may work with defaults out of the box, like the `opencensus` receiver, which can be configured to listen on port 55678 simply by listing it:

```
receivers:
  opencensus:
```

Other receivers, especially if they're pull-based, may require more configuration. For example, the `prometheus` receiver requires a `config` to be defined. This supports all options originally supported by Prometheus instances under their equivalent `scrape_config` block, which makes OpenTelemetry Collectors a viable drop-in replacement to scrape Prometheus targets.

```
receivers:
  prometheus:
    config:
      scrape_configs:
        - job_name: 'otel-collector'
          scrape_interval: 5s
          static_configs:
            - targets: ['0.0.0.0:8888']
```

In Chapter 10, we'll explore other options to configure scrape targets in `prometheus` receivers that allow collector `statefulsets` to scale horizontally while ensuring that targets are not scraped by multiple collectors.

At the time of writing, there are 77 different receivers in the contrib distribution of the OpenTelemetry Collector. The core distribution, however, contains only one, the `otlp` receiver. This receiver works for gRPC and HTTP transports, which can be enabled respectively by specifying them in the `protocols` config:

```
receivers:
  otlp:
    protocols:
      grpc:
      http:
```

If enabled, the default config stands up a server listening on `0.0.0.0:4317` for gRPC and `0.0.0.0:4318` for HTTP. This is configurable via the `endpoint` option, supported by both protocols. Each of them can also include connection related settings like TLS, mTLS, connection buffers, concurrent streams, etc. All these options are detailed in the relevant exporter documentation in GitHub.

Processors

Once data is received and transformed into in-memory data structures, it can be passed on to the next component in the pipeline, which is normally a processor. Processors are executed in the order they are defined in a pipeline and perform some action on the telemetry data that is passed to them or the pipeline itself. Although they are optional components, and it is possible to define a pipeline connecting receivers directly to exporters, some are strongly recommended. Processors are contained under the `/processor` path in the respective core and contrib repositories. Each of these processors contains documentation about its status, configuration options, and what signals the processor can apply to (i.e., not all processors are applicable to all signals).

In addition to providing features to mutate or enrich telemetry data, certain processors also provide general data flow management capabilities in telemetry pipelines. Processors expose properties that indicate their intent to mutate telemetry data, which informs the collector if the data coming out of a receiver should be cloned or not before passing it to the first processor in a pipeline. This ensures that each individual pipeline connected to the same receiver has an independent copy of the data, so that each processor in a mutating pipeline can have full ownership of the data while it carries out its function. It also allows pipelines that contain no mutating processors (and no receivers part of mutating pipelines) to provide a more lightweight approach to data management, as all components can have access to the same shared data representation.

Two of the recommended processors, contained in the core OpenTelemetry Collector distribution, are the memory_limiter and batch processors. As processors are executed sequentially on received telemetry, the order in which they're placed in a pipeline is crucial. Figure 9-2 shows the recommended order to place these processors in relation to other processors contained in the contrib distribution.

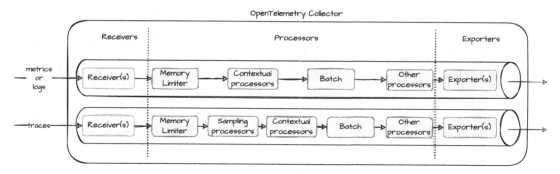

Figure 9-2. *Recommended order of processors within telemetry pipelines*

The memory_limiter processor is responsible for making sure that the collector process does not run out of memory and is thus killed by the underlying operating system or orchestration framework, which could result in extended telemetry interruptions. It achieves this by periodically checking memory consumption and reacting appropriately if certain soft and hard limits are reached. These are configurable using the limit_mb (or limit_percentage) and spike_limit_mb (or spike_limit_percentage) properties. The spike limit is used to calculate a soft limit as limit_mb - spike_limit_mb.

When the soft limit is reached, the processor starts to return errors to the previous component in the pipeline. If this is a receiver, as recommended, then the data will be refused by the pipeline and clients exporting telemetry to this collector will receive an appropriate backpressure response that allows them to retry their requests as required. When the hard limit is reached, the processor will continue to refuse data, but it will additionally force a garbage collection cycle to try to lower memory consumption.

It is important to understand that memory_limiter processors consider the full collector memory usage, not the memory usage of the individual pipelines in which they're defined. However, it is possible to define multiple memory_limiter processors with different thresholds or check intervals for each pipeline.

Another recommended core processor is the `batch` processor, which helps to reduce the throughput of exporters attached to a pipeline by grouping spans, metrics, or log records into batches. OpenTelemetry Collectors often receive or pull data from services in small amounts but at a very high throughput. For instance, all pods in a cluster may be sending spans to the same deployment of collectors. If the spans in each of these requests made their way through collector pipelines and then exported individually, this would result in an inefficient use of network connections. To solve this, the `batch` processor defines a minimum batch size to wait for in a pipeline (`send_batch_size`) and a maximum time to wait (`timeout`), and it keeps batching data in memory. When either of those thresholds is reached, the batch processor will pass on the current batch to the next component. It is also possible to configure a `send_batch_max_size`, disabled by default, which can help meet requirements of maximum payload sizes imposed by certain backends or network components when exporting data.

As the `batch` processor can aggregate data from multiple sources, it is key that it is placed after any processors that use the request `Context` present in the originating receiver operation to extract information about the source of telemetry. This is the case of the `k8sattributes` processor, which uses the IP address of the client to obtain other information like pod name, or namespace, which is then injected into the processed telemetry. After telemetry is batched, this context is no longer available to downstream processors. For similar reasons, it is also important that the `batch` processor is used after any sampling processors in order to achieve optimal batch sizes.

Many other processors (21 at the time of writing) are available in the contrib distribution of the OpenTelemetry Collector to process telemetry in different ways such as modifying attributes (e.g., `attributes`, `k8sattributes`, `transform`, or `resource`), filtering and sampling (e.g., `filter`, `probabilisticsampler`, or `tailsampling`), metrics aggregation (e.g., `cumulativetodelta`, `deltatorate`, `metricstransform`, or `spanmetrics`), and many others.

Exporters

One the main usages of OpenTelemetry Collectors is exporting telemetry to one or multiple backends, often in a different format than the telemetry they receive. Exporters receive data from the pipelines in which they're defined and send it to telemetry backends or other collectors. A pipeline must contain one or multiple exporters (i.e., having a pipeline with no exporter is not allowed), and an exporter can be declared in one or multiple pipelines. Exporters can be push-based (e.g., otlp, jaeger, prometheusremotewrite), normally requiring some configuration to point to the location where telemetry should be sent or written to, or pull-based (e.g., prometheus), which normally expose telemetry data on a configured port.

At the time of writing there are 42 different exporters bundled in the contrib distribution of the collector, each supporting one or more signal types under different levels of maturity. The core distribution of the collector provides three exporters: logging, otlp, and otlphttp. These can be found under the /exporter path in both the contrib and core repositories.

In Chapter 4, we configured a logging exporter in the collector used within our Docker Compose stack, which we later used in Chapter 8 to visualize the logs exported by our application. This exporter can be very useful in such debugging scenarios, setting its verbosity property to detailed, in order to visualize the telemetry being processed by a given pipeline. However, it is not generally used in production environments.

In order to export data in OTLP, either to other collectors or telemetry backends, the core distribution also provides otlp and otlphttp exporters for the corresponding gRPC and HTTP transports.

The otlp exporter has two required configuration properties:

- endpoint: The [<scheme>://]<host>:<port> to send OTLP data over gRPC. As explained in the OTLP section, if a scheme is used (e.g., https://otel-collector:4317), it overrides the tls.insecure setting.

- tls: TLS config for the exporter (enabled by default). This config is common to many exporters and receivers and documented in *https://github.com/open-telemetry/opentelemetry-collector/ blob/main/config/configtls/README.md.*

Additionally, the exporter allows to configure certain gRPC settings, common to other receivers and exporter documented under *https://github.com/open-telemetry/ opentelemetry-collector/blob/main/config/configgrpc/README.md.*

In turn, the otlphttp exporter only requires the endpoint config property. The resulting URL follows the conventions detailed in the OTLP section, that is, if the endpoint does not contain a path, the relevant path will be appended depending on signal type (e.g., /v1/traces). Optionally, the otlphttp exporter can configure other connection-specific settings like TLS, timeout, read/write buffers, or individual endpoints per signal type.

Different types of exporters have different memory requirements. For example, the `prometheus` exporter, being a pull-based exporter, needs to keep track of the value of sums and histograms to provide cumulative temporality aggregations. The higher the cardinality of the metrics exposed, the higher the memory requirements of this exporter. To avoid keeping references to expired metrics in memory, it provides a `metric_expiration` setting, defaulting to 5 minutes, which allows to control how long to wait for a time series not receiving any data to mark it as expired.

Push-based exporters, like the `otlp` or `otlphttp` exporters, need to implement mechanisms for queuing and retrying in order to reduce the side effects of sporadic service interruptions while exporting telemetry. To provide a standard approach to this challenge for all exporters, the core package provides an exporter helper, which implements common functionality and that can be used by any exporter. It exposes common configuration settings to control these mechanisms as documented under *https://github.com/open-telemetry/opentelemetry-collector/blob/main/ exporter/exporterhelper/README.md*.

Figure 9-3 summarizes the main behavior of queuing and retrying within push-based OpenTelemetry exporters. Each batch of telemetry data is exported individually, retrying the request in configurable intervals when retriable errors are received from the destination. If the sending queue is enabled (which it is by default), failed batches that can be retried later are added to the queue, to be picked up by a new consumer. Consequently, the larger the queue size, the more margin of error for sporadic service interruptions and the higher memory consumption when errors are received.

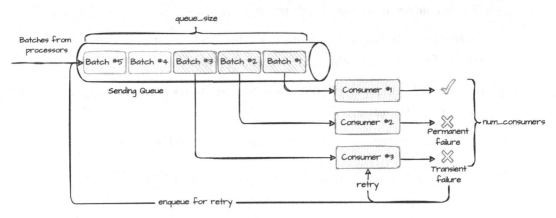

Figure 9-3. *Queuing and retrying within OpenTelemetry exporters*

After the queue is full, failed exports will not be enqueued, resulting in permanent data loss. In the "Telemetry" section presented later, we'll see how the OpenTelemetry Collector produces metrics that allow to tune these properties accordingly.

Extensions

OpenTelemetry Collectors provide capabilities outside of telemetry pipelines, but that can be useful under certain scenarios to operate collector instances. These can be configured under the extensions configuration block and enabled by declaring them in the service.extensions property as shown below. Their status and documentation can be found on their respective repository paths under /extension.

Examples of these extensions include memory_ballast, which can help optimize the amount of garbage collection happening on the collector by pre-allocating heap space, the zpages extension providing live debugging data for multiple components, or the healthcheck extension that enables an HTTP endpoint that can be probed (normally by orchestration systems like Kubernetes) to assert liveness and readiness of the collector instance.

Service

The service section of the OpenTelemetry Collector configuration defines what components are enabled and how they're positioned in telemetry pipelines. As shown previously in this chapter, it contains three properties:

- extensions: The list of extensions to enable. They must be declared and configured in the relevant extensions block.

- telemetry: Configures different aspects of telemetry instrumentation on the collector instance.

- pipelines: Configures different telemetry pipelines for each of the signal types.

Pipelines

The service.pipelines section of the configuration defines how different receivers, processors, and exporters declared in the configuration are placed within telemetry pipelines. Each pipeline processes data for one and only one signal type, namely, traces, metrics, or logs, although there can be more than one pipeline defined for a given signal type. The naming format is similar to that of other components defining multiple instances, that is, <signal>[/name]. For instance, the following configuration defines two separate pipelines for traces:

```
service:
  pipelines:
    traces:
      receivers: [otlp]
      processors: [memory_limiter, batch]
      exporters: [logging, otlp]
    traces/jaeger:
      receivers: [otlp]
      processors: [memory_limiter, batch]
      exporters: [jaeger]
```

Receivers in multiple pipelines, like the otlp receiver above, will "fan out" the data they receive to all pipelines on which they are configured, potentially cloning data in memory (if pipelines contain mutating processors) so that each pipeline can process data in isolation. After data is ingested, it is passed on from processor to processor in the order in which they're defined and ultimately exported in parallel by the list of configured exporters, each with their own configuration.

Telemetry

Operating OpenTelemetry Collectors is no different from operating any other service or application; it requires telemetry exposing its internal state in order to monitor its behavior and apply any necessary actions (manually or automatically) to maintain a reliable service. To facilitate this, OpenTelemetry Collectors allow to configure certain capabilities that are provided out of the box, defined under the `service.telemetry` section. These are as follows:

- `resource`: Allows to configure Resource attributes to be included in any exported telemetry.

- `metrics`: Exposes Prometheus-style metrics on a configured `address`. The `level` (`none`, `basic`, `normal`, or `detailed`) controls the number of indicators and dimensions added to the collected metrics.

- `logs`: Controls settings for the Go Zap logger. The settings are compatible with `zap.Config` configuration.

- `traces`: Allows OpenTelemetry Collectors to propagate trace context to downstream components. If the `batch` processor is used, context will not be propagated from receiver to exporter.

The following example showcases some of these configuration options in a sample `telemetry` definition:

```
service:
  telemetry:
    resource:
      service.name: my-collector
    metrics:
      level: normal
      address: 0.0.0.0:8888
    logs:
      level: DEBUG
      development: true
    traces:
      propagators: [tracecontext, b3]
```

Some of the most important metrics to monitor in a collector instance, in addition to compute resource metrics like CPU utilization and throttling, and heap or memory usage, are those related to receivers and exporters. Each of them contains a tag indicating the `receiver` or `exporter` in question and includes the `<type>` in the metric name, which can be `spans`, `metric_points`, or `log_records`:

- `otelcol_exporter_queue_capacity`: Max capacity of a given exporter retry queue.

- `otelcol_exporter_queue_size`: Current size of a given exporter retry queue. If this metric is close to its capacity, it indicates that data may be dropped soon.

- `otelcol_exporter_enqueue_failed_<type>`: Indicates that data could be not added to the sending queue, normally because it's full, and it's thus dropped. This is an irrecoverable error that is also accompanied by log messages in the collector.

- `otelcol_exporter_send_failed_<type>`: Indicates errors exporting data. It does not imply data loss unless the queue is full (or queueing is disabled), but sustained errors may indicate problems communicating with the backend where data is exported to or within the data itself.

- `otelcol_exporter_sent_<type>`: Number of spans, data points, or log records sent by an exporter.

- `otelcol_receiver_accepted_<type>`: Number of spans, data points, or log records received by a receiver.

- `otelcol_receiver_refused_<type>`: When this metric is greater than 0, it indicates that telemetry is not being accepted by a given receiver, and errors are being returned to clients. An increase in this metric normally indicates that the `memory_limiter` is kicking in and the collector is not accepting any more telemetry until the current data is processed and memory utilization decreases.

Monitoring these metrics can help OpenTelemetry Collector operators tune processors and exporters like the `memory_limiter` or the `sending_queue` for exporters that support it or assign the necessary resources to handle the throughput received by their collector instances.

Summary

This chapter introduced OTLP, the OpenTelemetry protocol, as a standard for data transport in telemetry systems. We have seen the main characteristics of the protocol and how clients and servers can implement it over gRPC and HTTP transports to provide a reliable service. We have also explored the main components of OpenTelemetry Collectors, one of the most useful components for observability engineers and application owners, that provide a solution to aggregate, transform, enrich, and export telemetry data in a highly performant manner.

Along with processors and exporters implemented in OpenTelemetry SDKs, OpenTelemetry Collectors are the final necessary piece to implement telemetry transport architectures that can meet the data processing requirements of teams and organizations, able to provide fast and reliable pipelines while reducing transport, computing, and storage costs. This will be the focus of Chapter 10, starting with advanced sampling techniques, one of the advantages of tracing data.

## CHAPTER 10

Sampling and Common Deployment Models

The flexibility of OpenTelemetry Collectors cannot be overstated. As we saw in Chapter 9, they can cater to many custom telemetry transport scenarios using different telemetry data processing techniques and deployment patterns. In this chapter, we'll explore some of the most common deployment models in cloud-native environments, also taking into consideration services instrumented with and without OpenTelemetry. With these tools in mind, we'll then explore some advanced trace sampling techniques, useful to increase observability while avoiding high transport and storage costs.

Common Deployment Models

Within an organization, the decision on what telemetry backends or observability platforms to use is normally conditioned by factors like cost, feature-set, support for legacy systems, etc. However, throughout this book, we have seen how OpenTelemetry puts the decision on *how* telemetry is exported to those backends in the hands of application owners, without affecting the underlying instrumentation. With so much choice, it is sometimes difficult to visualize the different ways in which OpenTelemetry can be adopted in an organization to support new and existing requirements. The following examples cover some of the most popular deployment models in cloud-native environments, along with their benefits and challenges.

We'll start from a system without OpenTelemetry, depicted in Figure 10-1. In order to focus on the telemetry processing and export pipelines, rather than its storage or querying, we'll assume all telemetry is ultimately exported to an external observability platform, which could be a third-party vendor, or an open-source solution deployed outside the cluster. Our example includes an application running in a Kubernetes cluster generating metrics using a Prometheus client. These metrics are scraped, along

179

© Daniel Gomez Blanco 2023
D. Gomez Blanco, *Practical OpenTelemetry*, https://doi.org/10.1007/978-1-4842-9075-0_10

with other common Prometheus metric producers like node-exporter or kube-state-metrics, by a Prometheus-compatible agent (quite often a Prometheus instance would be doing this job). Application logs are output to standard out/error and redirected by the container runtime to local files on the same node, from where they're tailed by a FluenBit agent. Finally, traces are exported directly to the backend using a vendor-specific OpenTracing tracer implementation.

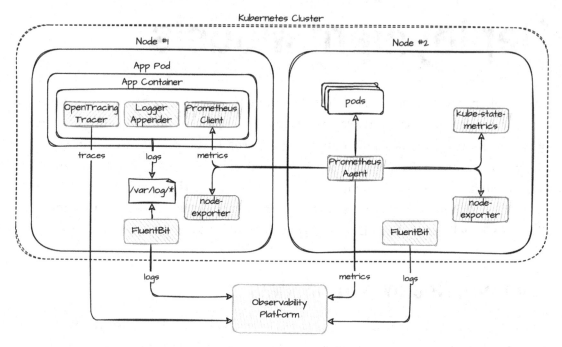

Figure 10-1. *Example pre-OpenTelemetry telemetry pipelines*

Collector-Less Model

Although OpenTelemetry Collectors are recommended components for multiple reasons we'll explore across this chapter, they're not absolutely necessary to implement OpenTelemetry. Our previous application could use the OpenTelemetry API to standardize instrumentation and the OpenTelemetry SDK to export data directly to our observability platform as illustrated in Figure 10-2. As we've seen in previous chapters, it would also be possible to configure the SDK to provide a Prometheus-compatible endpoint to be scraped instead, with no change to other components, or to keep using standard out logging appenders while benefiting from OpenTelemetry instrumentation (recommended until logging is declared stable).

Tip   In Kubernetes environments like this one, keeping standard out/error logging appenders can have other benefits like better integration with native Kubernetes tools such as `kubetcl` or providing a standard approach to logging in multi-tenant clusters.

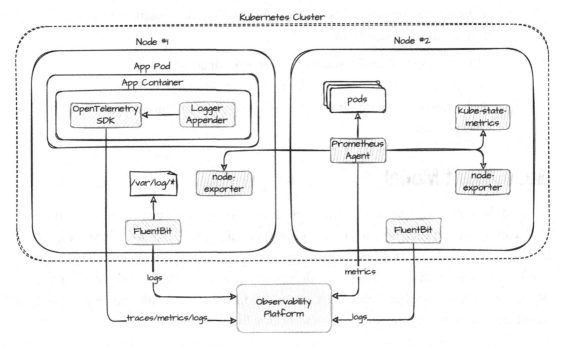

Figure 10-2. *Collector-less deployment model in a Kubernetes cluster*

The benefit of this approach is simplicity, as there are no added components to maintain. All that's required is configuration at the OpenTelemetry SDK level to export telemetry data in the required format. However, there are few drawbacks:

- The application container incurs the cost of aggregating and processing telemetry data, including batching, compression, and retries. Although this is normally negligible, saturation on the application can impact metric export or collection at the time it's most needed (when the application may be misbehaving). Sending queues used by telemetry exporters can also increase memory utilization if the backend is unstable.

- There is no central configuration point, which makes it more difficult to roll out changes to export options like backend URLs, authentication, protocols, and other settings that can affect all services in a cluster.

- There are no central data management pipelines that can process data, so any telemetry produced by our application needs to contain all the necessary attributes and be in the right format, aggregation, cardinality, or temporality.

- Although OpenTelemetry-instrumented applications can export data in multiple formats, we still need to run other agents to collect and export data for components that are not instrumented with OpenTelemetry.

Node Agent Model

Some of the preceding drawbacks can be circumvented with the use of OpenTelemetry Collector agents running on each node, represented in Figure 10-3. In Kubernetes, this is normally deployed as a daemonset. These agents can export telemetry from local targets, like Prometheus endpoints or log files, directly to telemetry backends. When using the opentelemetry-collector Helm chart, introduced in Chapter 9, this can be deployed by installing the chart with the following mode option in the chart values:

```
mode: daemonset
presets:
  logsCollection:
    enabled: true
  kubernetesAttributes:
    enabled: true
```

The previous presets configuration sets up some common pipelines, normally used in this agent mode, which enable the necessary receivers and processors to collect logs from container log files and automatically add resource attributes about the telemetry producer from information obtained from the Kubernetes API.

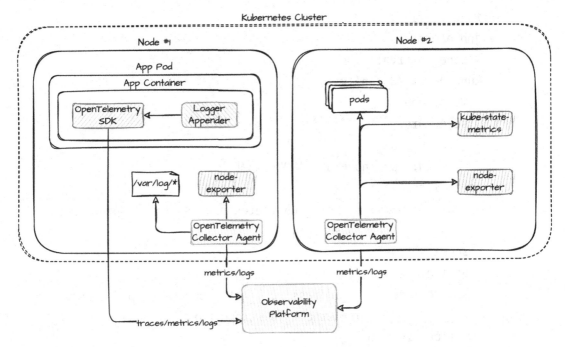

Figure 10-3. *OpenTelemetry Collector agent model in a Kubernetes cluster*

In our example, we left `node-exporter` and `kube-state-metrics` running to focus on telemetry export, but OpenTelemetry Collectors provide other receivers like `hostmetrics`, `kubeletstats`, or `k8scluster` (run in a single replica to avoid duplicates), which can provide similar functionality to `node-exporter` or `kube-state-metrics`. In order to configure a `prometheus` receiver to scrape only pods running on the same node as the collector (rather than all pods in the cluster), we can pass the node name from the collector pod spec as an environment variable and use that value in a Prometheus service discovery selector. This can be done with the following chart values:

```
extraEnvs:
- name: NODE_NAME
  valueFrom:
    fieldRef:
      fieldPath: spec.nodeName
config:
  receivers:
    prometheus:
      config:
```

```
scrape_configs:
- job_name: k8s
  scrape_interval: 10s
  kubernetes_sd_configs:
  - role: pod
    selectors:
    - role: pod
      field: spec.nodeName=$NODE_NAME
  relabel_configs:
  - source_labels: [__meta_kubernetes_pod_annotation_prometheus_
                    io_scrape]
    regex: "true"
    action: keep
  - source_labels: [__address__, __meta_kubernetes_pod_annotation_
                    prometheus_io_scrape_port]
    action: replace
    regex: ([^:]+)(?::\d+)?;(\d+)
    replacement: $$1:$$2
    target_label: __address__
```

This config also allows pods to specify if they want to be scraped or not, and on what port, reducing unnecessary scraping, by using pod annotations. Pods will be scraped only if prometheus.io/scrape=true, and they will be scraped on the /metrics path on the port specified on prometheus.io/scrape_port.

Deploying collectors as agents in every node provides value in addition to enabling telemetry export, especially to infrastructure operators:

- There is no need to maintain multiple agents for different telemetry types, reducing maintenance toil for operators. Telemetry exported by different frameworks can be collected in a standard way and exported to the desired backend.

- OpenTelemetry Collectors provide a lightweight and performant approach to scrape telemetry at the node level, reducing the blast radius of regressions or incidents within telemetry pipelines.

- Collectors can process and enrich telemetry, adding default resource information to the telemetry produced.

However, these advantages may not be so clear for application owners, as applications still need to handle telemetry export and configuration from within the application container, presenting the same challenges mentioned previously in the collector-less model.

Sidecar Agent Model

OpenTelemetry Collectors can be deployed as container sidecars, sitting alongside main application containers and consuming a very limited amount of compute resources to handle and export their telemetry, as shown in Figure 10-4. The sidecar container can be defined manually by the application owner as part of their pod definition, or it can be automatically injected via the mutating admission webhook provided by the opentelemetry-operator mentioned in Chapter 9. Applications can export all telemetry in standard formats, like OTLP, to a default local endpoint and then handle all telemetry processing and export configuration in the sidecar.

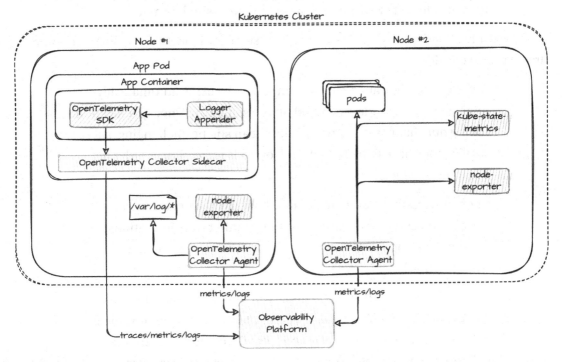

Figure 10-4. *OpenTelemetry Collector sidecar model in a Kubernetes cluster*

Having a collector sidecar brings many advantages to application owners and Kubernetes operators:

- The application container does not have to handle aggregation, sending queues, compression, etc. This decouples telemetry pipelines from applications as early as possible, reducing the impact of application saturation on telemetry export, and vice versa.

- Collectors can enrich telemetry data with resource attributes from the environment or apply other transformations to the data produced by the application before it's exported. This configuration can be applied independently from the application instrumentation.

- Using the `opentelemetry-operator` provides a central configuration point that can be applied across clusters, automatically injected into application pods. Application owners in multi-tenant clusters can configure OTLP exporters using core OpenTelemetry libraries and rely on collectors to export telemetry in the desired format.

These advantages justify the use of collector sidecars. Nonetheless, there are some drawbacks to consider:

- Although configuration can be centralized by using automatically injected collector sidecars based on the same container specification, rolling out changes to export pipelines can still be challenging, as applications have to be redeployed, or pods recreated, in order to apply any changes.

- There is no global view of the data, which may be necessary for certain processors providing sampling or other transformations that must be applied globally (e.g., limits and security related configuration).

- Depending on the cluster and deployment size, the use of sidecars can result in an inefficient use of compute resources. For instance, collectors with 100 milli-CPUs and 128 MB memory requests can still represent a sizable amount to reserve in clusters with tens of thousands of pods. Additionally, funnelling all data through a common point could optimize network transfer and connection management on the telemetry backend.

Gateway Model

The gateway model provides a funnel between applications (or other collectors) and observability platforms or telemetry backends, which is capable of processing telemetry in a centralized way, as shown in Figure 10-5.

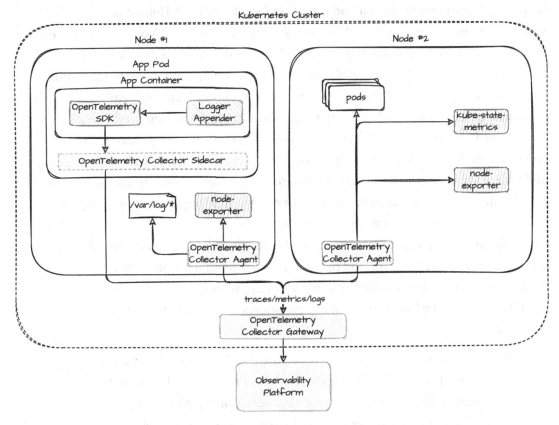

Figure 10-5. *OpenTelemetry Collector gateway model in a Kubernetes cluster*

When using the opentelemetry-collector Helm chart, a gateway can be deployed by using the deployment or statefulset mode in the chart values, for example:

```
mode: deployment
replicaCount: 3
autoscaling:
  enabled: true
  minReplicas: 3
  maxReplicas: 20
  targetCPUUtilizationPercentage: 60
```

These values configure a Kubernetes deployment with a minimum of three replicas and a maximum of 20, which is horizontally scaled to maintain a target of 60% average CPU utilization across all pods. Collectors deployed this way are stateless, with ephemeral storage. In order to benefit from certain features that require state to be retained between pod restarts (like the persistent queue in the `otlp` exporter that can keep data in the queue even if a pod is ungracefully killed), the Helm chart also offers a `statefulset` deployment mode. This uses Kubernetes Persistent Volume Claims (PVC) to provision backing volumes that are reused between restarts of the same pod.

A gateway of collectors is useful to receive data from applications, sidecars, and agents that use push-based exporters with a default cluster local endpoint. Pull-based exporters, on the other hand, present a challenge for collectors deployed as a gateway: target allocation. Without extra configuration, every collector using a `prometheus` receiver with the default Kubernetes service discovery would scrape all pods in a cluster, and having multiple collectors scrape the same target would result in duplicate data. To solve this, the `opentelemetry-operator` provides the TargetAllocator, an optional component currently under development that shards scrape targets across available OpenTelemetry Collectors. This can be used in the `prometheus` receiver config to obtain scrape targets dynamically instead of having a static configuration, resulting in a given target only scraped by one collector replica simultaneously.

Having a gateway between telemetry producers and a backends has many advantages:

- It provides a central place to configure the "last hop" of telemetry export. This keeps telemetry within clusters shielded from outside changes, like migration between backends or export formats. Application owners and Kubernetes operators can use the most standard way of exporting telemetry from their respective components, which could be OTLP or Prometheus, pointing their exporters toward a default endpoint backed by a collector gateway. This can then be transformed and exported to the desired telemetry backend.

- They provide a global view of the data, which is necessary for some advanced sampling techniques and other processors that benefit from having access to data before it's exported, such as processors that control policies or limits.

- Depending on the topology of clusters and other factors like the scale of deployments, application owners may decide to run without sidecars, instead relying on a local gateway deployment (preferably in the same availability zone) to export telemetry.

Tip   Providing a common endpoint for all telemetry within an organization, which resolves to the best/closest collector gateway for a given instance, is a great way to minimize migration requirements from teams when changes to telemetry backends are implemented.

While it is true that maintaining a new service requires extra engineering effort, the benefits outweigh the costs. Medium to large organizations can benefit from having a telemetry enablement team that, among other responsibilities, supports centralized telemetry pipelines behind collector gateways. As we'll see in Chapters 11 and 12, the engineering effort spent on these teams is quickly paid back when inevitable changes happen in business, technology stack, or third-party services.

Trace Sampling

In Chapter 6, we mentioned trace sampling as a necessity in any deployments serving production traffic at a reasonable scale. The amount of telemetry data collected can be overwhelming both technically and financially, as tracing instrumentation focuses on providing very high granularity insights that allow to correlate telemetry context across services and form the basis of transactional correlation across signals. Additionally, most of the data is normally captured when the system is behaving as expected, not relevant for debugging purposes, which is the main purpose of traces and logs.

In statistics, sampling refers to the process of selecting a subset from a statistical population in order to estimate characteristics from the whole population. There are multiple ways to approach this problem aiming to provide reliable representations of the population, but, in general, they can be divided between probability and non-probability sampling techniques. In *probability sampling*, every element has a certain chance to be selected. This may vary depending on the element properties, but it has some pre-established probability. For example, if we randomly pick one apple from one in ten of our apple trees and one pear from two in ten of our pear trees, we know the probability that a given apple, or pear, comes from a given tree (10% for apples, 20% for pears).

On the other hand, in *non-probability sampling*, the chances of an element being selected are affected by external factors not known beforehand. A form of non-probability sampling called purposive sampling can be used to focus on groups that match certain characteristics within the population, biassing sampling toward them, to form a case study. For instance, if we want to study apples or pears dropped in the early summer, which affects fruit production and indicates trees are running low in carbohydrates, instead of picking trees randomly in our previous example, we can pick the first apple or the first two pears to fall from a tree in the month of June (in the northern hemisphere). The probability that a given apple comes from a tree is no longer easy to calculate, as there are many factors that could affect it, like tree pruning, soil nutrients, weather, etc. We can no longer answer the question "what is the probability that this apple came from this tree?" reliably. The worst affected trees will have more chances of being selected, and there may be trees with no June drop, which have zero chances of being selected.

In observability, the population to consider refers to the collection of spans, logs, or data points processed by a system. Probability sampling is normally simpler to implement. For some signals, like traditional logging, it is usually the only possible option. Every log record can only be considered individually, and it can either be stored or not depending on the existence of some attributes (e.g., store 100% of error logs and 10% of debug logs). Tracing, however, allows for advanced sampling mechanisms that allow to take into consideration trace context information when deciding if a given span should be stored. For example, we can decide to sample a span if the parent was sampled, as this information is passed along with trace context. This results in a complete and contextual view of different services and operations involved in a sampled trace, rather than operations considered in isolation. Probability sampling can be implemented early, in the application itself, or later in the telemetry export process, in OpenTelemetry Collector processors.

Tracing also allows the use of external information, like the duration of a whole trace, to decide if a trace should be kept or not. This is a form of non-probability sampling that normally happens outside the application process, for example, in a collector, as it requires a complete view of the data. The probability of a given trace to be sampled is not known beforehand and depends on external factors.

Probability Sampling

Within OpenTelemetry-instrumented systems, the simplest form of sampling to configure is usually referred to as *head-based sampling*, as it is done in-process with no external components required. In this form of sampling, the decision is made up front, when the trace (or span) is created, using any available information to the sampler at that point in time. This has the benefit of reducing the tracer overhead, as well as the final storage and analysis costs. The Tracing API uses two main properties to decide if a span is exported and stored or not:

- IsRecording: A property of a Span that indicates if a span is recording events, attributes, status, etc. When a span is non-recording, it is not passed to a SpanProcessor and thus not exported. This is the default no-op type of span used when no TracerProvider is configured for the API, and it's useful to allow for context to be propagated correctly between services without processing the spans of a specific library or application and to allow instrumentation libraries to be decoupled from implementations.

- Sampled: A property of a SpanContext that is propagated along with other fields like span or trace IDs, as seen in the W3C TraceContext specification described in Chapter 6, and that indicates if a span should be exported or not. A span can be recording and not sampled. In that case, the span can be processed by a SpanProcessor but not forwarded to its SpanExporter. This allows spans to be considered for other processor features, like generating metrics from spans, or being consumed in-process (e.g., via zPages, a way to visualize in-memory telemetry for a single replica, currently in experimental state in OpenTelemetry but previously used in OpenCensus as documented in *https://opencensus.io/zpages*).

When we explored the Tracing SDK, we saw how it is possible to configure a `Sampler` when creating a `TracerProvider` within an OpenTelemetry-instrumented application and how the default sampler would be equivalent to setting the following sampler during creation:

```
SdkTracerProvider tracerProvider = SdkTracerProvider.builder()
  .setSampler(Sampler.parentBased(Sampler.alwaysOn()))
  .build();
```

This sampler is called upon span creation, and it must make a sampling decision based on certain properties like traced ID, span name, parent context, span kind, attributes, or links. The decision determines if a span should be sampled, recording, or both (although spans cannot be non-recording and sampled, as non-recording spans are not passed to processors). OpenTelemetry provides a few built-in samplers:

- `AlwaysOn`: Always returns a sampled (and thus recording) span.

- `AlwaysOff`: Always returns a non-recording (and thus unsampled) span.

- `TraceIdRatioBased`: Spans are sampled depending on the result of a deterministic function that accepts a trace ID and a ratio of traces to sample (e.g., 0.01 would sample 1% of traces). The details of this function are not yet detailed in the OpenTelemetry specification, and it may be implemented differently in individual languages, but it must result in the given ratio of traces sampled.

- `ParentBased`: This is a composite sampler. If a parent span context exists, it replicates its sampling decision on the span being created. If not, it calls another configured sampler (required during sampler creation) called the root sampler. Optionally, this sampler allows configuring individual samplers for each parent locality (if parent was created in this service or elsewhere) or sampled flag (if parent was sampled or not). The default is to use `AlwaysOn` if the parent is sampled and `AlwaysOff` if the parent is unsampled, regardless of the parent locality.

Using these built-in samplers provides a simple approach to reduce the number of traces stored. Using a `ParentBased` sampler is normally recommended to avoid traces where some spans are sampled and some are not, which can hinder observability.

Tracing platforms normally represent these spans that have a parent that was not sampled (or that failed to be exported for other reasons) as orphaned spans. As illustrated in Figure 10-6, having orphaned spans can interfere with debugging as the causal relationship between operations is broken or there are key operations missing.

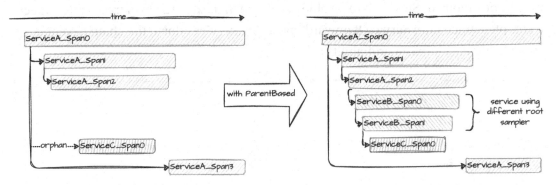

Figure 10-6.   *Trace with orphan spans due to a lack of* `ParentBased` *sampling*

Using Tracestate for Consistent Probability Sampling

Propagating the `sampled` flag along with trace context and taking the parent span sampling decisions into consideration in head-based sampling results in complete traces, but it also affects the effective sampling probability for a service. For instance, if Service A is configured to sample 12.5% of all traces and it is the only client of Service B, which is configured to sample 25% of all traces, Service B will end up sampling 12.5% of its spans if it uses a `ParentBased` sampler, as it must respect the parent sampling decision. This makes it difficult for span-to-metrics pipelines to calculate the original number of spans that were generated by a service before sampling occurs. This is called the *adjusted count*, that is, the number of spans in the population that are represented by an individual span. This is the inverse of the effective sampling probability. For instance, spans in Service B would end up having an adjusted count of 8 (as its parent sampling probability is 12.5%, there is one sampled span for every 8 unsampled spans) rather than its configured ratio of 1 to 4. Propagating the parent sample probability along with trace context can support accurate calculations of span counts in span-to-metrics pipelines.

Another area where the current `TraceIdRatioBased` definition lacks support is in allowing individual samplers to make independent sampling decisions in order to produce traces that are complete after a service in the call chain decides to sample it. As we've seen, the implementation of the sampling algorithm is not defined, which means it must be used with `ParentBased` samplers from the root of a trace to guarantee complete traces, even if all callee services in a trace are configured with the same or higher tracing ratios than their caller; otherwise, sampling decisions down the call chain may depend on implementations. Figure 10-7 showcases a scenario where Service A is configured to sample 12.5% of traces and calls Service B which is configured to sample 25% of traces. It may be desirable for Service B to be able to sample that extra 12.5% of traces and expect a complete trace from Service B onward (as long as services down the chain have the same or higher sampling probability).

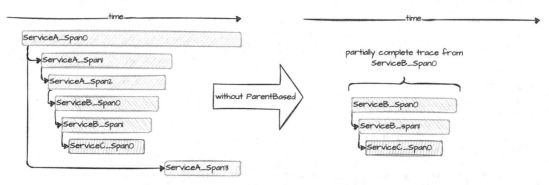

Figure 10-7. *Partially complete traces using consistent probability sampling*

To address both of these challenges, the OpenTelemetry specification proposes the use of a new sampler called ConsistentProbabilityBased and the use of the tracestate header in the W3C TraceContext specification. This is detailed in *https:// opentelemetry.io/docs/reference/specification/trace/tracestate-probability-sampling*, and although it's still in experimental state, and thus subject to change, some implementations are already available (e.g., Java provides one in the opentelemetry-java-contrib repo). In general terms, this sampler uses two propagated values (p-value and r-value) to enable consistent head-based sampling while supporting services to make independent sampling decisions.

The *p-value* is a value between 0 and 63, which represents the negative base-2 logarithm of the parent sampling probability (except 63, which represents 0% probability) configured when creating a ConsistentProbabilityBased sampler. This means that the possible sampling probabilities are limited to powers of two:

p-value	Sampling probability
0	1
1	½ (50%)
2	¼ (25%)
…	…
n	2^{-n}
…	…
63	0

For instance, Service A would have a p-value of 3, which represents a sampling probability of 12.5% (2^{-3}=0.125). This limit in possible p-values allows them to be encoded as small unsigned integers while providing increasingly smaller sampling ratios. Although it is recommended to choose powers of two when configuring `ConsistentProbabilityBased` samplers, if non-power-of-two probabilities are used, the sampler will select the closest one. When a sampler of this type decides to sample a trace, it includes this p-value in the `tracestate` to be propagated to its callee. The callee can use the incoming p-value to add information to its exported span data and accurately represent its adjusted count so that it takes into consideration the parent probability.

The *r-value* represents which one of a series of 63 possible probability values was used to sample a trace. The set of supported probabilities includes the integer powers of two between 1 and 2^{-62}, in a similar way as done for p-value detailed previously. This means an r-value of 0 has a 100% probability of being chosen, an r-value of 63 has a 0% probability of being chosen, and any r-value n in the middle will follow a 2^{-n} probability. The function to generate these r-values is irrelevant, as long as it can guarantee that its resulting probabilities are consistent. For instance, a common approach is to generate r-values by counting the number of leading 0s in a substring from the trace ID containing 32 random bits (note: trace IDs may not always have random leading 0s, e.g., when adapted between legacy propagators):

r-value	Probability	Example
0	1	11001100... (fixed 100%)
1	½ (50%)	01101100...
2	¼ (25%)	00111101...
...	...	
7	2^{-7}	00000001...
n	2^{-n}	00000000...
...	...	
63	0	00000000... (fixed 0%)

To guarantee consistency, the r-value must be generated at the root of the trace and propagated along with trace context with no modification from any sampler (unless it's invalid or nonexistent, in which case a new r-value is calculated, but the trace may be inconsistent). When a ConsistentProbabilityBased sampler makes a sampling decision, it compares the current r-value to its p-value (configured when creating the sampler) and decides to sample a span if $p \leq r$. In other words, it will sample the span if the probability of the r-value occurring is lower than its configured sampling ratio. Having the same r-value propagated across a trace guarantees that services configuring higher sampling probabilities than their callers will always result in complete (although potentially partial) traces. For instance, a trace with r-value 3 (12.5% chances of happening) will be sampled by services configuring p-values of 3, 2, 1, and 0, which correspond to sampling ratios of 12.5%, 25%, 50%, and 100%, respectively.

These two values are propagated under the ot vendor tag in the W3C TraceContext tracestate header. For example, an incoming trace context may look like this (traceparent header has been shortened for clarity):

```
traceparent: 00-6cd...-01
tracestate: ot=r:3;p:2
```

In this case, the parent span was sampled by its sampler because its p-value 2 (sampling ratio of 25%), was less than its r-value 3 (12.5% probability). If a sampler configured with p-value 3 (12.5% sampling ratio) picks up this trace, it will decide to sample it too and adjust the p-value to 3 to inform the next sampler of the effective adjusted count. If a sampler with p-value 4 is in the chain, it will not sample it and remove the p-value from the `tracestate` (it becomes irrelevant to the child span).

There is a parent-based version of this sampler called a `ParentConsistentProbabilityBased`. When the parent contains valid p-value and r-value, it propagates them to child spans and honors the sampling decision made by the parent. This still results in consistent traces as the sampling decision is forwarded.

Collector Processor for Probability Sampling

OpenTelemetry Collectors provide an out-of-process form of implementing probability sampling via a processor called `probabilistic_sampler`. This processor uses a hash generated from the trace ID, and a configurable sampling ratio, to decide if spans for a given trace should be kept or dropped. For instance, the following config samples 12.5% of all traces:

```
processors:
  probabilistic_sampler:
    hash_seed: 42
    sampling_percentage: 12.5
```

In order to produce consistent traces, the `hash_seed` must be the same in every collector processing spans for a given trace. The most typical way to implement this is to use this processor in a gateway model, where spans from all services are exported to the same endpoint and then load balanced across a set of collectors.

This processor does not support partially complete traces or different sampling ratios depending on services or attributes, although it does support the legacy OpenTracing `sampling.priority` span attribute, which informs the processor to sample a given trace (this takes priority). Its advantage is simplicity. There is no state to maintain or routing to be implemented.

Tail-Based Sampling

The probability sampling techniques we've seen so far go through different levels of complexity to provide a consistent approach to trace sampling according to a probability function, but they all have one major caveat: they're completely random. This is a desired property in many statistical representations. The higher the sampling ratio, the more accurately we can estimate characteristics of the whole population from the resulting subset. However, in observability, not all traces are considered equal. Some traces, like those exposing error or latency regressions in the systems they instrument, are more valuable than others for the purposes of debugging. We're normally interested in storing all or a big percentage of those "bad" traces, and we don't particularly care if a big percentage of the "good" traces is dropped.

Sampling spans according to characteristics of the whole trace is a form of non-probability sampling, as we cannot assert the probability of a span being sampled before its creation. After spans are sampled this way, the distribution of errors or duration will no longer be representative of the whole population but rather of a particular subset, which is the one we're interested in when debugging regressions. Spans from a service may be sampled because another service in the trace is failing, or they may be sampled because they're part of traces with the longest duration. This may affect any conclusions that service owners extract from analyzing the duration of particular groups of spans, as the distribution will be skewed toward the worst cases.

Tip   Metrics, rather than tracing, should be used to accurately aggregate measurements across dimensions, for reasons mentioned in Chapter 7. When using tail-based sampling, this is especially important, as span distributions will be biased representations of system behavior.

In order to consider the characteristics of a trace for sampling, the algorithm requires a complete view of the trace. Let's say we only want to sample traces that contain one or more errors. As samplers are invoked by the SDK on span creation, this wouldn't be achievable with in-process sampling (we don't know the status of a span until it finishes). We could create an out-of-process sampler in an OpenTelemetry Collector processor that only keeps spans for traces that contain an error, but as spans are processed in the order they arrive, spans could have already been dropped before an error span arrives. This is illustrated in Figure 10-8, where the spans in dotted lines represent the spans that would have been dropped by the time the first error arrives (assuming that they're processed in the order they finish), which is the first point at which we'd be able to make a decision. A trace with six spans would only be able to sample two.

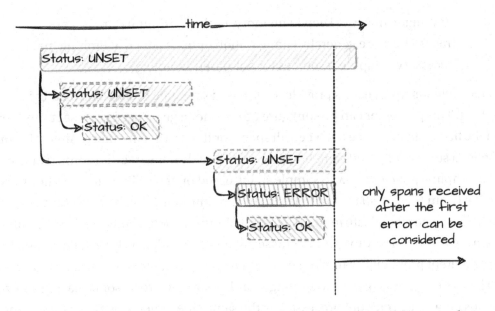

Figure 10-8. *Previous spans dropped before the trace is selected for sampling*

To avoid this, we need to wait for all spans in a trace to be received (or a reasonable amount of time) before making a sampling decision. This is commonly referred to as *tail-based sampling*. In Figure 10-8, this would mean waiting for the root span to finish and then deciding to sample all spans under it.

Some observability vendors provide features that allow exporting all spans to a common endpoint (local or remote), providing configurable tail-based sampling capabilities before ingesting traces into their platform. These normally allow to configure thresholds or conditions to select certain traces for storage, but they all have limits that are unavoidable when using tail-based sampling:

- How long to wait for spans before considering a trace complete? There is no standard way of asserting when a trace is finished, as traces are logical groupings of individual spans. Some implementations use a timer from when the first span is received for a trace; others use a timer that gets reset every time a span is received. Waiting too long to make a decision (regardless of the trace having finished or not) may result in data being delayed for analysis, which has side effects in the debugging experience (e.g., having traces delayed by 5 minutes is not great in the middle of a production incident).

- How many traces to keep in memory, or the maximum duration of a trace? These are generally configuration options aimed at limiting the necessary compute resources for tail-based sampling.

OpenTelemetry Collectors provide a tail-based sampling processor called `tail_sampling`. This processor can be configured to wait for a given `decision_wait` duration from the first span in a trace and keep all spans for that trace in memory. After this time, it applies a set of configured sampling policies to decide if the trace is sampled or not. These sampling policies allow to sample spans based on trace characteristics like trace duration (from the first span start to last span end timestamp), span status (any span matching a given status), attributes (spans matching attribute conditions), rate limiting, etc. It also provides a way to combine these policies in multiple ways, which allows the use of different probability sampling depending on traces matching certain conditions.

The most challenging part of running a `tail_sampling` processor is making sure that all spans for a given trace are processed by the same OpenTelemetry Collector instance. This is a strict requirement, as tail-based sampling needs to consider all spans in a trace to be able to make a decision and to sample any spans after a decision is made. There are two approaches to this problem:

- Using a single collector replica to receive all spans. This may be the simplest one, but it clearly cannot scale to large systems with thousands of service replicas communicating with each other.

- Load balancing spans according to their trace ID. By using a two-tier approach, one set of collectors (which could be a sidecar) can receive spans for all traces and then route all spans for a given trace to a single collector, part of a second tier of collectors, as depicted in Figure 10-9. OpenTelemetry offers the `loadbalancing` exporter for this purpose, which can route spans according to trace IDs to a configurable set of collectors. The routing can be static (a list of hostnames) or dynamic (a DNS resolver that returns a list of IP addresses).

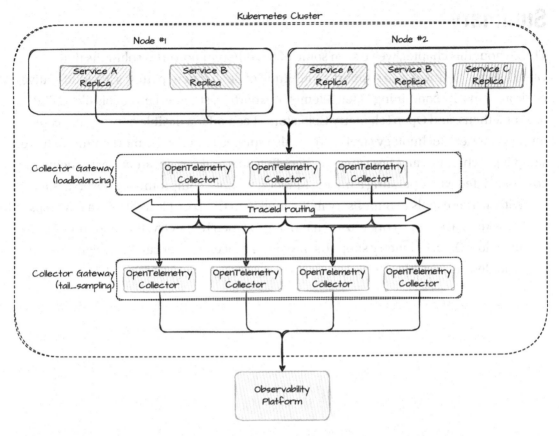

Figure 10-9. *Load balancing spans to tail-based sampling collectors*

Maintaining tail-based samplers is not trivial, especially in multi-cluster environments that require a central point outside the cluster to process all spans, but the outcome is usually worth it. It not only provides a way to reduce processing, storing, and analysis costs, but it also reduces telemetry noise (i.e., uninteresting traces that fall within the expected behavior of a system are not kept) to allow engineers to focus on the transactions that matter. Sometimes, less is more, and observability is not an exception.

Summary

Throughout this chapter, we've seen some of the different powerful solutions that OpenTelemetry provides to support a multitude of deployment patterns in cloud-native environments. By combining OpenTelemetry exporters, standard protocols like OTLP or Prometheus, and OpenTelemetry Collectors, it can offer a flexible approach to cater for most modern technology stacks. We've also studied some of the most common trace sampling techniques and how they can benefit teams and organizations by reducing the cost associated with operating a tracing function without compromising observability.

With all these tools in our observability toolkit, in Chapter 11, we'll take a few steps back to a key stage for any organization moving to OpenTelemetry: the migration. We'll examine how OpenTelemetry supports migration processes that can be designed to be as frictionless as possible.

PART III

Rolling Out OpenTelemetry Across Your Organization

## CHAPTER 11

Maximizing Adoption by Minimizing Friction

Interoperability has been an area of focus for the OpenTelemetry project since its conception. The pre-existing diversity of telemetry frameworks, instrumentation libraries, transport formats, and protocols meant that any adopted solution had to support easy ways to integrate new and old instrumentation to provide uniformity and standardization in telemetry pipelines. Even though OpenTelemetry Collectors can go a long way in helping to integrate legacy systems with OpenTelemetry-instrumented applications, past chapters in this book have taught us of the advantages of relying on OpenTelemetry APIs and SDKs at the instrumentation layer and standard formats and protocols like W3C TraceContext or OTLP to transport in-band and out-of-band data. At some point, which depends on external factors as well as stability of individual signals, and in order to fully benefit from OpenTelemetry features, teams and organizations should consider a gradual migration toward these open standards.

Migrations can be tedious. As any change in a system, they have potential for unwanted side effects and can add substantial work to engineering backlogs, slowing product delivery. It is important to minimize these migration requirements and gradually ramp up the value of technology adoption.

Investing in Telemetry Enablement

When teams and organizations take the important step of starting a migration process toward the open standards proposed by OpenTelemetry (hopefully this book and plenty of other great publicly available content has convinced them to do so), they normally ask themselves "what is the best place to start?" There are three main factors that normally weigh in on this decision:

© Daniel Gomez Blanco 2023
D. Gomez Blanco, *Practical OpenTelemetry*, https://doi.org/10.1007/978-1-4842-9075-0_11

- **Stability**: The general recommendation is to wait until a signal specification and its relevant implementations are considered stable before rolling it out across an organization. Although enablement teams should start to test a signal in experimental/beta status sooner to understand constraints and plan a migration path, backward compatibility is not guaranteed. Breaking changes may affect telemetry reliability or require additional migration work for early adopters, who should be rewarded, not penalized, for helping an organization move toward open standards.

- **Effort**: Depending on the environment, one signal can be easier to roll out than others. For instance, for a team that does not use tracing at all, adding tracing may be the easiest migration, especially with auto-instrumentation. For other teams, it may be logs, as they only require changes to appenders. For most, metrics is rarely the easiest, as it is usually the signal used to drive custom dashboards and alerts that need to be adapted to conform to any changes in semantic conventions. This normally requires simultaneously exporting old and new metrics to allow teams to change runbooks, alerts, and other critical resources needed to determine the health of a system.

- **Value**: Depending on existing conditions, focusing on a particular signal may provide more value than others. Tracing, for example, can be incredibly valuable for service owners to debug regressions, especially in teams with poor logging practices, where it can also help reduce cost, thanks to sampling. Organizations having to maintain multiple metrics clients and backends may find it more useful to focus on metrics first, to reduce maintenance costs, or to correlate metrics with other existing signals.

Putting aside stability, which should be a strict requirement, striking a balance between effort and value is key. Engineering teams will normally welcome a migration that involves little effort and adds clear value to their daily operations. Who wouldn't? If the only task to get instant observability was upgrading a library or a Docker image, the word "migration" would not convey the negative connotation it usually does for engineering teams. Unfortunately, this is rarely the case. Migrations require effort, and, in some cases, the value is not always clear.

Migration value is sometimes difficult to communicate, especially in the field of observability, where value increases exponentially for all services with every service that starts to form part of a set of contextually correlated signals. A single team, accustomed to using metrics and traditional logging, may not see the value in integrating tracing into their application or making sure that context is propagated correctly through their service and does not result in disjointed traces. They don't use these capabilities and may not see the benefits to start using them. However, apart from slowing down their own debugging experience using uncorrelated and uncontextualized signals, they also impact the observability of other services and teams, part of the same system, which would benefit from correct context propagation and the use of semantic conventions. When we consider correlation and context propagation as requirements to implement observability, the responsibility of a service owner does not end at their own service boundaries; it extends to making sure their service is part of a whole observable system.

This is where a *telemetry enablement function* is crucial for technology adoption within an organization, focusing on reducing migration effort, establishing sensible defaults that allow for telemetry to be correlated across services and signals, promoting open standards, and making sure that the value of observability is realized. Essentially, to effectively implement observability across a whole organization, there needs to be a set of internal, opinionated standards, which should be as easy as feasibly possible to adopt.

Tip   Telemetry enablement should focus on maximizing the value from increasing observability across an organization while making sure that the path of least resistance is the one following best practices for instrumentation.

In medium to large organizations operating in modern environments, telemetry enablement is normally embedded within platform engineering teams. Investing in platform engineering can improve the velocity of product teams by offloading the work necessary to research new technology, develop toolchains and workflows, assert integration with existing tooling, ensure security standards, etc. These teams are in charge of providing a layer of abstraction (in the form of internal libraries, templates, or Docker images) on top of existing technologies to implement an opinionated approach to common concepts. When we consider telemetry, this layer of abstraction can include the following:

- Telemetry exporters, with default configuration regarding endpoints, protocols, format, or aggregation temporality. For instance, using a default hostname resolving to a collector gateway benefits both service owners, who are shielded from any telemetry backend changes, as well as platform engineers, who can process telemetry as required before exporting it to backends, including sampling, rate limiting, obfuscation, etc.

- Context propagators, ensuring that the selection and order of these results in correct context propagation between services running different versions.

- Out-of-the-box configuration for instrumentation packages, metric views, and resource attributes that are catered to the environments where services are deployed while keeping unnecessary telemetry transfer and processing cost in mind.

- OpenTelemetry Collector gateways, agents, or automatically injected sidecars that are pre-configured with all the configuration mentioned previously and that allow telemetry maintainers to easily roll out changes to pipelines.

- API shims and bridges to legacy instrumentation that allow teams to gradually migrate to OpenTelemetry APIs at their own pace while benefiting from standard telemetry transport and instrumentation.

To help in providing some of these features, some vendors offer their own *OpenTelemetry distros*. These are useful for all types of organizations but especially for smaller ones that may not have the engineering workforce to be able to dedicate a whole team to telemetry enablement. Distros should not be confused with vendor-specific implementations or forks of OpenTelemetry SDKs or instrumentation packages, and they do not contain any plugins or any other functionality that is not available in public OpenTelemetry repositories under its Apache v2.0 license. Client distros simply configure OpenTelemetry SDKs, plugins, and instrumentation libraries with a set of opinionated defaults that are recommended by a particular vendor to integrate with their features, ensuring compatibility. In a similar fashion, collector distros contain a set of suggested receivers, processors, and exporters that have been validated by vendors to export telemetry to their backend.

Adopting OpenTelemetry

Having chosen a signal to focus on, and aided by distros offered by vendors or other integrations provided by enablement teams, service owners can start their OpenTelemetry adoption. The way to approach this depends on any existing instrumentation within the service in question.

Greenfield Environments

New services, and those that are not currently instrumented for a given signal, are normally less constrained, and they can adopt OpenTelemetry natively without requiring a migration. In this case, and provided OpenTelemetry libraries are stable in a particular language, service owners can follow the advice given so far in this book to use OpenTelemetry APIs and SDKs and configure instrumentation libraries and plugins.

As a general rule, evaluating the telemetry produced by instrumentation libraries, or native OpenTelemetry if libraries are already instrumented for that purpose, is a good place to start. Automatic instrumentation should always take precedence. It not only saves the effort to instrument a service, but it also ensures that its generated telemetry is as intended and can be maintained as part of library upgrades. In large deployments, these may need to be adjusted via metric views or attribute/resource processors to make sure the volume and cardinality of telemetry produced does not produce unforeseen costs or load on telemetry systems. One way of doing this is to enable instrumentation libraries in developing or staging environments and extrapolate the volume produced to production traffic.

Most services have custom business logic that requires its own instrumentation. To instrument these concepts, service owners should follow best practices and always consider the purpose of a given signal before proceeding. Different signals in the OpenTelemetry API can be analogous to instruments in a song. Each has its own strengths, and overusing one of them is not usually the best way to cover for a lack in others (as a drummer, I'm very conscious of this).

When it comes to instrumenting a set of services, as we'll discuss in Chapter 12, it is a good idea to start small and expand instrumentation outward, connecting services part of the same subsystems.

Compatibility with OpenTracing

A large part of the design of OpenTelemetry Tracing API was influenced by OpenTracing. As such, the OpenTelemetry community has acknowledged, since early stages, that a migration from one to the other shouldn't be painful, and backward compatibility should be supported when feasible. The decoupling of the tracing API from its implementation was already present in OpenTracing. This enabled the creation of a tracer implementation that can bridge calls to the OpenTracing API into OpenTelemetry API equivalents, called the *OpenTracing Shim*. In Java, this functionality is provided under the opentelemetry-opentracing-shim Maven artifact. An OpenTracing-compatible tracer can be created from a configured OpenTelemetry instance and registered with the OpenTracing API as follows:

```
# Create OpenTracing-compatible tracer
Tracer tracer = OpenTracingShim
  .createTracerShim(openTelemetry);

# Register tracer in OpenTracing API
GlobalTracer.registerIfAbsent(tracer);
```

Figure 11-1 describes the general behavior of the OpenTracing Shim, acting as a tracer implementation that relays calls to the OpenTelemetry Tracing and Baggage APIs. Under the hood, a single OpenTelemetry instance will handle all functionality, allowing to use both APIs within the same codebase.

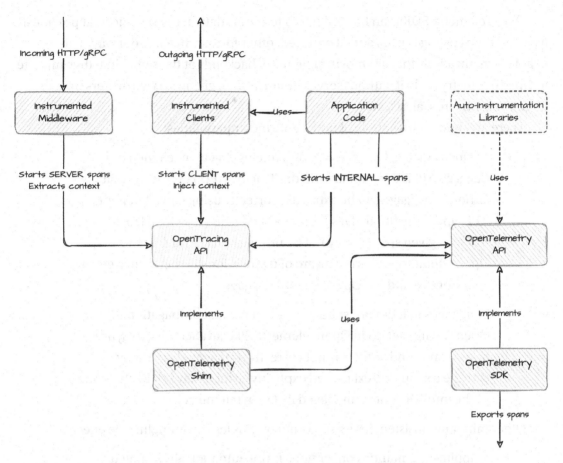

Figure 11-1. *OpenTracing Shim providing a bridge to OpenTelemetry*

With the shim in place, any OpenTracing-instrumented server and client libraries extract and inject context using the underlying OpenTelemetry Propagators API. This means they're able to use multiple propagators simultaneously (not supported in OpenTracing), allowing for a seamless transition to W3C TraceContext while supporting multiple services in a single trace that are yet to migrate, all without "breaking the chain." It also allows the integration of optional OpenTelemetry instrumentation libraries, or application code, using both OpenTracing and OpenTelemetry APIs within the same trace. Service owners can progressively replace OpenTracing instrumentation libraries for its OpenTelemetry equivalents and modify application code to use OpenTelemetry APIs, before completely removing OpenTracing.

OpenTelemetry SDKs can be configured to export data in the same format previously used by OpenTracing tracers and, if required, other formats in a fan-out way. This enables organizations that are moving telemetry backends at the same time they migrate to OpenTelemetry to do it without service interruption, giving service owners time to migrate dashboards, alerts, etc.

There are, however, a couple of noticeable incompatibilities:

- In OpenTracing, baggage is part of tracing. In OpenTelemetry, the Baggage API is decoupled from the Tracing API. This means that although baggage can be extracted correctly using OpenTelemetry APIs under the hood, if it's then modified using the OpenTracing API on a given span, it may not be propagated forward, as the OpenTelemetry API is not aware of the relationship between a given span context and its (OpenTracing) baggage.

- Languages that did not support implicit context propagation in OpenTracing but do in OpenTelemetry, like JavaScript (via async hooks), may find context is not correctly propagated after they activate a span context passed explicitly (which may not be the same as the implicit context managed by OpenTelemetry).

Other minor inconsistencies exist, normally with less meaningful side effects:

- Mapping of semantic conventions is not automatically handled, except for the `error` tag, which is translated to OpenTelemetry span status.

- In OpenTracing, the span kind could be modified after span creation; this is not possible in OpenTelemetry.

- The `FOLLOWS_FROM` reference between spans is translated into a span `Link`.

Compatibility with OpenCensus

As the other precursor project merged into OpenTelemetry, OpenCensus users can benefit from a backward compatible method to perform a gradual migration. This can be achieved via the *OpenCensus Shim*. In addition to tracing, this shim also bridges the use of OpenCensus metrics to OpenTelemetry APIs. In Java, the `opentelemetry-opencensus-shim` Maven artifact contains both shims.

The OpenCensus tracing shim follows the same approach as the OpenTracing Shim, configuring a tracer implementation that translates calls from OpenCensus to the underlying OpenTelemetry instance. Depending on the language, the way to configure this tracer may differ. This is because OpenCensus provides an implementation along with its API, while OpenTracing requires a given implementation to be globally registered. For example, in OpenCensus Java, a `Tracing` class is responsible for handling the global instance of the `TraceComponent`, initialized on class load, which in turn holds instances and configuration for all tracing components. When the OpenCensus shim dependency is included in a Java application, it is loaded by reflection during `Tracing` initialization, overriding the default `TraceComponent` implementation. There is no other action for service owners, except removing OpenCensus exporters in favor of OpenTelemetry ones.

There are also a few known incompatibilities:

- In OpenCensus, parent spans can be specified after span creation. This is not possible in OpenTelemetry, where the parent of a span is passed when building the span and it is not modifiable. This may lead to inconsistencies in parent-child relationships.

- Span links are also not allowed after span creation in OpenTelemetry. Any OpenCensus span that gets links added a posteriori will not have them applied.

- There is no support for span-scoped samplers in OpenTelemetry (supported in OpenCensus). This can only be configured when building a `TracerProvider`.

- Some OpenCensus APIs support `debug` and `defer` flags, in addition to the `sampled` flag, as part of span context. These are handled on a best-effort basis by individual implementations.

Although the OpenTelemetry specification for OpenCensus metrics is not yet stable, and it relies on experimental Metrics API components like `MetricProducer`, some implementations have started to provide experimental packages. For instance, in Java, OpenCensus metrics are supported via an implementation of a `MetricReader` that attaches itself to an existing `MetricReader` and uses a `MetricProducer` to pull measurements from OpenCensus to translate them into OpenTelemetry. Some of the known incompatibilities include no support for the GaugeHistogram type, context-based attributes (tags), or the SumOfSquaredDeviation field, which are dropped by the shim.

Other Telemetry Clients

Although the OpenTelemetry API only provides backward compatibility for OpenTracing and OpenCensus, OpenTelemetry Collectors can help migrate from other telemetry clients by enabling pipelines to receive data in multiple formats, process them to adopt naming conventions and other standards, and export them in a common format.

For instance, an application using a Prometheus client would not be able to automatically migrate to using OpenTelemetry Metrics SDKs internally. Every metric that is manually instrumented needs to be adapted. The difference in pull vs. push metrics exports used by Prometheus and OTLP makes this process more intricate. However, as depicted in Figure 11-2, it would be possible to use a collector sidecar to scrape Prometheus metrics from the application container, receive OTLP data for newly adapted metrics (or Prometheus data on different port), process them in common pipelines to standardize naming conventions, and export in the format supported by the telemetry backend in use (which could be pull or push-based, like Prometheus Remote-Write). This allows service owners to migrate metrics one by one, rather than in a single release, and validate their behavior without changing any consumers of these metrics, which can still pull metrics from the same Prometheus endpoint. Additionally, although dashboards and alerts would have to be adapted, annotating metrics with a `telemetry.sdk.name: opentelemetry` attribute would allow to produce the same metric via Prometheus and OpenTelemetry clients without aggregation conflicts (each would be a different time series) and assert correctness on the destination backend.

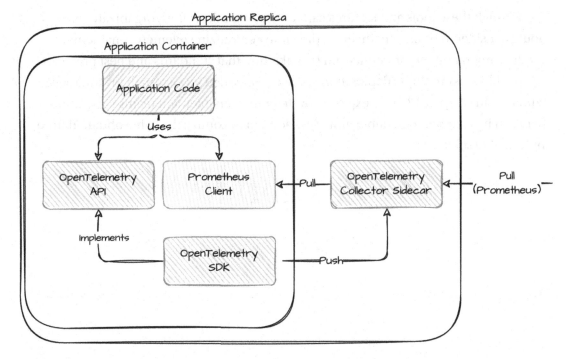

Figure 11-2. *Gradual migration of metrics produced via a Prometheus client*

Other migrations may be more straightforward, although this depends on individual environments. For example, Statsd sidecars being replaced with OpenTelemetry Collectors or logging frameworks enabling OpenTelemetry appenders and instrumentation to enhance their value for observability.

Summary

OpenTelemetry's interoperability features make it easy for organizations to gradually consolidate instrumentation into open standards, simplifying deployments and achieving a greater degree of correlation between signals and services. Services using OpenTracing and OpenCensus can benefit from backward compatibility, while OpenTelemetry Collectors can help merge export pipelines from telemetry exported by other clients.

Although these tools and features can reduce migration effort, organizations should consider investing engineering time into centralizing telemetry enablement to reduce migration requirements and to make sure that standards and best practices are upheld across multiple deployments. Having provided an easy path toward these standards, in Chapter 12, we'll explore how telemetry enablement teams can promote change in instrumentation debugging workflows to maximize the value obtained from observability solutions.

CHAPTER 12

Adopting Observability

The initial chapters of this book focused on why observability matters in modern distributed systems and how OpenTelemetry standards help to provide the building blocks to implement a holistic approach to understand distributed systems, correlating telemetry across signals and services, breaking those silos they've traditionally been confined to. Each of the individual signals we've explored (traces, metrics, and logs) has specific characteristics that make them a better signal for a particular use case, but using them in isolation, without context, reduces their usefulness. The value of observability can only be fully realized if engineering teams take advantage of all signals, not only to instrument their services accordingly but using telemetry context within their debugging workflows to troubleshoot regressions faster.

Shifting Debugging Workflows

Changing the way engineering teams debug production services is not easy. Telemetry has conventionally been custom to individual applications, mostly instrumented by their owners, who apply their knowledge of the system to describe it in a meaningful way. These experienced engineers are normally the ones building dashboards, alerts, and runbooks that can be followed by teams in the middle of an incident. It is of no surprise that, when approached with a new troubleshooting workflow, a typical reaction is to question its usefulness. After all, if it's worked until now, why change it? As explained in Chapter 1, there are many reasons why this assumption is flawed, especially in modern distributed systems. We cannot simply predict every single failure mode an application may encounter, regardless of the level of expertise.

One could have the most advanced telemetry tooling and instrumentation or large amounts of data being automatically correlated by observability frameworks. If engineers follow preestablished debugging workflows that rely on querying logs in an isolated browser window, and observing custom dashboards in another, it is not going

© Daniel Gomez Blanco 2023
D. Gomez Blanco, *Practical OpenTelemetry*, https://doi.org/10.1007/978-1-4842-9075-0_12

to improve the time taken to detect and identify the cause of regressions (the MTTD and MTTK metrics mentioned in Chapter 1). In order to change this, we need observability "champions" to challenge these conventions across an organization and to do so with evidence.

This does not mean that all preexisting knowledge goes out the window. Quite the opposite. Observability can *enhance* these workflows by shifting the debugging starting point and following an optimized path to find the root cause. Let's say a team have a runbook that guides engineers to react to a specific alert on an elevated number of 5xx responses by checking a Kubernetes dashboard for increased memory utilization (which could be fixed by temporarily scaling out the deployment) and then running specific queries against a log backend to find errors when calling dependencies (which could result in getting another team involved in an incident call to debug their service). Provided with the right data, observability platforms can automatically present memory utilization metrics and trends in other signals that correlate to those 5xx responses based on resource attributes like `service.name` or give exemplars of traces that contribute to those errors, which then may lead to the same logs. This is portrayed in Figure 12-1, where both debugging workflows arrive at a similar conclusion, one relying on context, correlation, and automated analysis and the other relying on experience from known failure modes. Only an experienced engineer could reliably troubleshoot a system without context propagation and automatic signal correlation, unless the preestablished steps written in a runbook are somehow always correct and up to date, which is rarely the case.

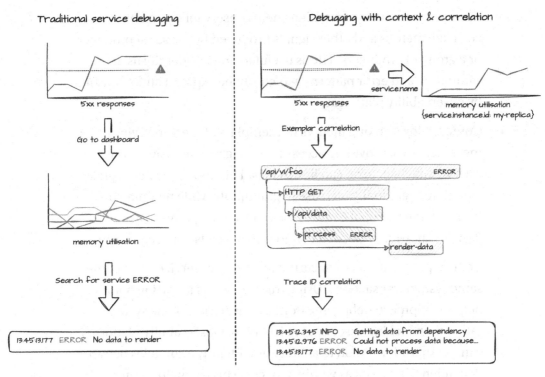

Figure 12-1. *Effective observability in debugging workflows*

Tip   One way to assert the effectiveness of any observability solution is to debug a regression with zero knowledge of a system. If the outcome reached is the same as the one reached by service owners in a similar or shorter length of time, that is a good sign.

Previous chapters detailed the purpose of each of the signals in the observability toolkit. Although every deployment is different, when it comes to alerting and debugging, they all have their particular strengths. In summary:

- Alerts and dashboards driven from metrics (even if a telemetry platform supports other signals) tend to be more reliable, as they provide a constant, complete, signal, and telemetry export and transport pipelines can be built to tolerate short service interruptions.

- The use of semantic conventions helps observability systems correlate metrics and other signals produced by the same producer or a group of producers. This is useful to quickly identify usage, saturation, and error patterns, which can be exposed automatically by observability platforms.

- Context allows linking metrics to exemplars of the underlying measurements, providing access to more granular insights via tracing, which, in turn, can link to logs. This allows the debugging workflow to gradually increase in granularity while retaining the frame of transactional context, reducing the cognitive load and domain knowledge needed to find the root cause of a regression.

- Context propagation connects the telemetry of services part of the same system transactions. Using tracing data as a starting point helps to approach debugging from a holistic view of the system, rather than looking at services in isolation. Observability platforms can use this information to analyze and identify anomalies between dependencies as well as within services. This can help during incident response, especially in organizations where different parts of a system are owned by different teams. Identifying what part of a system is causing a regression no longer has to involve multiple teams passing the buck on an incident call.

- Logs linked to traces can enhance debugging by contextualizing legacy instrumentation in libraries that use standard logging frameworks, and they provide key telemetry from processes outside distributed traces, like orchestration, startup, shutdown, background processes, etc.

When companies have a postmortem process in place to analyze and discuss past incidents, they are in a great position to start optimizing observability workflows and reduce their time to resolution. In order to be useful, these discussions need to be focused on *learning and improving*, keeping blame aside, and asking the relevant questions needed to optimize the process, not an individual's actions. In Albert Einstein's words, "failure is success in progress."

A good practice for postmortem analysis is to measure and document incident lifecycle metrics. We talked about these metrics in Chapter 1 and, in particular, the metrics that observability helps optimize. Although gathering every metric mentioned may not be possible, or efficient, having target times for some of the main metrics like MTTD or MTTRes can prompt engineers to ask some meaningful questions during this process, including the following:

- Why were engineers on call not alerted sooner?

- Are SLOs accurately representing the service reliability requirements?

- What was the impact on other services? Were they notified?

- How did engineers identify if the regression was caused by a dependency or if it was isolated to a single service?

- What signals were used to debug this incident?

- Would other existing signals provide a faster way of reaching the same conclusion?

- Is there custom instrumentation missing that could have enhanced the debugging experience?

Although there may be people in a team that can answer these questions and guide the rest of the team toward better approaches, this is not always the case. External input is often needed and should always be encouraged. One way of formalizing this is via the creation of a guild or a group of people across an organization can share knowledge and best practices in observability. Discussing postmortems in guild meetings or other forums, focused specifically on how MTTD or MTTRes could have been improved, can be beneficial for all teams, not only the team affected by the incident. These sessions can also be used to talk about near misses, success stories, or any news in the observability space that can foster a culture of sharing and learning.

Telemetry enablement teams can help by contributing to guild conversations, providing examples, or crafting a set of observability standards to follow across an organization. Having a list of dos and don'ts that can be easily consumed by engineering teams, to be used as a guide to useful instrumentation and debugging, can save a great amount of collective engineering time. Nonetheless, for this approach to be scalable to larger organizations, these standards and best practices need to be "championed" by a set of individuals with a particular interest in observability, that understand the value, and can communicate it to all areas of the business.

Expanding Context

When a team is ready to adopt observability in their instrumentation and debugging practices, the logical approach is to start from an individual service in a system, either because of its significance or because it is prone to failure, and follow the advice presented so far in this book. Unfortunately, a single service in a distributed system cannot normally implement effective observability on its own. Of course, the benefits from auto-instrumentation libraries, standard APIs, and semantic conventions to correlate signals are still of great value, but when services are part of a mesh of interconnected services, often managed by different teams, their failure modes are also conditioned by their dependencies. It is important then to think about a system as a whole, rather than a collection of independent services.

In order to achieve effective correlation and context propagation, a set of standards needs to be established. Services that are part of the same system must agree on matters like context propagation formats or domain-specific semantic conventions. Telemetry enablement teams can facilitate this task and possibly even make it practically transparent to service owners, providing default settings or common constants as part of their core libraries or OpenTelemetry distros. However, enabling automatic instrumentation and context propagation by default across a whole organization can be a double-edged sword. On the one hand, out-of-the-box telemetry can instantly enhance observability for all services, with little or no effort required. Most services can seamlessly propagate trace context, helping telemetry analysis and correlation for the whole system. On the other hand, if faulty instrumentation makes context get lost between async tasks in one service, this will produce disjointed traces, affecting observability. For instance, if a service receives a request and uses an async HTTP client to call a dependency without internally propagating context in order to connect SERVER and CLIENT spans under the same trace, this "breaks the chain." Whatever happened before SERVER span and after that CLIENT span will be part of different traces. Even worse, if context is incorrectly handled within a service (e.g., an unclosed scope), the result may be operations incorrectly assigned to a given trace. This can have damaging effects to observability, adding noise that gets in the way of debugging.

One way to manage this situation is to gradually build up telemetry context, focusing on key transactions, ensuring its correct propagation across services starting from the entry point to a particular system. This allows to form a use case that can clearly showcase the value of context propagation to multiple business areas. For instance, for web applications, this entry point may be the initial load of a page document or individual requests starting in user browsers. The opentelemetry-js instrumentation packages provide experimental instrumentation for XMLHttpRequest (XHR), able to create CLIENT spans and propagate trace context from browser to backend services (this is not possible for initial page loads, as there's no JavaScript loaded to initialize a tracer provider). Instrumentation on user devices, like browser or mobile applications, is still experimental, but as support for these clients develops, we'll see a better integration between traditional real user monitoring and backend services, thanks to standardized context propagation. In any case, even if the first instrumented component is a component within a system's backend, the earlier context starts to be propagated, the more accurately traces will represent the system as experienced by end users.

Once the earliest feasible component to start propagating context has been identified, service owners can start to add OpenTelemetry instrumentation and evaluate the telemetry produced. During this process, it is important to use local or integration environments to assess if the telemetry volume and cardinality produced by default instrumentation libraries are within the expected limits of telemetry backends. On larger deployments, this will avoid undesired surprises when these changes are deployed in production at a reasonable scale.

Telemetry enablement teams can vastly reduce the effort required during this telemetry adoption phase. In addition to common config and helper libraries, they can provide services with a *standard monitoring, alerting, and debugging* experience across a whole organization. This is currently outside the scope of OpenTelemetry and thus this book. It can include a set of predefined dashboards, templated alerts, and other resources than can get teams up and running quickly. Having a uniform observability user experience facilitates incident response, particularly during incident calls involving multiple teams. Cross-team collaboration becomes considerably easier if there is a common understanding of a given graph, a system view, or the significance of a particular alert. When these common resources are built and maintained by observability experts, they minimize the chances of having alerts that won't fire under the conditions they're expected to fire or graphs that may lead engineers to wrong assumptions about a system's health.

After a service adopts new telemetry standards in production, a typical way to decide the next area to focus on is to examine traces containing specific SERVER or CONSUMER spans. If a service is the entry point to a system, these will normally be root spans, unless a browser or mobile app `CLIENT` span starts the trace. It is important to validate that server span names represent meaningful operations (i.e., not too general, not too granular, as seen in previous chapters discussing semantic conventions) when real traffic starts to be served.

Examining the slowest traces for those previously identified key operations, or the ones containing errors, can help corroborate assumptions about a service against real evidence, guiding the next instrumentation efforts. For instance, if a given operation or external call within a trace is usually the one contributing to the longest trace durations, this is a good area to focus on. When external calls are inspected, if the corresponding `CLIENT` spans have no associated `SERVER` spans, this normally indicates that context is not being propagated correctly (unless spans from the receiving service are not being exported for some other reason). This is where service owners can start expanding context propagation, either by instrumenting the service at the other side of a `CLIENT` span or by reaching out to the owners of the service to do so. This process can then be repeated for the rest of dependencies, adding more services to traces, making sure that context is propagated along the full call chain where appropriate.

As represented in Figure 12-2, it is also possible that the process mentioned in the last paragraph was followed in different subsystems within an overarching system. This can be due to preexisting differences in technology frameworks or instrumentation capabilities, which can now start to form part of the same telemetry context thanks to the power of open standards. For instance, before OpenTelemetry, Node applications had to handle context explicitly, manually passing context objects from function call to function call or using other custom context propagation mechanisms. This resulted in black holes within context propagation. Thanks to async hooks, context can be handled implicitly and automatically propagated by instrumentation libraries. Propagating context between Service C and Service D in the example contained in Figure 12-2 provides more value than straightforward service-to-service communication. It connects multiple subsystems under a unified context.

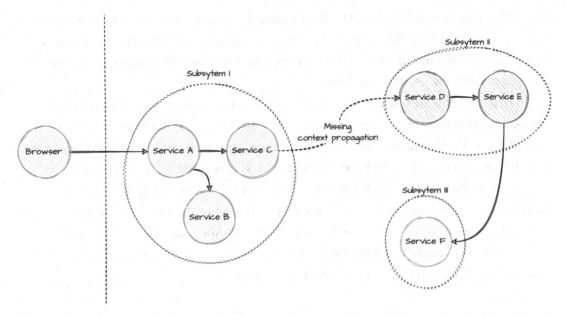

Figure 12-2. *Connecting subsystems part of the same trace via trace context*

Effective trace context propagation in large distributed systems is not trivial. The diligence to make sure that context is propagated correctly where it should and split into new traces where it shouldn't (e.g., fire-and-forget async tasks) has to be considered during the development process. In most cases, changes to application code will not require changes in instrumentation, especially if context is handled implicitly and propagators are configured appropriately. However, when changes are made to the way a given operation is handled in multi-threaded frameworks, or when new async tasks are implemented, there's potential to break context propagation, affecting observability for all services in a trace.

OpenTelemetry provides in-memory exporters that are specifically designed to be used within unit tests and that allow the retrieval of the telemetry generated within a test execution. These can be used to programmatically assert that internal context propagation behaves as expected and that it remains this way as changes are implemented into the codebase. This way, instrumentation can become part of the software development lifecycle, rather than an extra added on top.

In addition to unit tests, engineers that are familiar with their observability platform and the telemetry produced by the services are more proficient at debugging failures. Although one of the goals of observability is reducing the cognitive load necessary to debug production services, as any tool, it requires a minimum amount of training and familiarity to be used effectively. The fire brigade does not wait for a house to be on fire to learn how to use their fire engine. Furthermore, metrics and distributed traces can help teams understand the role of their services within a complex system, including usage patterns between dependencies

In large distributed systems, where different components are owned by different teams, it is not uncommon for engineers to be unaware of what happens before (or after) their service is called within individual transactions. Having a holistic view of the system based on real data can foster healthy discussions about general system design. Organizing sessions where multiple teams can examine traces for key operations together and share knowledge about their respective areas provides a useful framework to expand general knowledge of the overall system. Additionally, it allows identification of those black holes where telemetry context is not propagated or new instrumentation that needs to be added to accurately represent the system.

Keeping Telemetry Valuable

As distributed systems grow in number of services and traffic volume, the amount of telemetry produced in terms of data transfer and cardinality will follow a similar pattern. This is unavoidable. However, although teams typically pay attention to maintaining security standards and tackling technical debt as part of their engineering health processes, they rarely consider the state of their telemetry as part of this effort. Concepts that require manual instrumentation within an application are hardly ever reviewed again to assert if they're still useful, or used, even when the conditions surrounding them have changed. They can incur considerable costs while providing little or no value to monitoring, alerting, or debugging.

One way to manage telemetry data quality is via centralization, control, and limitation. No team can generate a new signal unless it's approved by maintainers of a given telemetry platform. Cardinality and volume limits are kept purposefully low and only raised upon approval. This, as the reader may have guessed, is not a recommended approach. It reduces velocity for engineering teams, generates toil for telemetry platform maintainers, and generally does not achieve its goal in the long term. After new data is added, these conditions are never evaluated again. Thus, telemetry should be easy to generate and to consume, but it must be done sensibly.

A different approach is to focus on enablement, rather than control. As previously mentioned, teams can be provided with default recommended instrumentation packages, sampling, and aggregations (e.g., metric views) that are designed to strike a balance between meaningful observability data and low data transfer, storage, and cardinality. It should then be as easy as feasibly possible for engineers to enhance this telemetry data with custom signals or change instrumentation packages and aggregations. Although having limits in place to safeguard the stability of a telemetry platform is still recommended (i.e., one badly instrumented service should negatively affect all other services), these limits should not be used to enforce good practices.

Tip   Incorporate the principle of least effort into telemetry instrumentation to ensure that the golden path is also the easiest one to follow.

This autonomy given to engineers to instrument their services as they see fit must come with *accountability*. The costs incurred by telemetry platforms are some of those infrastructure or compute platform costs that are usually hidden under multiple layers of abstraction and that are either not attributed to anyone or attributed to the team that operates the platform within an organization. Users of these platforms may have no understanding of how their usage (in this case telemetry) affects costs or performance. For instance, the compute costs from running a Kubernetes cluster, or any other multi-tenant compute platform where applications share resources (i.e., CPU, memory, network), can be distributed among services according to the share of compute resources they consume. The most typical method is to base this distribution on the amount of compute resources reserved. For instance, if a worker node with 2 CPU/8 GB runs two containers, one requesting 0.5 CPU/2 GB and another one requesting 1.5 CPU/6 GB, we could distribute the full cost of the node such that one container assumes 25% of the costs and the other 75%.

When it comes to distributing the infrastructure costs of a telemetry platform, it is not possible, or at least not easy, to estimate the required CPU or memory required to process and analyze the telemetry for a given service. One way to fairly distribute costs is using proxy metrics like data ingest volume, number of span/records/data points, or metric cardinality. The metric to use depends on the limiting factors for a given telemetry platform. For instance, for time series databases, we could distribute costs depending on the ratio between the cardinality of an individual metric and the total cardinality across all metrics. For a logging backend or tracing backend, this could be done on storage size.

One of the positive side effects of OpenTelemetry Resource semantic conventions is the clear *ownership* of telemetry data. As detailed in previous chapters, `service.name` is a required attribute for all resources, and `service.namespace` is recommended to group a collection of services, normally owned by the same team. These can be used to distribute costs among services and namespaces, which can then be attributed to individual teams. When teams are able to clearly see the impact that their services have on the overall cost or load on a telemetry platform, they can make informed decisions. For instance, the same metric, annotated with the same set of attributes, can be completely negligible for a small service running 100 replicas, but it may result in poor performance or astronomical costs for a service running 10,000 replicas. This is not to say that large-scale deployments should be instrumented "less" or that they should be penalized in terms of access to observability data. Large-scale deployments will always be more expensive to operate, and telemetry cost should always be factored into the budget of running such services, but having visibility over telemetry production allows their owners to understand the consequences of their changes (e.g., adding an attribute to a metric with an unbound number of values).

Cost distribution can also help teams prioritize the usefulness of different signals when compared to their cost. For example, when teams start to use distributed tracing, especially if sampling techniques are in place, they may see that the costs associated with it are lower than the costs of traditional logging if one were to try to capture the same granularity, allowing them to reduce their logging costs. They may also identify certain metrics with a high cardinality that are not used in any dashboard, or alert, and they were previously used for debugging use cases that may now also be fulfilled by tracing. These metrics can then be turned off or aggregated over lower-cardinality dimensions.

Telemetry cost and load optimization can deliver incredible results when compared to other optimizations like infrastructure or compute costs. One cannot easily save 80% of compute costs for a service (at least not without switching it off), but this would not be unthinkable for the telemetry costs of a service moving from traditional verbose access logging to distributed tracing, massively increasing the value of its telemetry data.

Summary

The focus of this last chapter has been placed on ensuring a responsible approach to adopting observability across an organization. It is certainly not an easy task, especially when there's a legacy of conventional instrumentation in place and teams are familiarized with traditional debugging workflows that do not take full advantage of observability platforms. It requires coordination and a model of gradual improvement and knowledge sharing that can scale across teams and business areas.

The path to adopting best practices must be one of enablement rather than excessive control. It must give teams autonomy to instrument their systems in the most meaningful way to easily identify and troubleshoot incidents in production while making them accountable for the telemetry they produce. Fortunately, the design of OpenTelemetry provides all the necessary ingredients to make this possible. When signals and context are used for their intended purposes, they can increase observability without compromising cost or load on telemetry platforms, forming a correlated web of telemetry signals that help us examine distributed systems holistically, rather than as a collection of isolated services.

Index

A

Access log, 144
addLink() method, 95
API, 27, 30–32, 39, 43, 47, 51, 66, 73
Application logging, 10, 78, 86, 143
Application owners, 16, 18, 30, 31, 34, 36,
      51, 54, 80, 81, 101, 106, 107, 114,
      131, 157, 160, 178, 179, 185, 186, 188
Application Performance Monitoring
      (APM), 7
asMap() method, 76
Audit logs, 144
Auto-instrumentation
    instrumentation libraries (*see*
        Instrumentation libraries)
    Resource SDK, 51–53
Automatic correlation, 10–12, 42

B

Baggage, 39, 75–77
Baggage API, 39, 73–76, 94, 212
Baggage data structure, 74
BatchLogRecordProcessor, 152
BatchSpanProcessor, 105–107, 153
buildAndRegisterGlobal(), 67

C

Call.Factory, 67
Cardinality explosion, 114
Carrier, 79, 80

Cloud-native environments, 179, 202
CNCF projects, 15, 20–22, 24
Collector-less model
    benefits, 181
    drawbacks, 181, 182
    Kubernetes, 180, 181
Collectors
    components, 163
    deployment, 166
    Docker Compose, 166
    exporters, 171–174
    extensions, 174
    Kubernetes, 167
    Linux, 167
    MacOS, 167
    naming format, 165
    otlp/otlp/differentport, 165
    otlp receivers, 164, 165
    pipelines, 163
    processors, 169, 171
        batch, 170, 171
        execution, 169
        features, 169
        memory_limiter, 170
        /processor path, 169
        telemetry pipelines, 170
    receivers, 168, 169
    repositories, 165
    service
        pipelines, 175
        properties, 174
        Telemetry, 176, 177

231

Collectors (*cont.*)
   standalone packages, 167
   status, 165
   TLS configuration, 164
   vendor agnostic solution, 162
   Windows, 167
   YAML configuration, 163, 164
Composite Propagators, 80
Config Store Proxy, 9, 20
Configure propagators, 82, 83
Constructors and plugin interfaces, 30
Context, 6–13, 29
Context API, 39, 69–75, 78
   wrapSupplier() functionality, 100
Context.current(), 72
ContextKey classes, 70
Context propagation, 10, 18, 20, 34, 37,
      39, 61, 68, 70, 78, 79, 82, 83, 85,
      87, 111, 207, 208, 218, 222,
      224, 225
Contrib packages, 30, 31, 33
Control systems theory, 3
Counter.add(), 121
Counter-productive pattern, 7
Cross-service context, 77–82
Custom instrumentation, 7, 23, 88,
      115, 221

D

Delayed telemetry, 12
Dependency Injection, 67, 89
Deployment models, 166, 179
Distributed systems, 8, 9, 11, 20, 77, 217,
      225, 226, 229
Distributed trace, 34, 35, 85, 87
docker-compose.yml, 55

E

Enablement teams, 64, 189, 206, 209,
      216, 221–223
Engineering teams, 206, 207, 217,
      221, 226
EventLogger interface, 150
Events API interface, 150, 151
Executor/ExecutorService, 73
Executor framework, Java, 73
Exemplars
   auto-configuration, 135
   ExemplarFilter, 135
   ExemplarReservoir, 135
   features, 134
   hooks, 134, 135
   informations, 134
   Prometheus, 135, 136
Exporters, 107, 157, 161–163, 169,
      171–174, 178
Extensions, 61–63, 163, 165, 174

F

forceFlush() function, 106, 126, 136, 151

G

Gateway model
   advantages, 188
   chart values, 187
   collectors, 188
   exporters, 188
   Helm chart, 188
   Kubernetes, 187, 188
   opentelemetry-collector, 187
   prometheus, 188
   telemetry enablement team, 189

get() method, 67
GlobalOpenTelemetry.get(), 67, 89
Google's Core Web Vitals, 146
Gradle dependencies, 67
Gradle project, 43

H

HashMap, 81, 82
Head-based sampling, 191, 193, 194
Histogram, 36, 37, 114, 120, 122, 128–130,
        138, 139, 142, 173
histogram.record(), 37
HTTP requests, 45, 76, 89, 108, 113

I

Implementation model, 54
Instrumentation agents, 22, 53
Instrumentation libraries, 40
    Docker Compose stack, 55, 58
    docker-compose.yml, 55
    simple telemetry pipeline,
        dropwizard-example, 57
    implementation model, 54
    Java agent (*see* Java agent)
    Java standalone
        instrumentation, 66, 67
    OpenTelemetry languages, 54
    OpenTelemetry project, 53
    otel-collector container, 56
    Zero-touch model, 54
Instrumentation scope, 88, 115, 117,
        118, 148
International System of Units (SI), 17
Interoperability, 108, 113, 157,
        205, 215

J

Jaeger, 21, 55, 57, 59, 79, 90, 96, 172
Java agent
    application, 58
    auto-instrumented JVM memory,
        metrics in Prometheus, 60
    download, 58
    exporter, 107
    extension, 61–63
    properties, 106
    resource, 63, 64
    suppress auto-instrumentation, 64, 65
    trace, /people operation, Jaeger, 59
Java application, 51, 60, 63, 68, 213
Java SDK, 52
Java Service Provider Interface (SPI),
        61, 62, 153
Java standalone instrumentation, 66, 67

K

Kubernetes, 179, 181, 182, 185–188
Kubernetes cluster, 51

L

Logger, 148, 149
LoggerProvider, 147, 151
Logging
    access, 144
    aggregate functions, 145
    application logs, 143
    audit, 144
    challenges, 144
    event monitoring, 146
    formats/frameworks, 146
    infrastructure components, 146

Logging (*cont.*)

    metrics, 145, 146

    observability, 143

    OpenTelemetry Collectors, 146

    operators, 145

    vs. spans, 145, 146

    tracing, 144

    transactions, 144

    use cases, 145

Logging API, 156

    definition, 147

    events API interface, 150, 151

    GlobalLoggerProvider, 148

    properties, LoggerProvider, 148

    LoggerProvider interface, 147

    loggers, 148

    logs API interface, 149

    OpenTelemetry, 147

Logging frameworks

    appenders, 154

    bootstrapping process, 154

    collector, 155, 156

    context injectors, 154

    Docker Compose, 155

    log message, 155

    OTLP to export, 155

Logging SDK

    attribute limits, 152

    exporters, 152–154

    implementations, 151

    Java agent, 152

    Logger implementations, 151

    LoggerProvider, 151

    processors, 152–154

LogRecord, 149

Logs, 6, 10–12, 15–18, 29, 35, 38, 41, 42, 45, 47, 48, 57, 78, 111, 143–147, 149–156, 165

M

mainOp() method, 99

mainOp span, 101, 102

makeCurrent() function, 71, 72, 75, 94

Mapped Diagnostic Context (MDC), 34, 70

Mean Time to Detect (MTTD), 5, 6

Mean Time to Fix (MTTF), 5, 6

Mean Time to Identify (MTTI), 5

Mean Time to Know (MTTK), 5, 6, 10, 11

Mean Time to Recovery (MTTRec), 4, 7

Mean Time to Resolution (MTTRes), 4, 5, 7, 221

Mean Time to Verify (MTTV), 5, 6

Measurements, 17, 35, 36, 111–114, 120, 126, 134

META-INF/services, 62

Metric cardinality, 7, 46, 114, 120, 227

Metrics, 35–37

    aggregations, 114

    backends, 112, 113

    clients, 112

    data flow, 113

    data points, 111, 139

    Gauge, 139

    graph plotting, 111

    http.status_code, 113

    http.url attribute, 114

    purposes, 142

    re-aggregated, 114

    signals, 112

    single request, duration, 114

    time aggregates, 113

    URL, 114

    uses, 111

Metrics API

    instrument registration

        duplication, 117, 118

        identification, 117

Java implementation, 117
monotonicity, 119
OpenTelemetry specification, 117
properties, 116
synchronous/asynchronous, 118
instrument types
advantages, 120
Attributes class, 120
Counter, 120
Histogram, 122
ObservableCounter, 121
ObservableGauge, 124, 125
ObservableUpDownCounter, 124
UpDownCounter, 123
use cases, 120
meters/meter providers, 115, 116
public interfaces, 114
SDK, 114
Metrics conventions, 46, 47
Metrics SDK
aggregation
bucket histogram, 128–130
default, 131
drop, 131
exponential histogram, 130, 131
functions, 127
instrument type, 127
last value, 128
sum, 127
aggregation temporality, 139, 140
application owners, 131
cumulative temporality, 139–141
delta temporality, 139–142
exemplars, 134–136
instrumentation author, 131
Maven artifacts, 126
Meter instances, 125
MeterProvider

configurations, 125
creation, 126
functions, 126
Java, 126
MetricReader
auto-configuration, 138
features, 136
Histogram, 138
instruments/metric views, 138
MetricProvider, 137
otel.metric.export.interval, 139
OtlpGrpcMetricExporter, 138
PeriodicMetricReader, 138
PrometheusHttpServer, 138
properties, 136, 137
values, 138
OTLP format, 142
processors, 142
push-based exporters, 141
responsibility, 125
Views
Java, 132
MeterProvider, 131
metric views, 133
multiple views, 132
properties, 131, 132
Migrations, 24, 41, 108, 188, 205–207, 209,
210, 212, 215, 216
Monotonicity, 119, 122, 127, 140
Multiple signals propagating context, 80
Multiple trace context propagators, 80
myExecutor.submit(), 73

N

Node agent model
chart values, 183
collectors, 184

Node agent model (*cont.*)
    Kubernetes, 182, 183
    mode option, 182
    node-exporter/kube-state-metrics, 183
    pods, 184
    presets configuration, 182
    receivers, 183
Non-probability sampling, 189, 190, 198

O

Observability, 143, 145, 217
    context, 7–12
    context propagation
        application code, 225
        cross-team collaboration, 223
        deployments, 223
        distributed systems, 225, 226
        enabling, 222
        exporters, 225
        instrumented component, 223
        Node applications, 224
        opentelemetry-js, 223
        operation/external call, 224
        server span names, 224
        service adoption, 223
        service owners, 223, 224
        services, 222, 223
        spans, 222–224
        subsystems, 224, 225
        telemetry context, 222
        Telemetry enablement teams, 222
        traces, 224
        unit tests, 225
        user devices, 223
    continuous deployment
        pipelines, 6
    control systems theory, 3

    correlation, 7–12
    debugging workflows, 219
        alerts and dashboards, 219
        context, 220
        data, 218
        engineering teams, 217
        engineers, 217
        external input, 221
        Kubernetes, 218
        learning/improving, 220
        logs, 220
        metrics, 221
        postmortem process, 220
        questions, 221
        semantic conventions, 220
        Telemetry enablement teams, 221
        troubleshooting, 217, 218
    distributed system, 222
    goal, 6
    incident response life cycle, 4
    incident response timeline, 5
    Kálmán, R.E., 3
    logical approach, 222
    microservice architectures, 6
    monitoring field, 6
    MTTD, 6
    MTTF, 6
    MTTK, 6
    MTTR, 4, 5
    MTTV, 6
    N+1 redundant system, 4
    performance regression, distributed
        system, 9
    services, 222
    telemetry, 6
        accountability, 227
        concepts, 226
        containers, 227

costs, 227, 228

data transfer/cardinality, 226

deployments, 228

enablement, 227

Kubernetes, 227

limits, 227

load optimization, 228

management, 226

metrics, 228

ownership, 228

sampling techniques, 228

teams, 228

users, 227

telemetry data, 6

transactional systems, 4

vendors value, 23

ofDoubles() method, 120–124

OkHttp instrumentation, 66

OkHttpTracing instrumentation, 67

OpenCensus, 20, 24, 28, 78, 83, 113, 168, 191, 212–215

Open-source projects, 21, 30, 35

OpenTelemetry, 24, 147, 150

APIs, 16

architecture overview, 31

changes telemetry landscape, 23

CNCF sandbox project, 22

distributed system, semantic conventions, 19

interoperability, 108

observability, 16

open-source, 16

open standards, 17–20

reality, 16

SDK, 16

semantic conventions (*see* Semantic conventions)

types, telemetry signals, 15

vendor added value, 21–24

vendor *vs.* open-source boundaries, 24

OpenTelemetry adoption

greenfield environments, 209, 210

OpenCensus, 212, 213

OpenTracing, 210–212

telemetry clients, 214, 215

OpenTelemetry Collectors, 41, 48, 55, 57, 60, 61, 86, 107, 141, 142, 156–159, 162, 163, 165–174, 176–178, 180, 182–185, 187, 188, 190, 197, 198, 200, 202, 205, 208, 214, 215

OpenTelemetry distros, 208, 222

OpenTelemetry Enhancement Proposals (OTEP), 28, 130, 159, 160

OpenTelemetry Logging, 156

OpenTelemetry Protocol (OTLP), 41, 57, 60, 66, 67, 106, 107, 118, 130, 136, 138, 141, 142, 153, 155, 157–159, 161, 162, 172, 178, 185, 186, 188, 205, 214

OpenTelemetry specification

APIs, 31

baggage, 39

collectors, 41

components, 29–31

Context API, 39

cross-language, 27

cross-platform, 27

design guidelines, 33

feature-freeze state, 29

instrumentation libraries, 40

logs, 38

long-term support, 33

mechanisms, 32

metrics, 35–37

open-source processes, projects, 28

OTEP, 28

OpenTelemetry specification (*cont.*)
  OTLP, 41
  Propagators API, 39
  resource, 40
  SDK, 32
  signal life cycle
    deprecated, 32
    experimental, 32
    remove, 32
    stable, 32
  signals, 29–31
  specification documents, 28
  traces, 34, 35
  version 1.0.0, 28
OpenTelemetry tackles, 113
OpenTracing, 20, 24, 76, 78, 80, 82, 83, 108,
    180, 197, 210–215
Operational monitoring, 6, 27, 111
otel-collector container, 56
otel-collector.yml, 56
otel.experimental.resource.
    disabled-keys, 64
otel.javaagent.extensions system, 63
otel.java.disabled.resource-providers, 64
otel.java.enabled.resource-providers, 64
otel.logs.exporter property, 154
otel.resource.attributes, 64
OTLP exporters, 66, 107, 138, 154, 161, 186
OT Trace propagator, 80

P, Q

Parent span, 89–91, 94, 99, 104, 109, 192,
    193, 196
Payment Service, 9, 10, 18–20, 33
Probability sampling, 189, 190
  collector processor, 197
  ParentBased, 192, 193

properties, 191
samplers, 192
sampling ratio, 197
spans, 198
trace/span, 191
tracestate
  adjusted count, 193
  consistency, 194
  ConsistentProbability
    Based, 194–196
  ot vendor tag, 196
  ParentBased sampler, 193
  ParentConsistent
    ProbabilityBased, 197
  p-value, 194–197
  r-value, 195, 196
  sampled flag, 193
  spans, 193
  TraceIdRatioBased, 193
tracing platforms, 193
Tracing SDK, 192
Processors, 63, 104, 105, 107, 135, 142, 152,
    162, 163, 165, 169–171, 175,
    177, 178
Prometheus, 16, 21, 35, 36, 55, 57, 60, 112,
    116, 118, 126, 130, 135, 136, 138,
    140–142, 168, 179, 180, 182,
    188, 215
Propagators API, 39, 108
  B3, 79
  carrier, 79, 80
  client/server package, 80
  composite propagators, 80
  consumer/producer instrumentation
    package, 80
  extract operations, 79
  HashMap, 81
  inject operations, 79

Jaeger, 79, 80
OT Trace propagator, 80
TextMapPropagator, 79
W3C Baggage, 76, 77, 79, 80
W3C TraceContext, 79
Protocol
    exporter configuration, 161, 162
    features, 157, 158
    OTLP, 162
    OTLP/gRPC, 159, 160
    OTLP/HTTP, 159, 161
    schemas, 159
Python, 40

R

Real User Monitoring (RUM), 146
Receivers, 159, 163, 165, 168–170, 172, 175
recordException() method, 98
Resource, 40, 51, 63, 64, 66
Resource conventions, 43, 44
Resource.getDefault() method, 52
Resource instances, 52
Resource SDK, 51–53
runAsync(), 101

S

Sampling mechanisms, 189, 190
SDK, 16, 22, 23, 27, 28, 30–33, 38, 40, 43,
    44, 47, 62, 85, 87, 103, 110, 111,
    113–117, 120–122, 128
Search Engine Optimization (SEO), 146
Semantic conventions, 30, 31
    cloud provider region, 42
    cross-cutting concern, 43
    define, 42
    goal, 42

metrics, 46, 47
resources, 43, 44
telemetry schemas, 48
tracing, 43, 45, 46
Semantics, 10, 19, 27, 30, 31, 112
service.instance.id, 44
Service Level Agreements (SLAs), 7
Service Level Objectives (SLOs), 7, 16, 221
service.name, 44, 53, 218
service.namespace, 44, 228
Service owners, 9, 54, 61, 64, 83, 91, 102,
    110, 111, 131, 198, 206–209,
    211–214, 222–224
service.version, 44, 63
setAllAttributes() method, 97
setNoParent(), 92
setRequestProperty(), 80
shutdown() function, 105, 126, 136, 151
Sidecar agent model
    advantages, 186
    drawbacks, 186
    Kubernetes, 185
    opentelemetry-operator, 185
SimpleLogRecordProcessor, 152
SimpleSpanProcessor, 105
slumber() method, 99, 101, 102
Software systems, 12, 17, 69, 111, 130
Spans, 34, 45, 86
    addLink() method, 95
    attributes, 90
    CLIENT, 91
    Context, 89
    end timestamp, 90
    events, 90
    granularity, 91
    innerMethod(), 94
    inner operation, 93
    INTERNAL, 92, 95

Spans (*cont.*)
  limits, properties, 104, 105
  links, 90, 95
  main operation, 93
  myMethod(), 93
  name, 89, 97
  parent, 89
  processors, 105–107
  SERVER, 91
  Span.current(), 94
  SpanKind, 89, 90
  start timestamp, 90
  status, 91
  transfer and storage costs, 91
SpanContext, 89, 90, 107, 108, 134,
    154, 191
span.makeCurrent(), 107
Split traces, fire-and-forget
    tasks, 101

T

Tail-based sampling, 198, 199
  approaches, 200
  limitations, 199
  maintenance, 201
  OpenTelemetry Collectors, 200
  sampling policies, 200
  spans, 200, 201
Telemetry, 7, 40
Telemetry backends, 113
Telemetry context, 69–73
Telemetry data, 11
Telemetry enablement, 207
  distros, 208
  engineering teams, 207
  factors, 205, 206
  layer of abstraction, 208

migration value, 207
  signals, 207
Telemetry enablement teams,
    189, 221–223
Telemetry instrumentation, 29
Telemetry noise, 11
Telemetry schemas, 48
Telemetry signals, 142
TextMapPropagator, 76, 79, 108
Time series, 35, 111, 112, 114, 124, 125,
    140, 141, 173, 214, 228
Trace, 6, 10, 12, 15, 16, 28–30, 34, 35, 37,
    39, 40, 42, 45, 47, 57–59, 61, 74, 86
Trace propagators, 30, 80, 108
Tracer, 88, 89, 108
  attributes, 88
  instrumentation scope, 88
  name, 88
  Schema URL, 88
  version, 88
TracerProvider, 88, 89, 104, 105
Trace sampling, 198, 199
  external information, 190
  observability, 190
  span, 190
  telemetry data, 189
  traditional logging, 190
Tracing API, 74
  add properties to existing span, 96, 97
  definition, 87
  dropwizard-example with job.title, 96
  errors, 98, 99
  exceptions, 98, 99
  Java, 92
  span (*see* Span)
  tracer providers, 88, 89
  tracers, 88, 89
  tracing asynchronous tasks, 99–103

Tracing conventions, 45, 46

Tracing SDK
 exporters, 105–107
 ID generator, 103
 resource, 104
 sampler, 104
 span limits, 103
 span processors, 103, 105–107
 W3C TraceContext, 107–109

Transaction, 9–11, 17, 19, 20, 29, 33, 34, 39, 59, 69, 70, 74, 77, 78, 80, 85–87, 89, 110, 144, 145, 201, 220, 222, 226

The Twelve-Factor App methodology, 38

Types of telemetry signals, 12, 15, 29

U

Usage Saturation Error (USE) method, 8

V

Vendor added value, 21–24

Vendor-specific APM agents, 78

W

W3C Baggage propagators, 64, 76, 77, 79–83, 108, 109

W3C TraceContext
 HTTP request headers, 108
 OpenTelemetry project, 108
 service, 110
 Span ID, 107
 trace context propagation via HTTP request headers, 109
 trace flags, 107
 Trace ID, 107
 trace state, 108

W3C TraceContext propagator, 60, 79, 82, 83, 89, 107–110, 191, 194, 196, 205, 211

X, Y

XMLHttpRequest (XHR), 223

Z

Zero-touch model, 54

Printed in the United States
by Baker & Taylor Publisher Services